WHOSE LANGUAGE IS ENGLISH?

WHOSE LANGUAGE IS ENGLISH?

JIEUN KIAER

Yale
UNIVERSITY PRESS
NEW HAVEN & LONDON

Published with assistance from the Mary Cady Tew Memorial Fund.

Yale University Press books may be purchased in quantity for educational, business, or promotional use. For information, please e-mail sales.press@yale.edu (U.S. office) or sales@yaleup.co.uk (U.K. office).

Set in Spectral and Shango type by IDS Infotech.

Printed in the United States of America.

ISBN 978-0-300-26405-0 (hardcover : alk. paper)
Library of Congress Control Number: 2024932816

A catalogue record for this book is available from the British Library.

This paper meets the requirements of ANSI/NISO Z39.48-1992 (Permanence of Paper).

10 9 8 7 6 5 4 3 2 1

To my father, Taehoon Joe,
and my father-in-law, Stanley Kiaer,
both of whom have given me such happy memories
of shared words

Contents

Acknowledgments

I am so grateful to the many people who have helped me with this project. A huge thanks to my editor, Jennifer Banks from Yale University Press, for her patience and openness to the ideas in this book. Thanks also to Louise Hossien, Abby Fletcher, Theo Knights, Amena Dancel Nebres, and Edward Voet for your invaluable help at various stages. Thank you, my family, who have been so patient with my endless questions.

WHOSE LANGUAGE IS ENGLISH?

Opening Words

At the peak of the British Empire in the late nineteenth and early twentieth centuries, James Murray, the primary editor of the Oxford English Dictionary, raised the question of the very identity of the English language.

> The English Language is the language of Englishmen! Of which Englishmen? Of all Englishmen or of some Englishmen? . . . Does it include the English of Great Britain and the English of America, the English of Australia, and of South Africa, and of those most assertive Englishmen, the Englishmen of India, who live in bungalows, hunt in jungles, wear terai hats or puggaries and pyjamas, write chits instead of letters and eat kedgeree and chutni? Yes! In its most comprehensive sense, and as an object of historical study, it includes all these; they are all forms of English.[1]

English as a language has absorbed words from all over the world. Even such common pantry items as eggs, tomatoes, bacon, and ketchup are instances of this absorption. Tea, to take an iconic example, has come to symbolize British national identity and culture, in spite of its origin being far from British; words have complex trajectories. English has many French words, but the origin of most of these words cannot be said to be purely French. They are words that have moved into French from somewhere else, and then into English. Take the word *sugar*, for example. According to the Oxford English Dictionary, it is derived from the Old French *çucre*, *çuquere*, *zuchre*, and *sukere*, and ultimately from the medieval Latin *zuccarum* or *succarum*, which likely came from the Arabic *sukkar.* Even the word *alphabet* is a combination of two Greek words.

The linguistic diversity in the English language is perhaps analogous to the diversity of our continually globalizing society. As President John F. Kennedy said, "everywhere, immigrants have enriched and strengthened the fabric of American life," so too have words enriched our language.[2] How do we define "American"? How do we define "English"? Over the past fifteen years, the percentage of students in schools in the United Kingdom whose first language is not English has more than doubled. In 2008, 7.8 percent of pupils spoke English as an additional language in the United Kingdom.[3] As of 2021, 19.3 percent of pupils have been reported to have a first language other than English.[4] More than half of the world's population is estimated to be bilingual, although this is difficult to measure precisely.[5]

I have personally been surprised by the number of bilinguals that I encounter in my daily life in the United Kingdom. The pupils at my twelve-year-old daughter's small primary school in Oxfordshire speak more than forty different languages at home. My daughter, who is now in Year 7, once told me that there are "no real English people" in her class, intending to convey to me that none of her classmates were monolingual English speakers. It's an exciting reality where everyone speaks English at her school, yet everyone has a different linguistic and cultural background.

> We have set ourselves to form a National Portrait Gallery, not only of the worthies, but of all the members, of the race of English words which is to form the dominant speech of the world . . .
>
> . . . Fling our doors wide! all, all, not one, but all, must enter: for their service let them be honored; and though the search for them may sometimes seem wearisome, and the labor of the ingathering more irksome still, yet the work is worthy and the aim unselfish. Let us, then, persevere.[6]

This is a quotation from Frederick James Furnivall (1825–1910), editor of the Oxford English Dictionary from 1861 to 1870, written in a circular to the members of the Philological Society, dated November 9, 1862. As Furnivall points out, English has opened its door to all words of the world. Since then, 160 years have passed, and today English has become the common language of the global population, in both the physical and the virtual worlds. Every word has the potential to become an English word, meaning that each word can acquire a second identity and take English as a second home.

This book explores words that take English as a second home, a trend that has been developing for centuries and now forms an extremely large collection. The British Empire adopted terms and expressions from inhabitants of the colonies into English. English became a more diverse language as a result—influencing the development of other languages, while simultaneously being influenced and changed by those same languages. Geographical variations of English became more strongly reinforced, as the rise of America as a global hegemon after World War II resulted in American English overtaking British English on a global scale.

Defining "English" words is no longer as straightforward as it once was, given that English is spoken by most people in the world; the words discussed in this book are those used in an English context or environment across the world. These words are not limited by regions or registers; if they are used in a linguistic environment where any form of English is dominant, they are within the scope of this book.

The development of worldwide English has been, in recent years, catalyzed by social media and technological advancement. In January 2019, 3.484 billion people globally were classified as active social media users. That is around half of the world's population. For many of these people it is commonplace to use WhatsApp and WeChat in daily life. Together with social media, the emergence of large language models such as ChatGPT and virtual realities has accelerated the process of creating what can be considered supersized English, by accelerating word traffic. Making, sharing, and mixing words and ideas in a borderless manner is easier than ever, and meanwhile the uptake of words is happening at an unprecedented speed.

This enormous word pantry allows for once marginalized, forgotten words to be embraced. Social media has brought about word democracy; ordinary people can participate in the making and sharing of words, tailoring them to their needs. However, it is also possible for corporations to monopolize our word pantry, and our understanding and usage of the words in it. Like us, words are in constant motion and difficult to pin down to a singular identity. They are all human-made and carry within them our emotions and history. Some people may view words as nothing more than words, but their significance should not be understated. English in 2024 is vastly different from its previous iterations, constantly evolving and shaped every second by anonymous speakers in both physical and virtual spaces. What will the future of supersized English and the words living in it be? This book explores the new realities of our increasingly expansive English language and the words that call it home.

Chapter 1

WHOSE ENGLISH?

More than One English?

Although we often tend to think of English as a monolith, it is more accurate to think of there being many Englishes. Around seventy-five countries are now using English as their official or first language.[1] The number of people speaking English around the world continues to rise. There are signs that the primary makeup of the English-speaking population is changing. Although the number of English speakers is increasing, the proportion of speakers for whom English is a first language is actually decreasing. In the mid-twentieth century, nearly 9 percent of the world's population grew up speaking English as their first language. By 2050, that number is expected to decline to around 5 percent. This decrease is not the result of population diminution among communities speaking English as their first language, but is rather due to the explosion in popularity of English as a second language. People who speak languages other than English have the fastest growing populations, and many of these people are now learning English as a second language.[2] In 2013, the British Council estimated that English was spoken "at a useful level" by 1.75 billion people world-wide, and that by 2020 the number of people using or learning English would pass 2 billion.[3] In other words, more people than ever before speak English as an additional language.

As more people learn English as a second language, the grow-ing number of diverse English-speaking communities around the globe will challenge the idea of who "owns" the English language. Just as migration led to divergence between the Englishes spoken by British and American speakers, so too should we expect differences between the Englishes spoken as a second language in newer communities of English speakers. Technology and social media may also have an impact. Because of social media, interactions between speakers of different varieties of English are more common than ever, and future technologies will increase our global connectivity even more. There is also the possibility of the development of an "International Standard English" that is "not recognizably British, American, or anything else," and will come to be used for communication between different global communities, in addition to a "variety of Standard English" people will learn in school.[4]

Even in countries where English is traditionally seen as the main spoken language, such as the United Kingdom and the United States, linguistic landscapes are becoming more diverse. In 2016, the American Community Survey revealed that native speakers of languages other than English make up about 20 percent of the U.S. population. Over the past twenty years, the percentage of students in U.K. schools whose first language is not English has almost doubled. In 2002, 10 percent of pupils spoke English as an additional language.[5] As of 2021, 19.3 percent of pupils have been reported to have a first language other than English.[6]

When people today think of languages, many imagine groups of monolingual speakers neatly arranged into distinct communities divided by national borders. This is an oversimplification: languages do not necessarily heed nation-state borders, and language maps are highly diverse. The common assumption about languages is likely to become more inaccurate as global connectivity increases. Indeed, "a new world order in languages" will accompany the next stage of global development.[7] One framework, albeit far from perfect, that has been proposed for making sense of the multiplicity of English speakers across the world is the linguist Braj

Kachru's typology of "World Englishes." In 1986, Kachru proposed that world English speakers belonged to three concentric circles: an inner circle of countries where English is used as a primary language, such as the United States, the United Kingdom, Australia, New Zealand, and Canada; an outer circle of countries where the use of English is a legacy of colonialism and often has some official status, such as India, Nigeria, the Philippines, and Singapore; and an expanding circle of countries where English is spoken but has no historical or official status, as in South Korea, Sweden, and Saudi Arabia. This model is now outdated, but it can still provide a useful basis on which to consider English in this world.[8]

The growing number of speakers of English as a second language, as well as bilingual speakers, inevitably leads us to question what it means to be an English speaker in the twenty-first century. Although English is increasingly being adopted as a lingua franca, this does not mean that other languages are in danger of being absorbed into or replaced by English. English sits alongside local languages rather than replacing them. It becomes a secondary language rather than a primary one. Globalization coupled with greater physical and virtual mobility has actually contributed to making all languages more visible than ever, including endangered languages.

English for Everyone

When my twelve-year-old daughter Sarah introduces herself, she says, "My mum is Korean. My dad is half Danish, a quarter Scottish and a quarter English, which makes me half Korean, a quarter Danish, an eighth Scottish and an eighth English." My husband is English, but his family history is equally complex: his father's grandparents were from Denmark, his grandmother was born and raised in Shanghai, and his mother was Scottish. It's not just us; most people's family histories are complex and diverse. My friend

Irene, for instance, is from Catalonia, and my friend Theo is from Denmark, but both moved to England. Because of this, their son Luke can speak Danish and Catalan, although he speaks mainly English when he goes to nursery. Their family speaks more than three languages daily, but they mainly use English. Because of the family's history, their version of English is a little bit different from ours, as they mix Spanish, Catalan, and Danish words into their English. Two of our other friends, Henry and Tess, are from Hungary and the Philippines, respectively. Tess's family is originally from the Philippines, but they moved to Los Angeles when Tess was a young girl. She then moved to the United Kingdom. Henry used to live in Budapest and speaks Hungarian and English, while Tess speaks English with a bit of Tagalog. Their son, Lorenzo, speaks English in nursery, but he can also speak and understand a bit of Tagalog and Hungarian, which he uses when visiting his grandparents. For my friends, English is the language that binds everyone in the family together, but it is not necessarily the language that each member, particularly the parents, finds the most comfortable or familiar. Families like these exist all over the globe. Just like us, English is full of words from different places.

At the end of March 2023, my younger daughter Jessie had a birthday party. Her friends come from various cultural backgrounds: Emma is Japanese, Ffi is Welsh, Olivia is Irish, Leilia is Moroccan, Rosa is Serbian, Valentine is French, and Jessie is of Korean and Danish heritage. During the party, they all spoke in English, though they occasionally used words from their parents' languages. Despite their diverse backgrounds, all of them are fluent English speakers, or more precisely, second or third generation diaspora English speakers.

How do we define an English speaker? Do I belong to the English-speaking populace? These are questions that arise when we discuss the complexities of language and identity. What about the following people:

Whose English?

"I mainly speak English in my everyday life but at home I speak a mix of Korean and English with my kids. English is not my first language. I only learned it when I was 13 years old, but I've lived in the UK for 20 years now. Although I still make grammatical mistakes and don't sound like those born in Britain and who speak only English, I still speak more English than Korean in my day-to-day life. Am I eligible to be called an English speaker?"

"I am German with Indian heritage. I live in Germany, but I use English a lot for work in order to collaborate with international colleagues. My English is fluent. I don't have a particular British or American English accent, but I have no problem working in English."

"I live in Beijing, China. I speak in Mandarin all the time and would say that my English is not very good. However, I use English to communicate on social media or WeChat with my friends in other parts of the world. Their English isn't good either but English is our common language."

(These quotations have all been sourced from my personal communications.) Although these people's place of birth, home country, native language, learned languages, and English proficiency are all different, they are all legitimate English speakers. One can be considered an English speaker if one uses English, regardless of any of these other characteristics, and this is especially true online, where users can often interact totally anonymously if they choose to. There are now a huge number of varieties of English, each resembling or departing from other varieties in various ways. People across the world use a wide variety of common Englishes alongside their local, regional languages. In social media spaces, English words belonging to global Englishes are made even livelier and more diverse through internet-mediated features, such as memes and emojis. Despite all of this, many of our ideas of what makes an English speaker are stuck in the past—why should we judge the many varieties of English spoken around the world against standards set by British or American speakers?

A paradigm shift is necessary so that we view English as a language belonging to everyone. Not speaking English in the modern world can be disabling, sometimes even limiting one's ability to navigate everyday life. One example of this is how an individual's intelligence and ability are often judged based on their proficiency in English. Many newcomers to the United Kingdom from Syria have been criticized in the media for their lack of English competence. Under David Cameron's government, gaining citizenship was made stricter, and required a higher level of English proficiency. Simultaneously, huge cuts to the funding of English as a foreign language education were made, leaving many feeling ostracized.[9] Not being able to speak English became a limiting factor in the lives of many Syrian newcomers, no matter how qualified they were in their professions. The whole experience can be depressing and isolating. In my personal experience in academia, I have seen people look down on a scholar's academic paper because their English skills were not up to standard. Often Asian scholars with great minds are undermined and overlooked because of their English ability. Perhaps we need to rethink the nature of English to make it more welcoming, which may be possible soon, thanks to the arrival of generative AI like ChatGPT or Google's Bard.

For English to maintain its status as the world's common language, we might begin to acknowledge that all varieties of English are languages in their own right when they are used by a community of speakers. They possess equal legitimacy as standard varieties. Wherever you are born, wherever you live, whatever your official nationality, and whatever your competence in a language, if a meaningful portion of your life is communicated through a form of English, then I argue that you should be considered an

English speaker. Rather than constantly trying to smooth our varieties of English into the type of English that is accepted in the United Kingdom or the United States, we should accept all the diversity that the English language has to offer us.

We should also be aiming to make English more accessible to everyone around the world. English is a capital asset, and it should be distributed fairly around the globe. I am currently working on a new initiative called "English for Everyone." It aims to combat the education bias around the world by providing local teachers with resources for English teaching, thus giving children, particularly those from the global south, refugees, and those without learning resources, the opportunity to learn a useful skill.

English: A Second Home to the World's Words

As a lexicographer working at the peak of the explosion of new words in the early twentieth century, James Murray struggled with the question of how best to classify words that had entered English from other languages. Were they English words or not? On what grounds? Like Furnivall and most editors of the Oxford English Dictionary (OED), in principle he held an "all welcome" view. Despite this, he often described foreign words as uncommon and referred to them as "aliens and denizens within the English language." There has been a significant shift since then. In the twenty-first century, we need to confront whether foreign-born words are still at the margin. English has emerged as the language where words from diverse corners of the world can find a home; it has become a sanctuary for words from different cultures and languages.

It's difficult to imagine English without words from other places. As people travel more, the words they carry with them spread far and wide. The pandemic has not stopped this process. In fact, as we continue to interact and communicate with one another, the exchange of words will only increase. It is no longer pertinent to classify certain words as foreign, just as it is difficult to define what it means to be a foreigner. The OED defines *foreign* as pertaining to countries other than one's own and related senses, but it is unsuitable to use this to describe us and words that are in constant flux.

Much like defining the identities of individuals, defining the identity of words can be a difficult task. Singular terms may not capture the full complexity of their origins, meanings, and uses. Words from other languages can be challenging to define and often carry a sense of otherness. Terms such as *foreign words, borrowing,* and *loanwords* may not always be neutral, much like the word *foreigner.* That said, I have previously argued that the terms *loan* or *borrowing* for foreign words are outdated, and no longer accurately describe the dynamic, cross-linguistic, and cultural interactions that occur between words of different heritages.[10] Such classifications may even be considered discriminatory in today's interconnected world. Instead, I propose the term *translingual words* to describe words that belong to multiple languages at once as a result of word migration. Because of their simultaneous existence in multiple languages, it is difficult to define translingual words as belonging more to one language than another, giving them complex, multicultural identities. These words do not lose their original meanings when they are adopted into another language, but rather exist at the boundary between two or more cultures and languages, taking on diverse nuances in meaning and enriching the lexicon of multiple languages all at once.

In Japanese, for instance, the character for *sake* can refer to any alcoholic drink—hence red wine is *sake* too. To many of us in the West, however, *sake* means "a Japanese fermented liquor made from rice," as the OED has it.[11] In a similar way, *kimono* is used in Japan to refer to any kind of garment. In the West, we associate the word with the traditional Japanese dress. Translingual words are ubiquitous in our lives. The most well known and widely adopted examples are perhaps not words in alphabetical form, but a set of ten numeral symbols, commonly referred to as Hindu-Arabic numerals: 0, 1, 2, 3, 4, 5, 6, 7, 8, and 9. With the rise of emojis and memes online, we are now seeing the emergence of translingual and transcultural words that, by definition, cannot be attributed to a single nation-state identity. In this book, I use terms such as "new words" or "immigrated words" (more precisely "trans-migrating words") or other more appropriate language when discussing words from other languages to avoid unnecessary discrimination or stigma. In principle, words of our time are not confined by language borders. The English language is now filled with words that have made English their second or third home, whether they have foreign origins or overseas heritage, much like the diversity present in the population itself.

Indeed, English, as we know it, is changing, and so are its users. Over the twentieth century, English has spread across the globe, becoming a shared language for billions. Consequently, English continues to go through a process of metamorphosis. The larger English becomes, the less it retains what previously constituted its Englishness. Forms and meanings will be added as the words move back and forth, crossing the boundaries of languages and cultures. In other words, as English is used more widely around the globe, the pantry of English words will be filled with words from all over the world, making it look different from the English that we used to know. Words that we explore in this book are from all around the world with roots from languages of Asia, Europe, Africa, Oceania, and South America. Some words are visibly hybrid, wearing their immigration life trajectories as part of their appearance. Others are born on social media, so their linguistic heritage is not clear. Every word that we will encounter is a word that has a home in English.

However, entering English is not a straightforward process for any word. First of all, a word has to receive its Anglo-romanization, unless it is an emoji or a meme. Its singular and plural forms must also be decided. It's worth noting that in many Asian languages, singular and plural forms of nouns are determined by the context in which they are used, rather than by inflections or other grammatical markers. European languages, on the other hand, are known for their rich inflectional systems, although they are not as prevalent in English. When translating Asian novels into English, publishers and editors often require that translators Anglicize Asian terms as much as possible. Asian people rarely use first names, for example, but in a translation of an Asian novel, you will see the frequent use of first names in direct speech. Additionally, English does not generally use diacritics, so English translations often ignore the distinction in vowel length in Japanese words (Tokyo, for instance, instead of Tōkyō). French words, on the other hand, are less likely to be simplified in English translations, exposing a double standard. Although English is less complex than many Western European languages, it still distinguishes between genders when using pronouns. One of the most challenging aspects of translating English into Asian languages is conveying gender. In *The Hen Who Dreamed She Could Fly*, for example, the acclaimed book by Sun-mi Hwang, the villain is a weasel. In the original Korean, its gender is not indicated, but in the English translation the weasel is referred to as "he." Only at the very end of the story is it made clear that the weasel is a mother, and the translation then changes its gender from male to female. This would have been surprising to an English reader, but to a Korean reader, it would have had little impact because gender was never specified anyway.[12]

Further adjustments in spelling, pronunciation, and meaning need to be made for words to enter English smoothly. It can be unclear whether to treat new words as local words or to treat them specially. Often, when a word enters English for the first time, it is capitalized or italicized after going through a probationary period. A word may be anglicized, and if it is, it could be anglicized in a range of ways. When looking at anglicized words of Chinese origin, some take on a romanized version of their Mandarin name (such as Beijing); others take the Cantonese pronunciation (such as chow mein or chop suey), seemingly without rhyme or reason.

Nevertheless, having a wide vocabulary may be a great asset for a language, much as a diverse population is an asset to a nation. The editors of the Oxford English Dictionary generally welcome new words, but this was not always the case. Sarah Ogilvie's book *Words of the World* shows that 17 percent of the entries in the 1933 Supplement to the OED were *deleted* by Robert Burchfield, the fifth chief editor of the OED. Daniel Salazar, the world English editor for the OED, reframes these words as a gift to the English language.[13] I agree; English alone is not capable of catering to the expressive needs of all those who need it. This is because English lacks expressions that convey delicate complex human relations like kinship terms. Translating the English second person pronoun, *you,* into Asian languages is difficult for this reason. In Japanese alone, there are dozens of different expressions to translate *you.* Using the correct pronoun is crucial, as using the wrong one can harm relationships because the level of respect is carried within the language itself. On the other hand, it can also feel liberating for those living in hierarchical societies, such as South Korea.[14]

Last year, while I was working with the OED, we added the word *skinship* to the dictionary. This term, used in Japanese and Korean contexts, refers to touching or close physical contact between a parent and child or between lovers or friends, expressing affection or strengthening emotional bonds. In the past, this word was looked down upon as being broken English. On the contrary I think that words like this can enrich the English lexicon. Without words from around the globe, English would be impoverished. Incorporating new words into English has made its lexicon more powerful and emotive. Without them, English would be less effective as a global language in our time.

New English

English has become a tool used by people all over the world, and the internet now allows these speakers to communicate with a global community of other English speakers. Device-mediated discourse, such as words predicted or suggested by smartphones, now makes up a large part of our daily communication. Many of us find it easier to text or use emojis to communicate than to talk in person, and the Covid-19 pandemic encouraged this trend further. Smart device initiated communication has its benefits, such as enabling us to communicate quickly and easily, and providing AI helpers that can suggest spelling corrections, but it can also have drawbacks. Some people, especially those who learned English as a second language, find it difficult to find the right tone, and spend time and effort polishing and censoring their writing to ensure it adheres to grammar rules. It can also feel constricting. If someone thinks too much about grammar, it may prevent them from being as creative as they'd like. Relying too much on AI devices can also be a problem if they interfere with the natural flow of writing and provide too many suggestions. With the International Baccalaureate now allowing pupils to use ChatGPT for their exams, some wonder whether relying too heavily on AI could limit our literacy skills in the long run. Will Generation Z and Alpha rely on AI devices to learn how to write and talk?

More than a hundred years on, James Murray's question "Of which Englishmen?" is more relevant than ever, but in a different way. The identity of English is once again fast evolving in the age of artificial intelligence, virtual reality, and social media. Worldwide social media has played a crucial role in making English the second home for words from around the world. Using English online and in virtual worlds has led to a supersized English. Keeping up with the expansion of the word pantry is no easy feat; Murray worked tirelessly to update the dictionary, receiving an average of thirty to forty letters a day, having to enlist the help of his eleven children to sort through these quotation slips. To record the ever expanding English words now, even a family of twelve working around the clock would struggle to stay on top of the rapidly growing English lexicon.

For many, English is neither a first language nor something they use in everyday life; instead it allows them entry into global discussions in online spaces. The English used on social media and other online platforms, which I will label *new* English, caters to these global citizens. *New* English, born out of the social media era, is both shared and shaped by global users with varied linguistic repertoires and life trajectories. A Chinese woman, an American K-pop fan, a British Filipino—speakers from a vast range are now diversifying the lexicon of this *new* English through their online interactions with other English speakers, both native and non-native. Yet this is not to say that native speakers do not also play a part in this process of diversification. Increasingly, English natives who become fans of foreign media adopt non-English words, assimilating them into their everyday lexicon. Western fans of Japanese *anime* have widened awareness of such terms as *senpai*, while K-pop fans have introduced words like *daebak* and have also added new meanings to existing words, such as *bias*. English native speakers and non-native speakers alike are working to diversify the English lexicon through their interactions online, enriching the language and providing subcultures with an increased sense of solidarity within their communities through shared varieties of language.

New English is also characterized by a different attitude toward the language. The decentralized structure of the internet and social media, coupled with the lack of linguistic censorship by language authorities, means that speakers are no longer passive recipients of an English judged against the standards of the United States and the United Kingdom. Instead, speakers are free to use English pragmatically according to their own linguistic needs and can reshape the language to these ends. Speakers now engage with a variety of languages and cultures in a borderless manner, becoming active participants in shaping the English language.

Whenever a language is evolving or changing, people with a conservative attitude about words and the way we speak often fear that the old forms will be tarnished or destroyed by new developments. Innovations such as text messages and social media have caused some to fear that the new forms of language accompanying them will damage "proper" grammar or spelling. Some have also raised concerns that social media has contributed to a linguistic generational gap, where older generations, unable to keep up with the rapid pace of online slang, find themselves not understanding the language that their children or grandchildren use. Some technologies encourage shifts in linguistic behavior through their design. Strict limits on the number of characters used in some social media, for instance, often force users to adopt a more abbreviated, snappy form of communication, while messages are exchanged so rapidly on instant messaging services that users may use abbreviations and slang terms to keep up. Similar trends can be seen in most places on the internet, where speed or succinctness of communication is prioritized over other attitudinal considerations, such as traditional spelling and grammar. These factors are often pointed to as reasons why social media may pose a threat to proper language. Yet these fears are not new; with every new generation, linguistic conservatives have criticized the slang used by young people, but the supposed deterioration of traditional spelling and grammar has not yet materialized.

Before we go on, however, I must first clarify an issue of terminology. In this book, I often make use of the term *native speaker*. However, this term is a problem in its standard usage; it is part of an ideology of native speakerism. This ideology constructs binary categories of native and non-native speakers of English that are held to be mutually exclusive. It has also been argued that the characteristics of native speakers are intrinsically linked to a matrix of language, race, and nationality, such as "born to the right language environment," as in the case of English for Caucasians and the United States.[15] In other words, this ideology entangles a term supposedly intended to measure linguistic proficiency with factors like one's language environment, race, and nationality, which is often used against ethnic minorities to exclude them from the privileged category of *native* English speaker.

Despite the decentralization of English, native speakers are still privileged. In many parts of the world, those who are proficient in English—measured against the standard of correct usage by native speakers—are rewarded economically through access to greater job opportunities. The close link between English proficiency and upward economic mobility has given rise to the phenomenon of "English fever" in many parts of the world, where children are tutored in English from a very young age to give them a competitive advantage over their peers. This is especially prevalent throughout Asia.

The core ideology behind the notion of native speaker also comes from a view of the world's speech community as being monolingual and monocultural.[16] Since the latter part of the twentieth century, a great number of studies have attempted to deconstruct this binary of native and non-native and have strongly argued that the native/non-native dichotomy is more of a social construct than a measurement of linguistic ability. For example, some see the rationale behind the popular use of such quasi-political terms as power-driven and laden with issues of identity.[17] The linguistics scholars Constant Leung, Roxy Harris, and Ben Rampton argue against this dichotomy, seeing it as an ideological construction of otherness.[18] Equating expertise with native speaker proficiency is a problem, as it is not always the case that having a language as one's mother tongue automatically guarantees a speaker the highest level of expertise in any given communication situation.[19]

In an attempt to move away from the binary notion of native/non-native speakers of English, a number of scholars have suggested alternative terms that aim to capture the more dynamic and complex linguistic identities of bilingual and multilingual speakers. The term *multicompetence,* for example, refers to all of the language knowledge a bilingual or multilingual person has.[20] The term *native user* may also be used instead of *native speaker*. The native speaker is intrinsically connected to the concept of language ownership and, by default, to the right to set standards and norms for language behavior and for being a native user.[21] In addition, the idea of the *proficient speaker* as an umbrella term has been suggested to describe a person who uses well-formed and appropriate language.[22] Similarly, David Graddol, a British linguist, proposed a model that focuses on the views of speakers of English, moving away from race and nativeness to the proficiency of language users.[23] The term *native speaker* is rarely used in this book, other than in referring to academic discussion about it, because it represents a common (and mistaken) way of thinking about language proficiency and ownership, so it is best to avoid the term. Instead, we will be examining the English spoken by people who may not fit the stereotypes surrounding what an English speaker looks like.

How Should I Use This Word?

New words must also negotiate how they fit into English grammar. For instance, should a word be pluralized as a mass or count noun? If it's a count noun, how should it be pluralized? And should it be spelled with a capital or a lowercase letter? In the past, these decisions were made by grammarians, but now there are simply too many words and too much diversity for traditional grammar rules to apply. Instead, powerful companies and social media influencers decide the fate of these words. Apple alone decides how to spell the names of Apple products. We consult their product manuals rather than dictionaries for guidance. I use an iPhone, and it gives me the option of "Face ID," but I'm not sure what it means. There are no instructions or verbs to guide me. I guess the meaning and hold my face close to it, and to my relief, it opens. However, this experience leaves me with a more complex feeling; who decides the meanings and usages of words? And how am I supposed to understand the meaning as intended when nobody explains it? Is it the corporation that determines this? Do I have to use English as corporations decide, and do corporations dictate how we should use the words?

Consider the following example. In 2022, #Wordle trended on Twitter almost every day. The aim of the game is to uncover the word of the day. Players guess a five-letter word. Any correct letter in the correct position will appear in green. Any correct letter in the wrong position will appear in yellow. Letters not in the word of the day will appear in gray. Users have only six guesses to work out the word. The word of the day is only available in that twenty-four-hour period. The aim is to guess the word in the fewest number of rows possible. The game keeps track of your number of guesses, streak of playing every day, and ratio of wins to losses. Celebrities and the general public take to social media to share their Wordle scores.

On days 207 and 235, the Wordles sparked outrage with some users. #Wordle207 and #Wordle235, respectively, were *favor* and *humor*. The use of American spellings enraged users of British English who thought *favour* and *humour* were six-letter words.

On the day of #Wordle235, Robert Peston, host of the ITV political commentary show *Peston*, tweeted: "Thank you Wordle for helping me to understand with dazzling clarity what it is to be British. I solved you, but I felt cheapened in the process. I think I am done with you." Other tweets found under the Wordle235 hashtag include: "Less of the USA spelling please, it ruined my day" and "Wordle needs to start using proper bloody spelling!" So, what is it—*favor* or *favour*—that is the question.

Pluralization is another tricky issue when using terms that have been directly imported into English from their original languages. This is particularly acute for words in a language like Italian, and many other European languages, where pluralization conventions are different from those in English (they do not simply add the letter *s* as we do). Words such as *calamari* and *panini* have fitted neatly into English without too much meaning or pronunciation confusion. But in the original Italian the letter *i* at the end is used for plural masculine nouns; in their adopted English context, however, these words are frequently used to refer to singular items. How should these words be made plural in English then? Should *panini* remain *panini* in plural, or should it be fully anglicized as *paninis*? And if we leave the plural as *panini*, then should we not follow Italian conventions to their logical conclusion and refer to the singular as *panino*?

This question is only further reinforced by the entrance of words from diverse backgrounds. The same complexity would apply to words like *squid* and *octopus*. What would be the plural of these words? The dictionary would dictate *squid* and *octopi*, but in our daily use, we frequently come across *squids* and *octopuses*. People decide how to pluralize words. In the past, pluralization conventions were defined according to the Greek or Latin origin of a word. Now, words have more diverse trajectories, so these rules are much less useful. There is no logical or scientific criteria to help us pluralize words. If we take countability as the criterion, then it should be applicable to non-European items. We have no problem saying "two cookies," but would you say "two *gyoza*" or "two *gyozas*"?

The End of Grammar Rules

English grammar rules may already be coming to an end, as instinctive grammatical knowledge was long considered the defining characteristic of English speakers who learned the language at a young age and built their competence through life-long practice. For those who learned English after a certain age, grammar can be a significant hurdle, particularly if their home language has an Asian, African, or indigenous background. This is because these languages operate differently from English and other Western European languages. Most Asian languages do not use morphological markers to specify gender, tense, or plurality and lack agreement between subjects and verbs. Although English is simpler than other Western European languages in its inflectional repertoire, it still relies on the singular-plural match and the use of articles, among other rules. Even if your output makes perfect sense, grammatical mistakes can render it unpresentable. Grammatical censorship is starting to break down. Through social media and text messaging, short, instant communication is becoming the norm, and speed is becoming the most important factor. Speed matters more than perfection, and a quick answer with simple grammar or spelling mistakes may be much better received than a late answer with perfect grammar. In the past, when we sent letters, we waited for a response. Even with emails, we may wait for hours or days to get a reply. Widespread access to the internet and social media, however, has caused us to become impatient. If someone reads your message but does not reply, or replies only with a smiley face, you may feel hurt and ignored.

This rapid spontaneous communication culture, whereby people from all around the world can simultaneously interact in social media spaces, has made English grammar ever simpler. The other significant reason for the end of grammar's reign is the development of AI technologies such as automated language processing, language translation, and ChatGPT, Bard and other generative AI bots, which have made it easier than ever to communicate in English without having to worry about grammatical accuracy. As *new* English embraces this supersized word pantry from all corners of the world, social media and automated language processing will speed up, loosening or ending the reign of grammar.

The more we use English as our common language across the globe, the more we will need new words to help its users express themselves more effectively. On the other hand, the more we interact, the more words we will share. I often use the analogy of a sunflower. How a sunflower grows is akin to that of our lexicon. At the center is a brown disk of florets, and around it are its petals. The central disk florets can be classified as the English language; the petals are its numerous varieties. The core and the petals multiply at the same time. In other words, as our shared vocabulary expands, so do more niche words (which may very well in turn become shared). The birth of translingual and hybrid words can be better understood through this analogy. After all, it is impossible to put systematic control on our lexicon, just as a wild sunflower will naturally grow on its own.

The linguistic cross-fertilization that takes place on social media makes English a richer, more innovative, and more inclusive language. These developments are helping us transcend an ideology that considers English an asset of the privileged few, fit to be used only by particular regions, ethnicities, and classes. I demonstrate the transformative power of English, looking at how it can amplify marginal voices, expedite the transfer of the linguistic and cultural repertoire of an individual or community, and bind together diverse voices across the globe, thereby creating solidarity. The *new* English that users are constantly shaping and evolving on social media is enriched by input from all the world's languages. This adds to its expressive power by creating new ways of expressing complex emotions, attitudes, and pragmatic sensitivity.

Chapter 2

WORD INJUSTICE

Which Words Have Prestige?

Words are everywhere. The average English speaker has about 50,000 words in their vocabulary, and it takes 600 milliseconds to find the right word. We produce two or three words per second and speak about 15,000 words in any given day. The Oxford English Dictionary currently contains 600,000 words from both the past and present, representing the English language from all over the world. This number is increasing. All words are born equal, just like us, however not all words are treated equally, just like us. There are celebrated words, marginalized words, and forgotten words—just like us. Word injustice in English was prevalent particularly during the reign of the British Empire. The global presence of the English language can be attributed, at least in part, to centuries of colonialism and imperialism. Even after the fall of the British Empire, the same injustice was persistent and at times exacerbated. The bigger English grows, the more varieties of English exist, but not all varieties are appreciated. Within each variety, there is the highly regarded standard variety and there are other vernacular varieties that are less esteemed. In principle, there should not be any hierarchy among them, but this is the reality. Many words are suppressed.

"Word injustice" refers to how certain types of words are discriminated against, erased, or classified as "other," "incorrect," or "improper." Many commentators have expressed their desire to preserve the English language against change and argued for a single "standard" model of English. The definition of "proper" English has been debated at least since the vernacular language was first widely set in print for circulation. Among the most common arguments put forward by advocates of "proper" English is that the language should be "purified" or "fixed" in some way. Their comments often show prejudice against so-called "foreign" words, hybrid words, and words from different regions and classes. Unsurprisingly, correct language is linked to ideas about national identity, class, and even morality. These attitudes often demonstrate a sense of superiority and implicit support for a top-down approach to language that does not reflect the reality of its everyday use.

From the seventeenth century onward, preserving English against change became a rallying cry among those English-speaking intellectuals. The English philosopher John Locke resolutely disagreed with language change, declaring "For Words . . . 'tis not for anyone, at pleasure, to change the stamp they are current in; nor alter the *Ideas* they are affixed to."[1] Locke believed that people who used words "without any steady meaning" led themselves and others into error. Only a few years later, Jonathan Swift, the Anglo-Irish satirist and author of *Gulliver's Travels*, attacked those who sought to "polish and refine" English, thus "multiplying Abuses and Absurdities." At the same time, he argued for the unchanging nature of English, suggesting that many words "deserve to be utterly thrown out of our Language; many more to be corrected, and perhaps not a few, long since antiquated, which ought to be restored, on Account of their Energy and Sound."[2]

It was not always a desire for mutual understanding or the restoration of an imagined more glorious past that motivated English-speaking advocates of a proper language. They were also driven by more troubling ideas, particularly related to class and regional differences. Samuel Johnson claimed that words relating to mercantile professions were transient and local, calling them a "fugitive cant" which must "perish." He concluded cruelly that what the laboring classes speak "cannot be regarded as any part of the durable materials of a language."[3] The eighteenth-century Irish elocutionist Thomas Sheridan held a similar view. He wrote that the English that would become fashionable was "the lot of that which prevails at court." Sheridan explained that this was because "All other dialects, are sure marks, either of a provincial, rustic, pedantic, or mechanic education; and therefore have some degree of disgrace annexed to them."[4] Samuel Johnson recommended that "unusual" and "foreign" words should be printed in italics.

By the nineteenth century, advocates used the vocabulary of nationalism to argue that language should not change. Henry Alford, a biblical scholar, wrote in *The Queen's English:* "The national mind is reflected in the national speech. . . . Every important feature in the language of a people has its origin in that people's character and history." Language became a point of national pride, national differentiation, and a reflection of national morality. As a result, "foreign nouns, adjectives, and verbs" became an invasion that threatened "to transform the *manly* English language into a sort of mongrel international slang," about which Alford even noted the use of "inappropriate French or Latin words."[5]

The desire to uphold proper English also animated debates on the emerging separation between British and American English. In the early nineteenth century the American linguist John Pickering attacked neologisms and perceived loss of purity in American English, saying, "we wish, if possible, to stem *that torrent of barbarous phraseology,* with which the *American* writers threaten to destroy the purity of the English language."[6] The English author George Frederick Graham also saw contractions and changes as "corruptions" and claimed that American spellings and neologisms "must be looked upon as abortions or deformations of our language."[7] Of course, not everyone was negative.

Archbishop Richard Chenevix Trench recognized local varieties of English, concluding that "the English language was in reality another name for the sum of a number of local languages."

What the arguments of all these historical advocates for "proper" English reveal is that at the heart of their thinking is an aversion to linguistic diversity and, for many, a hostility to change. They overwhelmingly condemn and ostracize any variation, not on the basis of sound linguistic reasoning, but because of an ideology stemming from their philosophical beliefs, class and regional prejudices, and nationalism.

The impact of linguistic racism did not cease with the end of colonialism; it persists even today. What does "proper" English mean today? There are many world Englishes that employ different spelling, grammar, and pronunciation. However, some Englishes are still perceived as "better than others," with privilege and prejudice based on certain words or accents. A study by Stephanie Lindemann asked seventy-five undergraduate students, all of whom were "native" American English speakers, to label a world map with their perception of the English spoken by international students from a given country.[8] These students widely associated a stigmatized "broken" English with all non-native speakers, except those from France, Germany, and Italy, whose English they described positively. The study also found that the students gave the most consistently stigmatized descriptions for Englishes spoken in East Asia and especially China. It is therefore evident that certain preconceptions continue to pervade our views on what constitutes a supposed "better" or "good" English. Social media means more freedom to adopt new words and spelling variations, but prejudices and injustices still exist, and words are still marginalized. Hybrid words continue to be considered temporary and transitional, often not included in the dictionary. Prescriptive nationalist views about the nature of language still influence us, and attempts at control and censorship by linguistic authorities remain.

In Britain, too, not all dialects and vernaculars are accepted as "proper." In the fourth episode of his podcast series for BBC Sounds, *People Like Us,* barrister Hashi Mohamed discusses how language can help or hinder social mobility. Hashi grew up bilingual, speaking Somali and Swahili. He knew no English when he first began attending school in London. When he did pick up English, it was not received pronunciation but rather Multicultural London English (MLE), which is influenced by Caribbean languages. Hashi quickly realized that this way of speaking was far from a neutral form of language. He noticed that many people had negative associations with MLE and tended to make assumptions about him based on the way he spoke. In other words, the content of his speech was undermined by people's prejudice against its form. He found that by adopting "standard" English associated with white middle-class speakers, he could dramatically change how people perceived and treated him, especially authority figures. In one anecdote, he describes how his parents were having trouble negotiating with the housing office, but when they put Hashi on the phone, he was able to quickly get the issue sorted with his "proper" English, which his current colleagues have described as coming "from the home counties." Hashi realized that language was an integral factor in social mobility, and attributes part of his success in becoming a barrister, a profession where he must now speak in highly formal, archaic language, to his ability to pragmatically adopt the appropriate language to suit his goals. Thus, it is not just so-called world Englishes that are subject to injustice, but also "non-standard" Englishes in places including Britain and America.

As I have already established, the lexicon of English is full of words from all over the map, but not all words with a foreign origin receive the same reception. In English-speaking societies, a speaker's knowledge and use of words with Latin, Greek, French, and German origins has long been interpreted as a sign of intelligence and a high level of education. At the same time, the English of speakers who frequently use non-European vocabulary in their speech has been derided as something less than English and was, and still is, often characterized as a form of pigeon, creole, or slang. This inequality can even manifest in the way words with foreign origins are adopted into English. Latin, Greek, French, and German words are almost always integrated via transliteration and sometimes with no alteration at all, even if the words employ accents or characters unfamiliar to English speakers. By contrast, non-European words will often be subject to calquing, where the components of a word or expression are translated rather than transliterated, obscuring the word's origin. Thus, the embrace or rejection of foreign-origin words in English has been premised on long-standing prejudices and an unstated hierarchy. It is time to move toward a non-hierarchical English, where the diverse origins of our lexicon are celebrated rather than discriminated against.

Word Exchange Injustice

Nelson Mandela famously said, "If you talk to a man in a language he understands, that goes to his head. If you talk to him in his language, that goes to his heart." This question is relevant not only in his time in South Africa but now in Britain. In the United Kingdom, European languages such as French, German, and Spanish have been the primary focus over the years. In the Language Census of 2021, however, French didn't rank in the top ten languages spoken in the United Kingdom. The emphasis on Western European languages is strong despite the significant number of Asian and Eastern European language speakers. This was highlighted by a conversation I had with a Pakistani taxi driver who was frustrated that his children could not learn his native language, Urdu, in Oxford. There are only a few secondary schools offering courses in Urdu. The government cites a lack of interested learners as the reason, but it seems like a weak excuse given that top-down decision-making determines school curricula. Why do we only rarely teach marginalized and low-resourced languages? Meanwhile, French continues to be the primary focus. Why do we mainly concentrate on Western European languages? The policy is outdated and may have roots in the country's post-colonial history. This approach is unhealthy for our growing generation.

Ernie Dingo, an Aboriginal actor and Yamatji man, argued:

> We all know how to say yes in Spanish don't we? We all know how to say yes in German don't we? We all know how to say yes in French don't we? Do we know how to say yes in any of the 360 Aboriginal dialects in this country?[9]

If we take a moment to pause and really think about Dingo's observation, he seems to draw attention to a serious problem with the modern English lexicon. Sure, we have words such as *kangaroo*, *koala*, and *boomerang* that can be traced to Australian Aboriginal languages, but the ever present bias toward Western European languages points to a more haunting reality. A significant proportion of Asian heritage words that have made their way into the English language are related to culinary terms, while words related to new ideas and technology tend to reveal a Eurocentric bias. Asian and African heritage words still make up a relatively small proportion of the overall English lexicon. Similarly, the words from former colonies also face the same issue. Many established English dictionaries published in the United States and the United Kingdom have limited inclusion of words from these other varieties. This raises the question of whether these dictionaries are inclusive enough and whether they adequately represent the linguistic diversity of the English-speaking world.

Historically, the initial waves of Asian migrants to Europe and America can be traced back to the early nineteenth century, following the emergence of nation-states, which changed labor recruitment patterns and encouraged new nations to attract migrants for the purposes of foreign labor and providing citizenship. An estimated 60 million people migrated to the Americas from 1820 to 1940, of which 3 million originated from Africa as well as India, China, and Japan.[10] Asians have resided in America for more than a hundred and fifty years, with the earliest migrants being of Japanese, Filipino, Chinese, and Korean descent.[11] The bulk of Asians arrived in America following the adoption of the Immigration Act of 1965, resulting in the Asian American population skyrocketing from 1.4 million in 1970 to 12 million in 2000.[12] Conversely, the presence of Asians in other English-speaking countries such as Australia, New Zealand, and Canada is a more recent occurrence, with large-scale migration taking place mostly only during the recent few decades.[13]

Following the advent of the twenty-first century and a globalized world economy, Asian migration patterns have become more dynamic than ever before. There has been a significant migrant outflow from Asia to Europe, with English-speaking countries in Europe being the most popular destinations for these Asian migrants from diverse ethnicities, including Thais, Chinese, Filipinos, and Indians.[14] In 2001, the traditional destinations for Asian migrants were largely four major English-speaking countries: Australia, the United States, Canada, and New Zealand, which accounted for more than 70 percent of these migrants, or around 10.7 million people.[15] Outflows to Europe and Japan were also significant, totaling almost 30 percent (or around 4 million) of the total Asian migrant population. The top countries where these Asian migrants hail from include the People's Republic of China, India, South Korea, Pakistan, the Philippines, and Vietnam.

More recent figures from 2006 to 2011 show that Asians continue to account for significant portions of immigrants to the five

Anglophone countries of Canada, the United States, Australia, New Zealand, and the United Kingdom. Of these, Australia and the United States receive the highest proportions. These immigrants have obviously had a major impact on the language landscape of their inner-circle host countries, increasing their number of Asian language speakers and the number of individuals who are natively bilingual in an Asian language and English. English no longer belongs to a small subset of people of a particular class and background, which demonstrates that it is time for us to pay greater attention to the increasingly dominant role that Asian populations and their languages are playing in shaping English.

When I go to pick my daughters up from their primary school in Oxfordshire, I hear an array of different languages in the playground. The school is so diverse, but how much do the students, or even parents, know about each other's languages? Do we truly know how to appreciate our diversity? A few years ago, I led a workshop at my daughter's school on the topic of linguistic diversity. When I asked which language is spoken in India, the answer I received was "Indian," a language that does not exist. Even the students of Indian heritage were not able to answer. Hundreds of thousands of people living in the United Kingdom are of Indian background, yet our young people are not even aware of which languages are spoken in India. If I were to go to an American primary school and ask which languages are spoken in China, I can imagine I might also hear "Chinese," with little mention of Mandarin, Cantonese, Hokkien, or any other Chinese dialects. This demonstrates a lack of appreciation for our languages and a blindness to the reality of the world we live in.

Ultimately, this kind of ignorance results in prejudice and hate. Lack of awareness demonstrates the need for change in education and academia, with greater attention and resources required to promote Asian languages and culture. Although Asian words are occasionally included in English dictionaries, they cover only a small number of entries. In the context of Asia-Europe linguistic interaction, the vast majority of words have moved from English into Asian countries, while only a handful of words from Asia have made their way into the English language. This phenomenon raises questions about the underlying cultural and societal factors that contribute to the lack of representation of Asian languages in English. By exploring the historical, social, and cultural influences on language development, we can gain a better understanding of the complex nature of linguistic exchange and its implications for cultural diversity and representation.

The majority of words found in English dictionaries are derived from Western European roots. However, with demographic changes, I believe this will and must change. Asian appearances were relatively rare in the English-speaking world and Europe until the nineteenth century. As demographics continue to shift, language will adapt and change to reflect the diversity of its speakers. This change will happen in our word pantry, but whether dictionaries will reflect this in time remains to be seen.

Indeed, on a global scale, we have seen word exchange injustice taking place throughout history, as in the linguistic exchanges between Japan and Europe. Compared with its neighboring countries, Japan opened its ports to Europe relatively early and peacefully. Contact between Japan and the West began as early as 1545, when a Portuguese ship reached the shores of Tanegashima Island, initiating the first meeting between Japanese and Europeans. A few years later, in 1549, a Jesuit mission was sent to Japan. The words that entered into Japanese in this period included religious terms such as *Misa* ("mass," 1591), and country names like *Igirisu* ("England," 1613) and *Oranda* ("Holland," 1698). Some of the first Portuguese words include *tempura*. *Tempura* is regarded as a typical Japanese word referring to a dish consisting of prawn, shrimp, or white fish, and often vegetables, coated in batter and then deep fried. This word is originally from Portuguese, *tempero*, "a meal taken on Fridays in Christian countries." After the closing of Japan, from around 1639, Dutch merchants were present in Dejima in the Bay of Nagasaki. This resulted in a more active contact and import of European notions and products in Japan and the rise of so-called "Dutch learning" (*rangaku*). The word *rangaku* came from *ran*, or "Dutch" (from "Oranda," for "Holland") + *gaku*, meaning "learning," and was used later to refer to Western learning in general. *Rangaku* introduced a lot of new words into Japanese:

> Food and drink: *koohii*, "coffee" (1615), *biiru*, "beer" (1724)
>
> Materials: *garasu*, "pane of glass" (1763), *gomu*, "rubber" (1822)
>
> Leisure: *orugooru*, "music box" (1803), *dansu*, "dance" (1831)
>
> Maritime terminology: *dekki*, "deck" (1857)
>
> Medicine and science: *korera*, "cholera" (1793), *pesuto*, "plague," or Black Death (1829)
>
> Foreign currencies: *doru*, "dollar," *pondo*, "pound" (1822)
>
> Place names: *doitsu*, "Germany" (1725)

Japanese has not only borrowed words from the West but has also contributed words to the English and European lexicon. One of the earliest examples is the Japanese liquor *sake*, which was recorded in European texts as early as 1687, and was defined in the OED: "Their ordinary drink is a kind of Beer (which they call Saque) made of Rice."[16]

Words from other Asian countries have been absorbed into the English language, although the number is relatively small.[17] This is surprising given the significant influence of Asian cultures on areas such as technology, cuisine, and art. The reason for this could be that established English dictionaries, mainly published in the United States and the United Kingdom, are not inclusive enough in their coverage of non-English languages. This leads to a lack of recognition and appreciation for the contributions of non-Western cultures to the English language. Furthermore, there may be a bias toward words from European languages, which are often viewed as more prestigious or sophisticated, at the expense of Asian languages. Henry Bradley, the editor of the OED between 1915 and 1923, continued to include foreign words in the dictionary but did not consider them "really English." His opinion on Chinese words was particularly illustrative: "China has given us tea and the names of various kinds of tea; and a good many other Chinese words figure in our larger dictionaries, though they cannot be said to have become really English."[18] Thus, we can see that linguistic diversity has been criticized by many on the grounds of class, region, and nationality.

Furthermore, it is interesting to note that in East Asia before the twentieth century, Chinese words were considered the primary social linguistic capital, reserved for the rich and elite. As the century progressed, however, this prestige and privilege were rapidly overtaken by English. Nowadays, English words hold significant value as a currency in many Asian countries, where there is even a term coined to describe the enthusiasm for English: English fever.

Since the nineteenth century, texts from colonial powers in the industrial West have been translated widely in non-European countries in the name of modernization. At that time, translation of such texts was often a matter of survival. The transmission of text was largely one directional. Non-European countries were the recipients of heaps and heaps of Western texts, while Europe received comparatively few non-European texts. Such relational dynamics remained in the twentieth century and were even reinforced as English became the global lingua franca. Non-European texts remained untranslated and, thus, unknown.

In the rare instances when a text was translated into English, naturalness in English was often stressed as being key to a good translation. No matter the source text, English readers were put first. An interesting example of this phenomenon is Ezra Pound's translations of Chinese poetry, particularly from the Tang dynasty. Famous for his modernist poetry, Pound also published a book of translations of Chinese poetry titled *Cathay*. Pound himself, however, could neither speak nor write Chinese. He received the draft translations of Chinese poems from Ernest Fenollosa, a Harvard graduate Orientalist who became the first chair in philosophy at Tokyo University, and Pound edited and then published them. The reception of these translations has varied, and Pound has been criticized for overemphasizing the so-called ideographic nature of Chinese and limiting Chinese characters to being purely "imagistic expressionism." Pound thought he was able to translate Chinese poetry without knowing the language.

Indeed, such Eurocentrism extends beyond translation and finds itself embedded in our very classifications of languages. The dictionary definition of *modern* is "of or relating to the present and recent times, as opposed to the remote past; of, relating to, or originating in the current age or period." In practice, however, what is considered "modern" is often associated with good things that originate from Western European cultures. Many people in the United States, the United Kingdom, and Australia speak Asian languages, but these are rarely referred to as modern. Languages are often classified into categories of Asian, modern, and classical. In the United Kingdom, "modern languages" really refers to French, German, and Spanish.[19] In fact, at the University of Oxford, the modern languages faculty offers only Czech, French, German, modern Greek, Italian, Polish, Portuguese, Russian, and Spanish. Meanwhile, Mandarin, Japanese, Arabic, Turkish, and Korean are offered by the faculty of Middle Eastern and Asian studies. Why can't Asian languages be considered modern even if the majority of their speakers are Asian? This demonstrates a larger issue of prejudice toward Asians in academia and the education sector.

As Michelle Yeoh said during her acceptance speech after winning an Oscar in 2023: "For all the little boys and girls who look like me watching tonight, this is a beacon of hope and possibilities. This is proof—dream big and dreams do come true." She was the first Asian woman to receive an Academy Award for best actress, and her win was a remarkable achievement. Yet it also highlighted the existence of a glass ceiling for Asian people and other ethnicities, both in the entertainment industry and beyond. This impediment extends to language, with many words of non-Western origin struggling to gain entry into English. Words that enter from Asia are mainly food words. Some words with Asian origins often have negative and condescending connotations. They may not receive the same recognition and respect as words with Western European origins.

One may initially think "BTS" is an abbreviation for "behind the scenes," but now an equally popular meaning for these three letters is the wildly famous Korean boy band Bangtan Sonyeondan. Why is "Beatles" in the dictionary, but "BTS" not? Shouldn't this expression deserve a space in the English word pantry? This reflects the larger systemic biases and prejudices that exist in our societies, perpetuating a narrow view of the world that does not accurately reflect the diversity and richness of the cultures and the people in it. The Stop Asian Hate movement, bringing attention to the racism and discrimination faced by Asian people, has made such injustices more visible.

Words of Asian origin are often arbitrarily adopted in English and used in other ways. *Xiangqi,* for example, a board game played widely in China, is often referred to in English as "Chinese chess." Although it is a strategic board game, it is distinctly different from chess. The term *Chinese chess* takes Western chess as the norm and suggests that xiangqi is a secondary version of the game. Both chess and xiangqi are old games, but why is xiangqi referred to as "Chinese chess," while chess is never referred to as "European xiangqi"?

Words can also be deleted. Recent research by the linguist and lexicographer, as well as a former editor of the OED, Sarah Ogilvie has traced changing approaches to words of foreign origin in the Oxford English Dictionary since the time of James Murray. Ogilvie has shown that the OED's chief editor between 1971 and 1986, Robert Burchfield, who was responsible for the four-volume second supplement to the dictionary, deleted 17 percent of the neologisms, adaptations, and foreign-born words that had been included in the first supplement published in 1933. This is particularly surprising both because Burchfield marketed the second supplement as a suitable replacement for the first supplement and because the loss of entries was a violation of the OED's long-standing policy of never deleting words from the dictionary, instead opting to indicate they had fallen out of use by placing a small dagger next to the headword. Ogilvie's analysis of the two supplements also revealed that, contrary to popular beliefs about changing approaches to words of foreign origin by English language lexicographers over the course of the twentieth century, the earlier supplement actually had a higher proportion of loanwords and world Englishes than the supplements published by Burchfield. Burchfield also opted to reinstate Murray's policy of marking the headword of entries for words that were "alien or not yet naturalized" in English but still used, which for complex reasons had been dropped by the editors of the 1933 supplement.

Decolonizing English

European imperialism in Africa had a devastating impact on the continent's linguistic diversity. Before the arrival of European powers, Africa boasted thousands of languages, each reflecting the distinct cultures, traditions, and histories of its diverse peoples. However, as European powers jostled to colonize Africa, they forced their languages and cultures on the local populations, often using violence and coercion to suppress indigenous languages and traditions. The colonial powers viewed indigenous languages as inferior and sought to replace them with their own languages. They established schools that taught European languages, such as English, French, and Portuguese, and discouraged the use of African languages in the classroom. This had a profound impact on younger generations, many of whom grew up speaking European languages rather than their native tongues. As a result, many African languages have become endangered or even extinct. Entire language families have been wiped out, taking valuable knowledge and cultural traditions with them. Furthermore, the imposition of European languages has led to a loss of identity and disconnection from cultural heritage for many African communities.

European colonizers also imposed their own interests or history in naming African places. The capital of the former Belgian Congo (now the Democratic Republic of the Congo) was named Leopoldville (now Kinshasa) after King Leopold II of Belgium, who was the primary instigator of the colonization of the region. Rhodesia (now Zimbabwe) was named after Cecil Rhodes, a British colonialist who played a major role in the colonization of southern Africa. These steps all diminished the identities of nations and communities on the African continent.

Today, the linguistic landscape of Africa is complex and diverse. Many African countries have recognized the importance of preserving and promoting indigenous languages and have taken steps to promote the use of local languages in education, government, and media. European languages, however, remain widely spoken and continue to be used in formal settings such as government and education. English, in particular, has become a lingua franca across many African countries and is often used as a medium of communication among speakers of different African languages. Many indigenous languages and words have been replaced with English and other European words. Conversely, the impact of words from Africa and Asia on the English language has been relatively small, despite the large populations of these regions. Although there are natural products originating from these regions, they are often understood as European words by birth. Who would think of *banana* as a foreign-born word? The linguistic impact of European colonization on Africa was so immense that it virtually wiped out the continent's original word fields. Although a few African words, such as *banana, rooibos tea, jumbo,* and *apartheid,* have made their way into the English language and European lexicon, the majority of the continent's linguistic diversity has been replaced by European words and languages.

The word *banana* entered English through Portuguese and Spanish. Its origins can be traced back to Wolof, a West African language spoken in Senegal, the Gambia, and Mauritania, where the word for it is *banaana.* When Portuguese traders and explorers arrived in West Africa in the late fifteenth century, they encountered the fruit and adopted the Wolof word *banaana.* From there, the word entered Spanish, and then other European languages, including English. The first known recorded use of the word *banana* in English was in 1597, in a book called *The Historie of Travell into Virginia Britania,* by John Josselyn. The book describes Josselyn's travels in the Americas, where he encountered the fruit and referred to it as "bananas." The word *banana* was also used by William Dampier in his book *A New Voyage Around the World,* published in 1697. Dampier describes his travels in the Pacific, where he encountered the fruit and referred to it as "the Bonano tree," noting that it was similar to the plantain.

Now turn to the word *apartheid. Apartheid* most commonly refers to the political regime of racial segregation in South Africa from 1948 to the early '90s. *Apartheid* has entered the dictionary of many foreign languages; however, its linguistic origins are complex. It entered English and many other languages via Afrikaans, spoken in South Africa. But its origins in Afrikaans stem from the Dutch colonial presence in South Africa. The word *apartheid* is formed through the combination of Dutch *apart* (from the French *à part*) and the suffix *-heid,* meaning "-hood." It therefore means "aparthood" or "separateness." However, it is not used to refer to a general state of being apart. The word as it has entered global vocabularies has now been fossilized with its political and colonial history as a descriptor of racial segregation and inequality. Because of the context through which it became known to the world, there is no other word that could be used in its stead. It's not used to refer to its direct meaning of general "separateness," because its use automatically makes the listener think of the context of South African segregation.

"Apartheid" is now the name of a crime under international law, but its political meaning is still fossilized within the word itself. Even when used to describe a context other than South Africa, the memory of and feelings about South African apartheid remain, lending an additional layer of meaning that often manifests as outrage at injustice. The term *food apartheid,* for example, refers to a lack of access to high quality and nutritional foods in certain communities as a result of active institutional and governmental processes intended to exclude them. Similarly, there was global discussion of "vaccine apartheid" as wealthy and predominantly Western countries received first access to the Covid-19 vaccine while less wealthy nations struggled to secure supplies. The meaning of *apartheid* has retained its South African history and its association with injustice, but it has developed alongside our understandings of the various forms of racial and economic injustice as well—and is now used to refer to forms of injustice with overt or underlying political intentions.

We must keep in mind that word injustice is not limited to English, as it can be found in other languages and cultures as well. English has been introduced to former colonies and has evolved into hybrid varieties, which require appropriate recognition and respect. To truly serve people worldwide, English needs to embrace diversity and overcome its Eurocentric bias. The word pantry also needs to be decolonized by welcoming more words from different parts of the world. On one hand, it is useful to be able to interact through a shared language, but on the other, it creates a great deal of injustice. The diversity of so many words, including their sounds and their meanings, has been lost in the process of anglicization. Non-English words are tuned to suit the English ear, so that we can all have an anglicized common vocabulary. Local voices and dialects are wiped out in the pursuit of building standard English, and so the diverse origins of our words are lost. Then, a more conscious effort is needed to decolonize and diversify present-day English.

The first entry under *lingua franca* in the OED states the following: "A pidgin language drawing its lexicon mainly from the southern Romance languages and formerly used as a trading language, first in the eastern Mediterranean and later throughout much of northern Africa and the Middle East. Frequently with capital initials. Now *historical*."[20] Many of us, however, will understand this term more in the following sense: "Any language that is used by speakers of different languages as a common medium of communication; a common language." Historically speaking, English became a lingua franca in the late nineteenth and early twentieth centuries as a result of colonization by the British Empire, which exported its own language to all corners of the earth. It is power and politics that have seen English become a global language.

At one time, the British Empire encompassed almost a quarter of the world, making English a significant language in many colonies. In Asia and Africa, English may not have been the people's language, but it was the language of trade. It was the language of the elite and afforded access to education and advancement. Eventually, the countries that made up the British Empire gained their independence, but they still needed to communicate with each other. English arose as the medium for communication because the most influential people already spoke it. It was inevitable that through economic influence, English would become the language of business and politics. More and more people are learning business English for this reason. It acquired a firm foothold and remains the dominant or official language in many territories.

English gradually became more and more significant globally, but it was not the first European language of colonization. As recently as the nineteenth century, it was more common for those with different native languages to communicate in French. History also shows that English would never have become the world's lingua franca had the United States not evolved into such a powerful nation. The American economy boomed after World War II, reinforcing English as the language of trade and finance. As a result, American influence spread far and wide. All nations needed to trade with the United States, and the ability to speak English was crucial to those seeking careers in business or politics. It was the power and influence of the British Empire and later the United States that resulted in English becoming a lingua franca, so it is fundamentally the output of colonialism. Although English has come to be a valuable tool for many people across the globe, we need to overcome colonial discourse by decolonizing and de-Westernizing linguistic resources. It's not so much about changing languages but allowing English to live more organically and as a more diversified entity. The great part is that we are already seeing it as our word pantries are changing to be more diverse.

Yet such changes are not limited to our lexicon. "The rain in Spain falls mainly in the plain" is a phrase used in the film *My Fair Lady* by Professor Higgins, a professor of phonetics, when trying to teach the film's protagonist, Eliza Doolittle, how to speak "proper" English. Doolittle, a young woman from London who originally speaks with a strong Cockney accent, learns to speak with an upper-class English accent after mastering this particular phrase. In the film, speaking "properly" is seen by most characters as an essential factor in becoming successful in one's career and endeavors in general. The film is based on the play *Pygmalion* from 1913 by George Bernard Shaw, the title of which is derived from a Greek mythological figure who falls in love with one of his statues that then comes to life.

The English language is often thought of as the linguistic capital of Great Britain. In other words, authority over the language's proper form and pronunciation is thought to reside in Britain. The influence of decolonization in the twentieth century contributed greatly to this view, with an upper-class southern English accent (sometimes referred to as the Queen's English) thrown into stark relief against the increasing number of world Englishes, all with vastly different pronunciation systems, developing as a result of the disintegration of the British Empire. These different local varieties of English were always known to English linguists. However, they have historically been, and often still are, considered peripheral. This hierarchical view of the English language treats a particular pronunciation as the most acceptable form, followed by other British varieties, then the accents of those for whom English is a first language (such as the United States or Australia), then those for whom English was introduced as a second language through colonial occupation (such as India or Singapore). The hierarchical view of pronunciation considers "peripheral" accents improper or informal, instead preferring and taking more seriously those with accents from the top of the hierarchical pyramid, often leading to better social and economic opportunities and thereby contributing to the perpetuation of social class distinctions. A shift in the use of global Englishes has accompanied the modernization and globalization of recent decades. With the increasingly interchangeable use of languages by users across the globe, new problems have arisen in pronunciation, particularly regarding what we deem proper, which must be addressed.

The nuances of language are constantly evolving, and this can be seen in the changing perceptions of certain dialects and slang terms. Multicultural London English (MLE), for example, which was once negatively viewed, has now become a powerful and dominant variety of English. In MLE, the greeting "Wagwan" is commonly used as a contraction of the Jamaican patois phrase "What's going on?" and is a casual way of saying "hello." Similarly, the slang term *peng* is used in MLE to describe someone as attractive and good-looking. It can also be used to describe something that is impressive or excellent. Once stigmatized, it has now gained acceptance and popularity, becoming recognized as a vibrant and cool variation of the English language among Britons. Similarly, John McWhorter's book *Talking Back, Talking Black: Truths About America's Lingua Franca* explores how Black English has evolved into a significant and influential form of communication in America, serving as a widely spoken and recognized lingua franca. This is a testament to how language nuances change based on the language users and environments they are used in.

English Language Conventions

Some English speakers, like me, learn their English abroad before coming to live and work for much of their lives in a country where English is the dominant language; others will learn and use their English in a non-native setting for their entire lives. Still other speakers will grow up learning English in places such as India, Pakistan, Hong Kong, or Singapore. These are outer circle English countries where the English language no doubt holds a special status and is extremely widely spoken, but which do not exercise the same power over the language as inner circle English countries that set global standards for fluency, spelling, and orthography. As we will see in this section, for English speakers like those described above, the selection of English language conventions, whether on a personal or national level, often extends beyond matters of personal identity to reflect pragmatic choices as well as the pressures of geopolitics and global trade.

Let me open this discussion by recounting my own experience with English language conventions as someone who began to learn English in the expanding circle but has now lived in the inner circle for many years. In South Korea at the age of twelve, I began to learn American English, and for the next ten years I learned and spoke American English. Twenty years ago, however, I moved to England and everything changed. I began to find it beneficial to employ British English conventions for my scholarship as well as in my daily life. But the reality is, like most second language learners of English, my life trajectory has meant that I have never had a strong opinion about, or affiliation with, a particular set of spelling conventions. Instead, I choose one or the other for pragmatic reasons, such as who my intended audience might be. For this book, my publisher is primarily located in the United States, so I have made the pragmatic choice to follow American spelling and grammatical conventions. For many English language speakers born outside Britain and the United States, personal pragmatism, like my own, will determine the selection of English language conventions, but in the following sections, I will also consider how other external pressures have shaped the way "proper English" is taught. Even so, I may not find it easy to choose everything from American English—simply because British English words are closest to my daily life. I feel uncomfortable using *soccer players,* for instance, over *football players.*

Let's pause to consider spelling conventions, another of the ways written Englishes often differentiate themselves. If different

Englishes often have different spellings, and as we heard before, James Murray, editor of the Oxford English Dictionary, considered the vocabulary of all forms of English legitimate objects for inclusion in his dictionary, what spelling conventions does the world's most prestigious English dictionary follow?

Well, the OED aims to be the global standard for English dictionaries and is used as a resource by writers, publishers, and academics across the English-speaking world. It has been setting the standard for spelling since the late nineteenth century. Yet what norms determine the spelling conventions it upholds in its entries? To analyze this question, we can interrogate the identities encoded within the name. It is the Oxford English Dictionary, produced by Oxford University Press, so one might hazard a guess that it is bound by the British English conventions of the esteemed and historic Oxford University.

If this were the case, what are the conventions of the Queen's English that we might expect it to follow? Some might be familiar to you even if you have never used British English, such as its preference for the "-ise" ending in words such as *recognise* and *organise,* "-our" spellings in such words as *colour* and *labour,* and its use of the letter "u" rather than "o" in the word *mum.* Others might be more unfamiliar unless you've lived in a location where everyday communication favors the conventions of British English, such as the use of "-yse" in words like *analyse* and *catalyse,* the almost francophone final "-e" in words such as *centre* and *programme,* the retention of "e" for pronunciation in *ageing* and *acknowledgement,* the use of a double "l" in *traveller, travelling,* and *travelled,* and the use of "c" rather than "s" in such words as *defence, licence, offence,* and *pretence.*

Yet you might be shocked to learn that although students and professors at Oxford are encouraged by the university to use exactly these conventions in their exams, dissertations, and published works, the Oxford English Dictionary and the Oxford University Press employ a different set of spelling conventions for their works. They call this alternative convention "Oxford spelling," and it differs from British English spellings in preferring "-ize" endings instead of "-ise," so *organise* and *organisation* become *organize* and *organization,* and *realise* becomes *realize*—but "-yse" endings and the other peculiarities of British spelling remain unchanged.

So then, are the OED's spelling conventions a dramatic betrayal of the Queen's English by the dictionary that has been setting spelling standards for English since the late 1800s? Not quite. The dictionary and the press maintain that their use of "-ize" endings has been consistent since its first edition, which was issued in parts between 1884 and 1928. They claim that their slightly different preference stands on firm etymological grounding because the "-ize" ending is more similar in sound to the Greek verb endings that the suffix descends from. In fact, in the earliest printings of the King James Bible and the printed works of Shakespeare, the "-ize" endings are used throughout; in commenting on the "-ize"/"-ise" debate in the past, the OED has noted that its earliest example of *realize* dates from 1611, whereas no example using the spelling *realise* has been found from before 1755.

Turning to economics and geopolitics on a more international scale, to illustrate the pressure these factors can place on the selection of English language conventions, let's look first at the issue of English language education in modern-day Singapore. The island of Singapore came under British colonial rule in 1819 and existed in some form of less than total self-government until mid-1959, after which it enjoyed home rule over all but issues of defense and foreign policy. Over more than a century of British rule, English was established as the island's lingua franca for commerce and inter-ethnic communication. English is one of the nation's four official languages, and it is the only language of instruction in public schools.

You might expect that given the influence of British colonial rule, Singaporeans would uphold the conventions of British English, and to some extent this was the case in the years immediately following independence. However, by 2011, the situation had broken down, and Prime Minister Lee Kuan Yew openly admitted that it was a challenge to determine whether Singapore should use British or American English. What motivated Lee to address this challenge? "The increasing dominance of the American media," their "sheer numbers," and "the dominance of their economy," he stated, were the primary reasons why Singaporeans needed to be familiar with American English. He also linked the nation's long-term economic success to its population's continued proficiency in English, crediting the English-speaking environment as an advantage over surrounding countries for attracting foreign talent, because it made living and working there easier.[21]

In response to these factors, Lee suggested a shift to teaching American English in Singaporean schools. Both American and British English spelling and grammar are now accepted in national student exams. Although the switch to American English has not yet been fully realized, the Ministry of Education's English grammar reference book for secondary school highlights regional variations in British and American vocabulary, although British English remains the default. Similarly, the ministry's English language syllabus accepts either American or British spellings as long as they are used consistently. What is clear from Lee's comments and the changes to Singapore's English language education designed to make American English more familiar to Singaporeans is that they were a pragmatic response to the reality of the commercial dominance of the United States over global media and trade, rather than by any deep-seated change in national identity.

Even though Singapore's selection of language conventions has been inflected by the legacy of British colonialism, for those in the expanding circle countries, decisions about spelling and pronunciation conventions have much less to do with historical experience. Unconcerned by the outdated pursuit of authenticity and purity, Singaporeans employ British or American English according to individual conventions and one's specific needs. It is a pragmatic choice based on consideration of power dynamics. In this way, such language choices are strategic decisions.

Indeed, second language learners mixing British and American English in their writing, and the alternative conventions used in English language speaking countries in parts of Africa and Asia, expose another issue with our existing metrics for English fluency. Beyond the inner circle of English, language proficiency is assessed by the International English Language Testing System (IELTS) and the Test of English as a Foreign Language (TOEFL). These globally recognized exams allow test takers to respond in either British or American English, but they continue to penalize examinees for mixing British and American English spelling conventions and pronunciations. There is an unconscious and unnoticed mixing of American and British standard English by even "native" speakers as a result of media influence and social media—so is what we class as "correct" changing? In this way the exams fail to reflect the reality that these distinctions are meaningless for the majority of English language speakers. Similarly, for those who inhabit countries traditionally in the outer circle of English, the ubiquity of IELTS and TOEFL requirements raises a number of other concerns. Given the relatively small number of former colonial possessions that the American and British governments classify as majority native English speaking, many first language speakers of English in places such as India, Pakistan, Singapore, the Philippines, and Nigeria are frequently required to prove their fluency in their primary language. Similarly, these speakers may wonder why their former colonial possessors get to set the standards of English proficiency, while local English conventions are dismissed as incorrect.

For most of us, "broken English" is a phrase that we would have heard plenty of times over the course of our lives, but can you think of any other language that can be called broken? We do not label speakers of other languages with less proficiency as broken language speakers. As such, it is an Anglocentric term. Although a regular part of common parlance in most English-speaking countries, "broken English" can have a distinctly detrimental effect on those learning and speaking English as a second language as a part of their everyday lives. The phrase "broken English" clearly suggests that there is a correct English and an incorrect English. Not only does this phrase stigmatize learners of English who speak with unconventional grammar or "foreign" accents, but it also upholds the view (unfortunately prevalent in many English-speaking contexts) that English is the most important language in any given speaker's arsenal, and that being unable to speak English fluently implies that one's linguistic ability (and, as an extension, general intelligence) is inferior to those who speak it fluently, regardless of how many other languages a person may speak. I therefore propose that not only is the phrase "broken English" a source of shame and stigma, and generally detrimental to the spread of language learning and intercultural communication on a worldwide scale, but it is also flawed in its conception as a manner of distinguishing an imagined "primary" group of speakers from "secondary" (or lesser) speakers.

How do we even define brokenness? In an article on the BBC website concerning the BAFTA film awards for 2021, an acceptance speech given by the Korean actress Yuh-Jung Youn for her supporting role in the Korean-American film *Minari* was described in the following way:

The supporting actress trophy went to South Korea's Yuh-Jung Youn for playing a grandmother in Korean-American drama Minari. Giving her speech in broken English, the 73-year-old said the award meant a lot because Brits were "snobbish" people.[22]

In many of Youn's various acceptance speeches and interviews over the course of the 2021 awards season, audiences appear to find humor in the way she uses the English language, such as in her Oscars speech, in which she stated that her two sons made "mummy work hard," and commented on English speakers' various incorrect ways of pronouncing her name, all in a playful way. Far from undermining her intention or hindering her self-expression, her interesting use of English acts as a source of fun and novelty, playing up to her audience and making her stand out among the vast swaths of native English-speaking award winners giving acceptance speeches in fluent English. Compared with the recent visit of King Charles III to Germany, during which he was praised in the media for merely speaking a few sentences of German, the expectation for a Korean grandma to speak English fluently in order to avoid accusations of "broken English" is hypocritical.

Youn's speech is an excellent example of the true diversity of the English language when it is opened up to speakers of various cultural and linguistic backgrounds and experiences as equals, without judgment or expectations of attaining a certain level of "proficiency" as determined by native speakers. This shows how the English that many may otherwise consider "broken" can in fact bring fun and interest into what may otherwise be a very standard speech. Furthermore, the foregrounding of various forms of English in the media in this way—without comment on its being "broken" or otherwise—helps to build solidarity among those speaking English as an additional language and between first- and second-language English speakers. Thus, English like Youn's should never be condemned as "broken," but rather seen as innovative and playful.

Where Are You *Really* From?

On a personal level, the question "Where are you from?" is frequently one of the first topics of conversation that I am engaged in when I meet someone for the first time in my day-to-day life. When asked this question outside of the United Kingdom, I say that I am from the U.K. However, this answer more often than not appears to leave the inquirer dissatisfied, so I eventually explain that I am "originally" from South Korea, upon which the other person says "aha" and nods. I often wonder to myself whether I would be asked the same question if I looked the same as those around me; I am confident that the same question is leveled at white Europeans living in Asia or Africa. However, to many of us, this question can sound rude and unwelcoming. In our increasingly connected global atmosphere, billions of us are living in locations where we could easily be considered "foreigners." However, nobody wishes to be pointed out as different or treated like an "Other" in the place that we live, that we seek to call home. From a linguistic perspective, being asked where one is from signifies that you are speaking a language that is not your own. It betrays an underlying sentiment that there is a "proper English" and a foreign English.

In the world of academia, I am often asked where I am from, sometimes even before I am asked my name. In the sciences, "proper English" is not such a big issue, as scientists have their own technical language through which to communicate. The humanities are different. I have to translate all of my work into English at all times. Academics who did not grow up in an English-speaking environment take on a huge burden to translate their work for the English-speaking world. So much great academic thinking gets lost because academics who cannot speak English have no way of taking their research to a wider audience. This is another form of language injustice.

I've also seen how the necessity to learn English troubles students in the higher education systems. In Turkey, for example, many of the country's top universities—such as Boğaziçi, Sabancı, and Koç—employ English as their primary language of instruction. In almost every class at these universities, students are expected to read, write, and discuss the course in English, and consequently these schools heavily weight the results of strenuous English language exams in their admissions processes. Students typically graduate with a level of fluency that allows them to comfortably operate in environments that demand academic and professional English, a fact attested by their high level of success at gaining admission to British and American graduate schools. Yet many students I've spoken to privately express concern that their English skills are insufficient for work or life in an Anglophone country, hyper-fixating on what they perceive as their failure to master small differences of pronunciation or minor grammar rules—issues that have no impact on their ability to express themselves or on my ability to comprehend them. In my time working as a professor, I have similarly seen cases where great academics who do not speak English well go without the recognition they deserve. Setting such standards for English proficiency thus seems unfair, as much knowledge exchange is blocked by them.

The idea that any of us lead truly monolingual lives seems increasingly antiquated. Despite this, many of our institutions stubbornly stick to these categories of "native" and "foreign." For instance, the Korean American director Lee Isaac Chung's semi-autobiographical film *Minari* was nominated not for "Best Drama" but for "Best Foreign Language Film," despite being a film set in America that tells the story of an immigrant family chasing the American dream. It was categorized with other "Foreign Language" films because it was judged to feature too much Korean dialogue. Although one could make the case that the decision was justified because the film does, indeed, feature primarily Korean dialogue, it raises the question, "Why do we need a foreign language category in the first place?" Foreign-language media has become such a normal part of so many of our lives that it seems strange to arbitrarily judge these films in their own separate category. In the case of *Minari*, this is especially jarring as it is an American film, taking place in America, featuring a mainly American cast, and dealing with American issues. Following the decision to place the film in the foreign language category, Lulu Wang, director of *The Farewell*, tweeted, "I have not seen a more American film than #Minari this year. It's a story about an immigrant family, In America, pursuing the American dream. We really need to change these antiquated rules that characterize Americans as only English-speaking."[23] In this case, language was the determining factor of the film's foreignness. This decision might make sense on some level, but questions about what is "foreign" are becoming harder to answer in a globalized world. We might even argue that the term *foreign* for language is no longer relevant. The Golden Globes have since renamed the Best Foreign Language Picture category to Best Non-English Language Picture, but whether English language and non-English language films should still be considered separately is contentious.

On the other hand, Australia may present different cases compared with other places. To start with, the label "foreign" is altogether dropped when describing languages. The term *foreign language* is not used in any official capacity. So as not to be exclusionary or hierarchical, languages are simply described as "languages," no matter whether they are commonly spoken in Australia or not. This might seem like a small action, but it is representative of a larger attitude that welcomes people of all backgrounds in Australia. When I went to Perth, Australia, I was surprised to hear Korean spoken to me when I put my passport down on the eGate. In Europe, eGates tend to use only English. I also noticed that the departure board showed destinations written in both English and their local script. Seeing this made me feel safe and welcomed, particularly compared with U.K. border control, where I have seen visitors grilled for their lack of English proficiency. Language binds or breaks us. It can make us feel welcomed, but it can also make us feel threatened and isolated. Having a common language, like English, has just as much potential to make us feel unsafe as safe.

Call for Word Diversity

We need to expand the English lexicon in order to better represent the diversity of the world. Words can enter the language in either translated or transliterated forms, and we need more of them. In the past, translated forms were generally preferred for the sake of making the language more understandable to English speakers, and familiar words were often chosen. However, in this era of diversity, we should focus on catering to not only an English audience, but also to a global audience. According to the British Council's Language Trends 2015 Report, the number of students studying languages has plummeted in recent years, especially in countries with English as their first language.[24] The main reason for this drop is that language teaching involves outdated teaching methods that have little connection to real-life situations. Such lessons are unstimulating to our youth, thus failing to spark their curiosity, but also many English-speaking young people don't necessarily see the point of learning a language when English is spoken everywhere. Language learning is typically quite popular among primary school children, but this drops considerably during secondary school. We need to review the factors that discourage them and find ways to encourage pupils to learn to have interest in diverse languages and cultures.

School is not only to blame, however. In my own study of children's books published in the United States, United Kingdom, and Australia, books dealing with languages and cultures other than those of the U.S. or Western Europe were in the sheer minority. For books that did touch on cultures outside of the Western world, the subject matter was stereotypical and lacking nuance.

Thus, these books had the potential to negatively influence children's perception of other languages and cultures. Both quantity and quality are needed. A greater range of high-quality books that present the linguistic and cultural diversity of the world are needed for our growing children. The earlier that an awareness and appreciation for diversity develops, the better—once our children have grown up, it is altogether too late.

Words mirror our identities. I was born in Korea, and I grew up there, but now I consider myself a member of society in the United Kingdom. When I look around, I see people of a variety of backgrounds and life trajectories. This is the reality in which we live, meaning that awareness and inclusiveness are of the utmost importance. The periphery feeds the English language, meaning that the English lexicon grows exponentially every year. This is a very positive thing, as it means that English has an enriched lexicon. "Foreign words," as some call them, enhance the English language. As such, we should drop the prejudiced view of foreign origin words and take a more inclusive and welcoming stance. Receiving a Golden Globe for his highly acclaimed film *Parasite,* the director Bong Joon-ho stated, "Once you overcome the one-inch-tall barriers of subtitles, you will be introduced to so many more amazing films."[25] From the perspective of this book, I would say, once we overcome word injustice, then we will be able to enjoy a more diverse and rich language.

English is the lingua franca of our time, and more and more people are using it as a means of communication. As the number of English speakers increases, the language itself inevitably becomes more diverse. While everyone speaks English, each person's usage of the language is slightly different from another's. No one's English is better or worse than another's, as each version of the language has its unique value, just like us. We are all different, but we all have our own values. No culture or language is superior or inferior to another.

Chapter 3

ORDINARY WORDS

Word Instinct

Ordinary words are ones that, like pedestrians, we come across daily. Rarely are these words planned by the literary elites; instead, they are often accidentally born in our daily lives. Ordinary words are different from refined and sophisticated words, the ones that sit in important seats with suits on and live in the linguistic establishment, such as a dictionary. For a long time in human civilization, ordinary words were, regardless of popularity and usefulness, largely overlooked in relation to the standard words. How ordinary people spell, abbreviate, and pronounce them has been labeled as non-standard and even "lowly." Yet ordinary words make up the bulk of the daily words that we have and use. Even though we might not find them in the dictionary, they are most useful to describe the objects of our daily lives. Ordinary words make us feel at home, relaxed and comfortable. They are words that are easy to remember and are used by many. Ordinary words live close to us. The best place to go to find new ordinary words is a supermarket, particularly in the food section. I often find myself lost among words and objects in the supermarket. Ordinary words are the common words we encounter on our streets, in shops and supermarkets, and on every corner of our lives. Ordinary words are often unappreciated and underprivileged. Many foreign-origin words, heritage words, dialect words, hybrid words, and subcultural words belong to the category of ordinary words. This echoes how society works. Just as foreign, hybrid, subcultural, or slang words are considered peripheral, there is a long history of people of foreign origin being marginalized.

This, however, is changing thanks to the rise of social media. A bottom-up revolution is taking place; words are made of the people, by the people, and for the people just like us. This isn't the end of the story. With the advent of generative AI, exemplified by ChatGPT, and the emergence of the metaverse, myriad possibilities have unfolded, offering ordinary words a journey from the tangible to the virtual domain. This remarkable progress, in my view, will trigger word evolution to an unprecedented level, surpassing anything we have previously witnessed in terms of scope and speed.

The Bible provides a fascinating insight into the origin of words. Genesis 2:19–20 describes how Adam was given the task of naming all the animals and birds that God had created. This story highlights the uniquely human ability to name things and shows that words are not just random sounds; they carry deep meaning and importance. Humans make words. At the dawn of modern linguistics, generative linguists were fascinated by humans' ability to continuously generate new sentences throughout our lives. Although it is true that we often reuse expressions and structures repeatedly in our daily lives, the capacity for syntactic competence is generally accepted as uniquely human. In the era of generative AI, however, we now question whether endless generation is exclusive to humans, as AI can also generate different sentences to a certain extent. One aspect that I still believe remains uniquely human is the ability to create words.

Even though AI capabilities have crept up on us, becoming far more advanced than we thought possible in a very short time, they have their limits. ChatGPT was developed by OpenAI, and released to the public on November 30, 2022. OpenAI's website describes ChatGPT as follows: "We've trained a model called ChatGPT which interacts in a conversational way. The dialogue format makes it possible for ChatGPT to answer follow-up questions, admit its mistakes, challenge incorrect premises, and reject inappropriate requests." ChatGPT is an AI chatbot that is an improved version of the GPT-3.5 (Generative Pretrained Transformer) language model. GPT-3.5 is one of several versions of what is called a large language model (LLM), which relies on a massive database (175 billion parameters, making it among the biggest language processing models currently available) to understand human language and produce human-like language.[1] These LLMs work by predicting upcoming words in a sequence of text (similar to the text prediction function in search engines and phone keypads). In the case of ChatGPT, this is further enhanced with the Reinforcement Learning with Human Feedback (RLHF), which aims to better understand instructions and questions sent by human users and to produce answers or results that are more closely aligned to what has been asked or requested.[2]

When photography was first invented by Nicéphore Niépce in 1822, it caused a stir in the art world. Yet the camera did not replace the role of the artist. Instead, it caused artists to reconsider the meaning of their craft. Cameras provided the opportunity for artists to engage in philosophical inquiry and sparked important questions about the future of their field. In his famous essay "Kleine Geschichte der Photographie," published in September and October 1931, Walter Benjamin argued that photography brought about a renewal of artistic language and intensified formal explorations: "As the scope of communications increased, the informational importance of painting diminished."

Advanced and accessible AI systems like ChatGPT have the potential to radically transform the ways in which we live. However, even with its 175 billion parameters and supersized database, ChatGPT does not create or suggest words that have been proven to be useful. It's a reminder that language is constantly evolving, and while technology can assist in processing and understanding language, the creation of new and useful words is still primarily driven by human creativity and usage. Despite remarkable technological advancements, there are still certain tasks that only humans are capable of doing. Even with advanced language models like ChatGPT, we cannot replicate the human ability to create new words.

Although all words are crafted by humans, not all words receive equal attention or recognition. Throughout history, certain words have enjoyed privilege and prominence, while others have been overlooked or marginalized. Not all words manage to survive and thrive over time. In the past, words were primarily created by the elite class, and these words carried a certain level of prestige and influence. However, with the advent of social media, a significant shift occurred. Social media platforms provided a space for ordinary words to gain recognition as common words. It was through social media that fandom words and slang, often associated with negative connotations, gained popularity, and became perceived as cool and trendy.

Endless Words

Our world is teeming with an abundance of words. Staying abreast of this linguistic influx has become an integral aspect of leading an ordinary life. But it sparks an intriguing epistemic question: Does the proliferation of these words genuinely contribute to the ease and happiness of our lives? It is noteworthy that many new words are intertwined with products, subtly nudging us toward their usage as we find ourselves implicitly coerced into acquiring the associated items. Some may argue that it boils down to personal choice, but the truth remains that our society is fervently driving us toward a smartphone-dominated existence. Devoid of the installation of various applications, the ability to navigate our world effectively becomes an arduous task. Resisting this prevailing trend results in a sense of disconnection, relegating individuals to a dwindling minority, with scarce opportunity for reversal—far too late to return to the status quo. The sheer number of technological and product-related words is indeed overwhelming, and being familiar with them has become crucial for our survival.

Recently, I received a document that required my signature. When it asked for my address, I initially imagined a postal address, but of course it meant my email address. Furthermore, it specifically referred to "DocuSign" as the preferred format for signing. When I typed "DocuSign" in Outlook, it didn't show any red lines, indicating that the word is accepted and recognized. Is "DocuSign" a common word? Yes, it is for many, but not for everyone. The invasion of technology-related words is an ongoing process that will only accelerate in the future. I can't help but feel a sense of confusion. Will the incessant increase in tech words eventually render ordinary life unbearable for ordinary people?

Indeed, there are certain words that have gained immense popularity and made a significant impact on social media platforms, yet their origins remain unknown. *Selfie* is one such word that skyrocketed to fame during the early days of social media. The first recorded instance of the term *selfie* in the Oxford English Dictionary dates to 2002, when it appeared in a forum post on September 13 on the website www2b.abc.net.au. The post read, "Sorry about the focus, it was a selfie." According to the OED, the word is considered colloquial and was originally of Australian origin. It refers to a photograph taken by oneself, typically using a smartphone or webcam, and shared through social media platforms. Therefore, the emergence of the word *selfie* closely aligns with the rise of smartphone technology. The popularity of *selfie* was recognized by the OED when it named it the Word of the

Year in 2013. In that year alone, its frequency in the English language increased by a staggering 17,000 percent. However, as with many trends, the use of the word eventually started to decline. A study conducted in 2018 revealed a drastic drop in its usage.[3] Looking at the crowd-sourced Urban Dictionary, the rate of new definitions for the word decreased by two-thirds within a span of two years. After making its appearance on Urban Dictionary in 2003, the word reached peak popularity in 2014 and 2015, especially after being embraced by celebrities like Kim Kardashian. Its popularity then dwindled in the following year.

What's more, it is great fun to think that some of the ordinary words we encounter daily are born accidentally. When we think of words, we think of nouns. There are two types of nouns—common nouns, which we use in everyday language, and proper nouns, which are names that give the maker total freedom. It's a free choice. We can make funny names, and nobody can stop us. The act of word-making doesn't always have to be a serious and deliberate affair with deep semantic meanings. Some streets in the United Kingdom, like Turn Again Lane, Christmas Pie Avenue, Folly Bridge, Silly Lane, and Frying Pan Alley, have whimsical and sometimes nonsensical names. These names remind us that language can be playful and fun, and not every word needs to have a serious purpose.

Curiously, too, some words are considered too insignificant to be classified as proper words and are referred to as "non-words." These include fillers such as "uh," "um," "ah," "er," and many more.[4] These expressions are not only prevalent in English but are present in all human languages. Despite their simplicity, they hold great importance. The writer Michael Erard put it in this way: *um* is about how you really speak. In fact, these expressions, often labeled as "disfluencies," may be what distinguishes human language and adds a certain charm to it. Just imagine listening to Siri, with its flawless voice, devoid of these words. It wouldn't take long for us to become disinterested and lose our attention. Although these non-words may be undervalued in the field of linguistics, I believe they lie at the very core of our everyday, conversational language.

Everyday words possess an inherent charm that instantly puts us at ease and provides a sense of comfort. These words often undergo abbreviations or are shortened, adding an extra layer of familiarity and making us feel more "comfy." What about the word *comfy* itself? We all know that *comfy* is an abbreviation of *comfortable,* but there is a difference in how we perceive these words. When we feel relaxed and at ease, we tend to use *comfy* rather than *comfortable*. Similarly, *veggie* is widely recognized as shorthand for *vegetable*. How many times have you heard your mom telling you to "eat your veg"? How often have you seen online or heard the phrases "5 portions of fruit and veg" and "veggie burger"? In all of those cases, a shortened form of *vegetable* was used. Some may argue that *vegetable* is the standard form, and *veg* and *veggie* are informal colloquialisms, but the truth is that different forms of the word are suitable for different contexts. All words have their place, and their suitability is determined by the context, much like how we choose our personal style and search through our wardrobes. Just as we would put on formal wear to work, and casual wear to a party, we choose our words according to the situation that we are in.

New words naturally emerge as our realities change. Often, words are created to depict concepts that are not yet widely familiar. In contrast, for things that are commonplace, we may not even require specific words. One term that has gained substantial popularity, especially in recent years, is *meat-free*. What it describes is widely acknowledged as the future of dietary practices, particularly as we try to tackle the challenges presented by climate change. According to the OED, the phrase "meat-free diet" was first recorded on November 30, 1906, in an article from the *Daily*

Mail. The article mentioned that Mr. Eustace Miles delivered a lecture on the merits of a meat-free diet, creating a stir in an environment filled with the aroma of carnivorous cooking.

At that time, meat eating was common, so dietary restrictions were not typically mentioned when someone consumed meat. Last year, however, I hosted a party where the majority of attendees were vegans, and I had to specify that there were nine vegans and one meat eater. I could have used the expression *meat eater* at the time, but I suddenly felt that it sounds a bit unfriendly. I instinctively made up the word *non-vegan.* Later, I found out that use of this word is growing. When meat eaters were in the majority, we didn't require a word like this, but now a specific term is necessary. In the OED, the first recorded usage of the term *meat eater* was in 1849, and it goes: "I am not much of a meat eater, yet I presume I have consumed about eight ounces a day." Additionally, there is the word *carnivore,* originating from French and Latin and meaning "flesh-eating." According to the OED, it is often used humorously or as mildly derogatory. This demonstrates how meat eating was once commonplace and ordinary. Google N-gram data, which is based on books from 1800 to 2019, also indicates that from 2002 onward, *vegan* began to surpass *carnivore.* Before that, both words—*vegan* and *carnivore,* and even *meat eater*—were not extensively used, as meat eating was considered the default. Not only words like *vegan,* but also other dietary or lifestyle terms have emerged, including *flexitarian, plant-based, cruelty-free,* and *environment friendly.* Although many of these originated before the turn of the millennium, it is around this period that they truly gained popularity.

Similarly, the term *face-to-face* made its initial appearance in the OED back in 1833. However, its true significance became evident during the Covid-19 pandemic, when physical meetings and interactions became practically impossible. Similarly, the term *contactless* experienced a similar trajectory. It was first recorded in 1861, in the sense of individuals adopting an independent and non-interfering approach, as illustrated by the quotation: "Groups [of Trappist monks] are ... housing themselves, with contactless individualism, into those straight-backed, marble-seated, spine-torturing stalls." Its technological connotation emerged in 2004. However, once again, it was the impact of the pandemic that propelled its widespread popularity. Nowadays, many establishments exclusively accept contactless payments as the common method.

It is clear that words have the ability to transcend time and be preserved through the ages. In ancient times, they were preserved not through written media but through oral traditions, such as poetry and songs. Melodic words and phrases are more likely to survive the test of time than non-melodic ones. Short and simple words are also easier to remember than longer, complex ones. What matters most, though, is whether a word has a certain sound or image that makes it more memorable.

Despite the preservation of certain words over time, their meanings may become lost or misunderstood as time passes. In the Lord's Prayer, for example, the word *hallowed* is recited, but its original meaning may not be familiar to many. The use of Latin in the graduation ceremony at Oxford University is a long-standing tradition that persists to this day. Despite the fact that many attendees may not fully understand the language, the emphasis is on the preservation of language and tradition rather than simply conveying information. Understanding the meaning of words is important, but the form and context in which they are used also matter. It's difficult to say whether preserving words in their original form is better or worse than translating them. We know that even when the same words are translated, nuances and other elements can be lost or altered. As such, translation is always a delicate and sensitive business.

In addition, words as a form of cultural currency is not a novel idea; it can be traced back to Pierre Bourdieu's work on the forms of cultural capital.[5] Language can be a social asset. We can construct our own identity and figure out another person's identity and background through the words we choose. Our lexical decisions can very well be an invisible indicator of the social groups we are connected to. In recent years, there has been a growing tendency to use the number of viewers or followers as a primary tool to calculate impact. The rise of social media platforms and digital content has significantly influenced this approach. Many individuals, organizations, and brands have become increasingly focused on such metrics as views, likes, shares, and followers as a measure of their influence and reach.

Remaining in the online realm, we see that ordinary words can take on specialized meanings. It takes time for words to come into existence and travel locally and globally, but the speed at which they now spread is incredibly fast. In many cases, it's too soon for them to be localized or translated. Words, as they are circulated, often maintain their original form, and most of the time, these words happen to be in English. The MeToo movement serves as a prime example. Shortly after its inception, the movement gained viral attention. Within a mere twenty-four hours of the actress Alyssa Milano's tweet on October 15, 2017, encouraging people to share their experiences using the hashtag #MeToo, the phrase went viral on social media platforms across the globe. This phenomenon extends to numerous other words and phrases that are hashtagged. They effortlessly transcend borders, spreading at the speed of light, unaffected by language or geographic barriers. In the United States alone, the hashtag #MeToo was tweeted more than 19 million times in the first year after it went viral in 2017, and in India, the hashtag #MeTooIndia was used more than 200,000 times in the first month after its launch in 2018, demonstrating the movement's ability to bring attention to the issue on a massive scale.

Menu Words

Everyone uses words and everyone creates words. Not all words manage to survive and thrive. Not all words receive praise and celebration. In my previous works, I conducted research to identify the words that flourish and endure in the English word pantry.[6] Among them, I found the everyday words we use in our daily lives, such as food-related terms, to be particularly resilient. Though the number of Asian words incorporated into the English language may not be extensive, the scope of their influence is significant. Asian words have made their way into various fields. However, it is worth noting that the Asian words that have endured and remain in active use are primarily common words, particularly those related to food. This shows the significance of culinary terms in our daily language and cultural exchange.

Although the English language has many words that are quintessentially British, given that its main origin and development was in Britain before it spread throughout the world, when I reflect on the everyday language that we use, some of the most fascinating words that come to mind are those used to describe menus and food. I find myself pondering the origins of such expressions as "full English breakfast," "afternoon tea," and "fish and chips" in the English language. These terms may seem somewhat arbitrary, but they are a reflection of how ordinary words develop and evolve over time. As English has been the language of England for many centuries, it is full of words that are intrinsically tied to the culture and heritage of the country.

Consider the following: *fish and chips* is defined in the OED as a dish consisting of fried fish and fried chipped potatoes. The first recorded appearance of this term was in 1876 in the *Listener,* where it was noted that fish and chip shops were a considerable source of nuisance. The history of fish and chips, for instance, is far from straightforward. Despite being a quintessential British dish, it actually consists of battered fish that was first introduced to England by Portuguese Jews in the sixteenth century. Known as Marranos, these Jews would fry fish in egg and breadcrumbs on Fridays to eat cold on the Sabbath, as cooking was prohibited then in their religion. The batter not only preserved the fish, but it also stopped the oil from ruining its flavor. This dish was called "fish" in the Jewish manner. It wasn't until later that chips were added to the dish. Some claim that fried potatoes were originally a substitute for fish during the winter months when fishing was more difficult.

English breakfast, now, is a substantial breakfast including hot cooked food such as bacon and eggs, particularly as contrasted with a Continental breakfast. The traditional components of an English breakfast include eggs (usually fried or scrambled), bacon, sausage, black pudding, baked beans, grilled tomatoes, mushrooms, and toast. Other variations may include hash browns or fried potatoes, fried bread, and blood sausage. The term *English breakfast* has been in use for several centuries. The earliest recorded use dates to 1773, in P. Brydone's *Tour of Sicily and Malta,* where he describes having an English breakfast after bathing at his lordship's. However, it wasn't until the Industrial Revolution that the English breakfast became a meal not only for the wealthy, but for the masses as well. The working classes began to regularly eat this dish, viewing it as a staple to provide them with the energy required for heavy manual labour. As a result, the term *English breakfast* became increasingly popular and widely used. This is a word that carries a rich history with it.

Erasing Class and Regional Differences

English is marked by class differences. The pioneering scholar of social dialects Alan Strode Campbell Ross even stated, "It is solely by its language that the upper class is clearly marked off from the others."[7] It is not surprising that many historical thinkers proposed a single version of English based on upper-class pronunciation. This reflected their beliefs that it is better to have one standard form of English, and that the upper classes and residents of London and the southeast are usually the best representatives for this standard form.

The English lexicographer Henry Wyld invented a category called "Modified Standard" English. He defined this as "standard" gone wrong, and "modified" by either a provincial or, as I prefer to call it, a regional dialect, or by "an inferior Class Dialect." He went on to say that "Received Standard" English is "the type spoken by members of the great Public Schools. . . . I suggest that this is the best kind of English." The elocutionist Thomas Sheridan also distinguished between "polite" pronunciation and the "provincial dialects" that should be avoided, following the idea that certain types of pronunciation are superior.[8]

John Walker promoted a form of single standard pronunciation for English, aiming for social unity by eliminating linguistic differences. Like Wyld, Walker also identified upper middle-class speakers as the basis of this ideal pronunciation model, and criticized deviations from this as "imperfections in pronunciation, which disgust every ear not accustomed to them."[9] Similarly, Henry Newbolt promoted the idea of some Englishes as superior to others, talking about "evil habits of speech contracted in home and street."[10] Many critics offered explanations for their choice—John Marenbon, for example, suggested that so-called standard English has a much greater range of functions than limited local dialects.[11]

Indeed, class division is most evident in one's pronunciation and choice of words. In shows like *Downton Abbey*, the language used by the characters reflects their social status, and members of the upper class speak quite formally, with a strong emphasis on "proper" grammar and vocabulary. This specific style of language was considered a symbol of education, refinement, and prestige, highly valued among the upper classes. On the other hand, shows like *Coronation Street* feature characters from working-class backgrounds, and their language tends to be more colloquial and informal. In *Downton Abbey*, you might hear upper-class characters using such words as *indeed, perchance, pardon, jolly good,* and *capital* to express approval or satisfaction. These words are commonly associated with the upper class. In contrast, in *Coronation Street*, working-class characters use words such as *ta, mum, pet, bloke,* and *chuffed*, which reflect their colloquial language and regional accents. Indeed, word choice often serves as an indicator of social belonging. Certain words have gained notoriety for being associated with specific social classes. The word *napkin*, for example, has long been linked to the upper class, while *serviette* is more commonly used among the general population. Similarly, *pudding* has been suggested to carry associations with the upper class, whereas *dessert* is the preferred term among those outside that social stratum.

I became aware of these nuances upon my arrival in the United Kingdom, where my father-in-law, a Cambridge graduate with a background in classics, kindly explained these distinctions to me. As I learned more about the differences between upper- and non-upper-class terminology, I began to feel conflicted, since I have never belonged to the English upper class myself. Though my father-in-law's English sounded upper class, he himself was of Danish descent. Among such complex life trajectories, what does class mean?

My journey through British English has now spanned more than twenty years, and it is evident that language evolves and changes over time. If you were to ask millennials and younger generations about the variations in words and their associations with specific social classes, many would likely be unaware of these distinctions. The generational gap is in fact much bigger in its scope than class or any other gap one can think of. In Britain, it is customary to say "bless you" almost instinctively when someone sneezes. I learned this expression when I first arrived in Britain, and now it has become so ingrained in my interactions that it is often uttered automatically. For Generation Z and beyond, however, this practice is rapidly fading, along with numerous other phrasal expressions. Many expressions commonly found in English textbooks may disappear, as the younger generation is unfamiliar with the phrasal expressions that were once widely shared among English speakers.

In parallel, we constantly witness the emergence of new slang words. The OED defines *slang* as follows:

> Words and phrases which are very colloquial or informal, typically consisting of coinages, arbitrary modifications of existing words, playful or colourful figures of speech, coarse or offensive words, etc., and often used among younger people or (in a distinctive variety) among the members of a given group; such words and phrases considered collectively as a category of vocabulary.[12]

But slang often makes up the very words that we live with daily. Millennials and Gen Z tend to use a lot of slang words—*glow up, ghosted, slay,* and *stan,* to name a few. Does this make their entire generations "disreputable"? It is time to change our outlook on slang. Slang words are just ordinary words, and it would be better to define them as a sociolect or idiolect. This simply means that slang indicates our social belonging and is part of our own individual identity. In this sense, there is no "high" or "low" language: there are simply different people with different idiolects. Slang forms part of our unique voices. *Dinner, tea,* and *supper* are all words used to describe a meal taken in the evening in England. Once, *tea* might have been seen as a "low" way of saying "dinner," but now it is simply an indication of your regional belonging—*tea* is more commonly used in northern England. As our societies move away from rigid class systems, our perception of language must follow suit, too. Rather than seeing "slang" as a scourge of "proper" language, we should see it as a creative and innovative tool that enables language evolution. Slang is a bottom-up method of creating language that allows ordinary people to spread their ordinary words.

Looking back into history, William Shakespeare, a literary giant of his time, left an indelible mark on the English language with his vast contributions. His influence on the language is immeasurable, and he is credited with inventing or introducing more than seventeen hundred words that are still in use today. He seamlessly integrated these words into his plays and sonnets, and they have become an integral part of the English lexicon. Among the many words Shakespeare coined, we find such familiar terms as *amazement, apostrophe, bloody, bump, critic, frugal, dwindle, gloomy, generous, hurry, invaluable, lonely, monumental, suspicious,* and the famous phrase *green-eyed monster*. These are just a handful of examples that reflect his linguistic creativity and innovation. What is remarkable is how these words, once considered exclusive to the realm of literature, have transcended their literary origins and become part of everyday language.

Shakespeare's plays often depicted the lives of commoners, their joys, sorrows, and agonies. These words, originally crafted to resonate with the masses, have endured and remained relevant through the centuries. The majority of his audiences were illiterate, and he crafted his plays to entertain and engage them. His words were designed to ignite emotions, put food on the table, and captivate the hearts and minds of his spectators. They were alive on the stage, where the power of performance brought them to life, evoking laughter, tears, and a wide range of human experiences.

Fandom Words

Words derived from literature, films, drama, and songs wield tremendous influence over our language. They serve as a testament to the enduring impact of literary giants who left behind a rich linguistic legacy. Lewis Carroll, the celebrated mathematician, logician, and master of nonsensical writing, stands among the notable word creators. His imaginative and iconic works, including *Alice's Adventures in Wonderland* and *Through the Looking-Glass,* brim with linguistic inventiveness. In these literary masterpieces, Carroll introduced a profusion of novel words that have since woven themselves into the fabric of the English language. Here are a few of the words Carroll birthed. *Chortle,* a clever amalgamation of *chuckle* and *snort,* captures the essence of a gleeful or triumphant laugh. Such examples serve as a testament to Carroll's linguistic ingenuity, showcasing his exceptional ability to forge captivating words that have endured the test of time.

The Harry Potter series of books, written by J. K. Rowling, captured the hearts of millions of readers worldwide and spawned a whole new lexicon of words and phrases that are now part of our everyday language. Some of the most famous super words related to Harry Potter include *Muggle, Quidditch,* and *Hogwarts. Muggle* refers to a person without magical abilities, while Quidditch is a sport played by witches and wizards on flying broomsticks. Hogwarts is the name of the wizarding school that Harry Potter and his friends attend, and it has become synonymous with magic and adventure. Harry Potter super words have become part of popular culture, appearing in movies, TV shows, and music. They are often used as references, inside jokes, and cultural markers that identify fans of the series. They have become so ubiquitous that even people who have never read the books or seen the movies are familiar with them.

What's more, the words of millennials, Gen Z, and Gen Alpha transcend the confines of nation-state boundaries in all corners of their lives. They have grown up alongside such terms as *Sudoku,* *Pokémon,* and numerous food names from all around the globe. To them, these words are not perceived as foreign; they are not seen through the prism of nation-state identities. These generations are most receptive to cultural products from a range of cultures and languages. The majority of K-pop fans, for example, are from the younger generations.

Fandoms are entities that are born and live in online spaces. People of all ages from all over the world take to social media to discuss their favorite singer, TV show, film, or any other form of popular media. #KpopTwitter was tweeted over 7.8 billion times in 2021.

Turning to the K-pop fandom, specifically that of BTS, the word *ARMY* (also found in other forms such as "army" and "A.R.M.Y.") has taken on a new meaning. To a person outside of K-pop circles, *army* is generally associated with notions of military force. However, scrolling through the YouTube comments of a live performance by BTS, you'll find countless references to "ARMY," their loyal fanbase. Thanks to social media and other online platforms, this word has established itself internationally, traversing cultures and languages, from young to old fans of BTS, and others who may have heard of one of the biggest K-pop groups in history.

You may have also come across the word *borahae,* particularly if you're scrolling through the comments of a BTS video. What exactly does this mean? Well, *borahae* is a term coined by the member V during a concert in 2016, meaning "I purple you," or "I'll love you forever," since purple (or violet) is the last color of the rainbow. The word combines two Korean words: for "violet" (*bora*) and "I love you" (*saranghae*). Since then, the phrase has rapidly grown in popularity among ARMY, the BTS fandom, as well as in other K-pop circles thanks to the influence of BTS. Although the Beatles can be described as the most famous boy band in history, it seems that BTS is giving them a run for their money—particularly in the realm of linguistics. A term such as *borahae* is not an individually owned word but one that has grown in a community of fans from all ages and backgrounds.

Another example is *hype boy*. "Hype Boy" is the latest song from the K-pop girl group New Jeans that has gained tremendous popularity in South Korea and globally. The track has been streamed more than 100 million times on Spotify, while its music video on YouTube has garnered over 100 million views. The term *hype boy* itself is a mix of Korean and English, so it poses a challenge for both Korean and English speakers to decipher its meaning. To discover the true meaning of *hype boy*, one needs to turn to dedicated fandom websites. In my search on HiNative, a language site used by many K-fans, I found that the term signifies "I hype you, boy," which can be interpreted as "I believe in you, boy." The word *boy* in this context can denote "friend" or simply "you."

In the domain of film, too, we see that the international success of the Korean film *Parasite* marked a turning point in the film industry; it helped to catalyze the movement of Korean words into the Anglophone sphere. We also sometimes see words born accidentally from the process of translation, such as *ram-don*. The film's translator Darcy Paquet explained that the original word, *jjapaguri*, would likely not be easily received by the international audience because of its complexity, and instead came up with the term *ram-don*. In an interview, Paquet said: "I was embarrassed because I made up this word 'ram-don.' I thought people would laugh at me for it, but it works in the film. The word is first used during a phone conversation. Later, as one character prepares the food, we see the packages on the screen, and I wrote 'ramyeon' and 'udon' over them to show how 'ramdon' came about. I did Google 'ram-don' actually before writing it, and nothing came up. It appears to not be a word in any language at all."[13]

Ordinary Word Makers

Without doubt, social media plays a pivotal role in the proliferation of everyday language. It serves as a communal platform
where linguistic innovation thrives. In some instances author-
ship is known, but there are also anonymous contributions that
contribute to the diverse array of online posts and entries. Moreover, social media breaks down borders, facilitating global communication between people from all walks of life. Most major
social media platforms embrace multi-modality, allowing for the
incorporation of various forms of media. Importantly, this space
exists outside the confines of grammar rules, enabling ordinary
individuals to freely create and employ words without censorship.
Applying grammatical standards becomes challenging in the personal realm of social media, where the true identity of writers
remains unknown.

Ordinary words go beyond mere alphabetical words, encompassing emojis and memes. This trend is not limited to the younger
generations; it has become the norm across all age groups. In
anticipation of the coronation of King Charles III, a new crown
emoji was designed to commemorate this significant event. The
emoji was inspired by the iconic Saint Edward's Crown, which
carries profound symbolism in the crowning of a new monarch.
Whenever a tweet contains a hashtag related to the coronation,
the emoji will automatically appear next to it. Buckingham Palace
took the initiative to create this emoji, featuring a yellow depic-
tion of a purple velvet cap adorned with four crosses. Measuring
sixteen pixels by sixteen pixels, the emoji seamlessly integrates
into digital conversations on the platform.

Power lies in the hands of ordinary individuals. In this world's
ever evolving landscape, a more diverse and appropriate lexicon
is needed; this is often achieved through the dynamic movement
of words. Consequently, many indigenous or local terms have

gained visibility through their travels in the online sphere. This linguistic shift is intertwined with the profound changes brought about by the fourth Industrial Revolution—a conceptualization of the rapid transformation of technology, industries, and societal patterns in the twenty-first century, driven by heightened interconnectivity and automation. Members of Generation Z and Generation Alpha, who are digital natives, have further democratized lexical creativity, placing it within the reach of ordinary individuals thanks to their countless online interactions.

It is still essential to acknowledge that linguistic progress does not come without challenges. The exponential growth of new words may give rise to issues, particularly in terms of intergenerational and socioeconomic disparities, as access to technology varies greatly across demographics. Thus, the pursuit of equality has become even more pressing and should be considered alongside the simultaneous development of language and technology. As we navigate new realities, the emergence of new words remains indispensable. Linguistic innovations reflect the evolving nature of our society and help us articulate and make sense of the changing world we inhabit.

Chapter 4

WORD PANTRY

Word Diversity

New words are added to the English language every day. According to the U.S. company Global Language Monitor (GLM), a new English word is created every 98 minutes, which amounts to about 14.7 words a day or 5,400 words a year. As of August 2021, the English language is estimated to have 1,066,096 distinct words.[1] Our learning of new words doesn't slow down, particularly as the world grows closer. Words of all origin enter into English; our word pantry knows no boundaries according to nation-state identity. We will never feel we have enough words. The more people use English as a common language, the more words people feel they need to express themselves.

Classifying words as "loanwords" or "borrowings" has become obsolete in our borderless pantry of words. Many words live without nation-state labels, and in the future, the distinction between nation-states will be less important. Instead, what will matter is the availability of common versus less common words in our word pantry. It's worth noting that the commonality of words is subject to rapid change and is time sensitive. In parallel, the boundary between culinary traditions is becoming increasingly blurred. Soy sauce, for instance, is originally from Asia, but it is now widely used, and people often use it in ways that differ from the original usage in Asia. The same is true for ingredients such as chilies and coriander, which are now commonly found in all kinds of cuisines.

Words are no longer limited to their original linguistic and cultural contexts. We can shape our words as we wish and imagine as our imagination desires, and this practice of mixing and matching and creating new words has become increasingly common. Our word pantry is becoming more diverse and colorful, just like our kitchen pantry.

Every word has an intriguing history, much like we each do as individuals. We use so many words on a daily basis, often without a second thought, presuming that they have always been with us. Every word was created by humans at some point in our history. As we embrace virtual realities and super-digital lifestyles, the diversity of words is continuing to expand. There are so many diverse words, but not all words are appreciated. Some are celebrated, while others remain underappreciated. The same is true for languages. According to the *Ethnologue: Languages of the World,* a comprehensive catalog of languages, there are currently 7,168 languages in use today.[2] This number is constantly in flux as we learn more about the world's languages every day. Languages themselves are also in flux. They are living and dynamic entities, used by communities whose lives are shaped by our rapidly changing world. This is a fragile time for language diversity, as roughly 40 percent of languages are now endangered, sometimes with fewer than a thousand users remaining. Meanwhile, just twenty-three languages account for more than half the world's population.[3]

Words come in different sizes—short or long, and in a broad sense, even a phrase can be called a word. Some are heavily weighted, either in sound or meaning, while some are light. What we used to call verbal blunders or slips, such as "uh," "eh," or "um," form the very essence of human words. Hyperscale AI cannot mimic these words, and thus, they betray our humanness. Yet, often these little one-syllable words are considered non-words, when in fact it is these small non-words that can be most powerful.

A word can have many meanings, and often we take their meaning from spoken or written language. This needs to be updated, with most communication now happening on our phones. We send or receive words by typing and tapping. Funny memes and moving images with text are some of the new words that we are embracing daily. It's a pity that we don't have a verb to refer to sending an emoji or a meme: *text* is not the right description, as it is too associated with written words. Words from all over the world are entering English through global social media platforms. The door is open to all—as long as a word is romanized, it can enter into English. As the diversity of English speakers increases, the diversity of the English language grows too. Just as our diversity and commonality are ever growing, our words are always changing too. In a world that is the most globalized it has ever been, our identities and origins are never straightforward. The term *English* applies to an increasingly broad array of people and languages. Even the star players of England's national football team are of diverse heritages, with Harry Kane and Jack Grealish of Irish heritage, Raheem Sterling of Jamaican heritage, Marcus Rashford of Jamaican and Kittitian heritage, and Bukayo Saka of Nigerian heritage. *English* no longer refers to only England: it is now a global affair.

I recall the time I sent an email to a student asking a question, but when I didn't receive a reply, I became a bit puzzled. Upon further investigation, I realized that my student had actually responded to me with a "Like" sign: a thumbs-up emoji. It dawned on me that this, too, was a form of communication, and that even emojis and symbols can be considered words. Whether we use letters of the alphabet, emojis, memes, or symbols, each represents a form of expression and can convey meaning. As long as it carries meaning, it's a word. The Oxford English Dictionary provides us with a definition of *word* that encompasses a range of meanings, from spoken to written expressions. In its singular form, *word* refers to an utterance, statement, or remark, while the plural *words* encompasses all forms of verbal expression, including discourse and written language. Specifically, *word* can also refer to any sequence of sounds or morphemes that constitute a basic unit of meaning in a language. According to the OED, the word is derived from the Germanic languages and has a long and rich history. It is cognate with Old Frisian, Old Dutch, Old Saxon, Old High German, Old Icelandic, Old Swedish, Gothic, and other languages, all of which have similar meanings denoting both "an utterance" and "an element or unit of speech, a word." The root of the word can be traced back to the same Indo-European base as Lithuanian *vardas* (name, forename, title), Latvian *vārds* (word, forename, promise), and classical Latin *verbum* (word), which shows an extended form of the Indo-European base of the ancient Greek word for "speaker" and "I shall say," and perhaps also the Sanskrit word for "behest" and "command."

Communication is not limited to just alphabetic words, and sometimes, meaning can be conveyed through a combination of characters, as in the case of "24hr," which combines numbers and letters to indicate continuous availability. Therefore, it is essential to acknowledge that every symbol, image, or alphabetic character that we encounter in our daily lives can be regarded as a word that carries a specific meaning.

Non-verbal communication is often more powerful than verbal communication. As such, it seems that the use of image words may eventually overtake traditional text words in both frequency and importance. This may seem unusual, since visual expressions are typically not included in the definition of words. Signs, symbols, emojis, and memes will be the future of our communications, particularly for younger people such as millennials and Generation Z (sometimes referred to collectively as Gen MZ) and beyond. Emoji or meme competence is necessary for future language users.

Consider the heart symbol. For centuries, the heart symbol has been synonymous with love and affection. Its origins can be traced back to the fourteenth century, when it was used as a representation of the heart ideogram, which symbolized the emotion of love. From the fifteenth century onward, the heart symbol found its way into romantic literature, jewelry, playing cards, and more, where it became an enduring symbol of love and affection. Today, the heart symbol has become ubiquitous in popular culture, particularly in online communication, where it is used to express endorsement or gratitude. The heart symbol has continued to evolve, with the emergence of heart gestures with hands or fingers, made popular by K-pop idols. The borders between symbols, gestures, and words are becoming blurred in online and offline communication.

Furthermore, without context, it is difficult to know what "SUP" and "PYO" might mean, and you could find yourself left out of the conversation if you do not know. To an academic in the humanities or social sciences, *SUP* might mean the influential Stanford University Press, but for many living in warmer climates near a body of water it is the name for the increasingly popular sport of stand-up paddle boarding. If you are driving through a rural area and see a sign reading "PYO Berries," it almost certainly refers to a farm that lets members of the public "pick your own berries," but if you are in Philadelphia, it is just as likely the acronym used for the talented Philadelphia Youth Orchestra, and if you are chatting to a London lawyer he might be referring to the legal term for a persistent young offender. The very nature of acronyms is that they can make communication more convenient for people who know the meaning, but they can also make certain forms of communication exclusionary and labyrinthine for those who do not. Of course, what acronyms refer to also changes as our history changes. Since the death of Queen Elizabeth II in 2022, the use of "HM" in Britain has changed. It used to mean "Her Majesty," but now that Charles III is the king, it means "His Majesty."

Abbreviations and acronyms have become ubiquitous in online communication, from text messages to social media posts. They are intended to save time and effort but can also lead to confusion, especially for those unfamiliar with them. Examples include *fr* (meaning "for real"), *POV* ("point of view"), *rn* ("right now"), *smh* ("shaking my head"), *sus* ("suspicious"), *tbh* ("to be honest"), and *tfw* ("that feeling when"). Keeping track of the abbreviations can be challenging, however, as their meanings frequently change. It is not always clear whether an abbreviation has the same meaning as the original word. For example, *sync* is commonly used as an abbreviation for "synchronize," but the definition of *synchronizing* does not seem to fully match the process of online data backup. So, the question arises whether the abbreviation and the original word are truly interchangeable. Determining ownership of an abbreviation can be a complicated matter. *NFT* illustrates this point: originally standing for the British National Film Theatre, it now primarily refers to non-fungible tokens. The OED has recorded three meanings for *NFT*, with the earliest dating to 1965 in the *New Statesman*, where it referred to the British National Film Theatre. The second meaning, relating to neurology and standing for "neurofibrillary tangle," was first seen in 1980 in the journal *Science*. The third meaning, non-fungible tokens, was first recorded in 2017 on the website GitHub, where it was described as "incredibly awkward."

The Railway to Digital: Online and Offline

Words like *online* have become so ubiquitous in our daily lives that it's easy to forget that they haven't been around forever. The term *on-line* was first used in a 1918 issue of the *Yale Law Jour-*

nal and referred to something situated on the route of a railway line or relating to railway lines, such as the carrying of messages along the common line of two companies. In 1947, M. B. Baker used the term to describe something situated or occurring on the current authorized routes of an airline or relating to routes or services provided by the same airline, as opposed to interline. The term *on-line* was also used in telecommunications in the late 1940s to describe something transmitted via an electronic circuit or involved in or relating to such transmissions. While this meaning is now considered rare, it paved the way for the use of *on-line* in modern computing. Interestingly, the term *offline* also has its roots in the railway industry. Now, the word *online* is mostly used in computing contexts rather than railway contexts. In the digital world, *online* is a more popular term than its opposite, *offline,* as our lives have become increasingly intertwined with the internet and digital technologies. Predominantly, *online* is more popular than *offline* according to Google N-gram data.

In particular, the language used by Generation MZ is rapidly evolving, with a growing emphasis on visual communication. The language of Gen MZ is diverse and adaptable, reflecting the complex and interconnected nature of their world. The blending of different languages and cultural influences has become a hallmark of their communication style, as they navigate the globalized and virtual landscape that defines their generation. As they spend more time in virtual spaces for interaction, play, and socializing, visual language has become increasingly powerful. National boundaries are less significant to this generation compared to previous ones. This is reflected in the language they use. For example, the language of K-pop is not solely focused on the Korean language. While the "K" in *K-pop* and *K-wave* is related to Korea, the lyrics of K-pop songs often incorporate a mix of Korean, English, and other languages. Hearing a K-pop song will quickly demonstrate linguistic diversity.

According to the OED, the first instance of *K-pop* appeared in 1999 in an article published in *Billboard:* "The rock-oriented J-pop scene is not what melody-oriented K-pop listeners are asking for."[4] Offline K-pop fandoms sprung up in the 1990s in East Asia and Southeast Asia before expanding even farther afield. In 2009, *K-pop* as a word began to appear more than *J-pop*. Eventually, as our lives migrated to social media platforms, *K-pop* exploded in popularity across the globe. From the mid-2010s, K-pop groups like BTS, BlackPink, EXO, and Twice gained global success. A decade later, K-pop has become an international mainstream phenomenon.

Now, K-fans are a transnational, transcultural, and translingual body. This means that they engage in matters of nationality, culture, and language without limitations from nation-state borders. Thanks to social media, K-fans are able to communicate across regions and nations with increased ease. Their impact now goes beyond the expressions of loving fans, and extends into popular culture, socio-political affairs, and linguistic developments. K-fans are vital to the Korean Wave. They actively construct the meaning of K-pop and the significance it has in the world. They have changed the "K" in *K-pop, K-variety shows, K-dramas, K-beauty,* and more to mean something bigger than "Korean." Meanings snowball and change, becoming more transcultural and translingual. Whereas "K-" could be very much defined by nation-state boundaries, its meaning has diversified. *K-ness* is being shaped globally. Although the practice of combining words is not unique to Gen Z, as individuals throughout human history and across various generations have utilized it, what sets Gen Z apart is the speed and broad scope at which they are incorporating words of diverse origins and hybrid varieties into their everyday vocabulary.

Traveling to Taiwan, we see that pineapple cake is a Taiwanese sweet delicacy, romanized in Pinyin as *fènglísū*. In Taiwan, it is also romanized under Péh-ōe-jī as *ông-lâi-so.* The word for pineapple in Taiwanese Hokkien, *ông-lâi*, sounds phonologically like a phrase that means "prosperity arrives, or go forth and prosper," which conveys the idea that many children will be born to a family. As a result, pineapples are given as engagement gifts. From there, the cake evolved beyond being an engagement treat and became a Taiwanese delicacy. Despite historically being a ceremonial treat in Taiwan, a Google search shows the overwhelming prominence of the English translation of *pineapple cake* over the romanized forms of *fènglísū* or *ông-lâi-so*. One potential reason for this could be the immense popularity of pineapple cake among Japanese tourists. In Japanese, it is transcribed using katakana as *painappuru keki*. Pineapple has been known to grow in Taiwan since as early as the seventeenth century, but it wasn't until the Japanese occupation in the nineteenth century that Taiwan became the third largest producer of pineapples in the world. Japan's role in the introduction of pineapples to Taiwan in contemporary history could have contributed to the popularity of the term *pineapple cake*, close to *painappuru keki* as opposed to other Chinese forms.

Moreover, not many would recognize that such words as *karaoke* have English components. The word *karaoke* (meaning "empty orchestra") is made up of the Japanese *kara*, meaning "empty," and *oke*, from the English "orchestra." This word entered the English lexicon in the 1970s and later was introduced into a number of European languages via English. Likewise, the word *anime*, which most English speakers recognize as a word of Japanese origin, is in fact formed through back clipping or shortening from the English word *animation*, which of course has roots in Latin and has undergone significant semantic shifts up until the present day. There are many instances of words that are recognized as simply being Japanese, but in fact have complex, translingual identities that have been made through contact with English words of various pedigrees, as the examples of *karaoke* and *anime* demonstrate. As discussed previously, it is often difficult or meaningless to make judgments regarding the origin of words. Just as our lives become increasingly diverse and globalized, our lexicons become increasingly dynamic and fluid. Words end up as hybrid, translingual things. Indeed, many newly made culture or commercial terms are hybrid words with blurred identities.

What's more, words are like people in that they each have their own unique nuances and meanings—no two words are exactly alike. This is particularly evident when it comes to emotional words, which can vary significantly across languages and cultures. A recent study examined nearly 2,500 languages to determine the degree of similarity in the linguistic networks of twenty-four terms for emotions across cultures.[5] The results found a high degree of variability in the meaning of such terms. The similarity of terms for emotions could be predicted based on several factors, including the geographic proximity of the languages they originate from, and the physiological arousal they evoke. These findings have contributed to ongoing debates about the universality and diversity in how humans understand and experience emotions. The study also found that in some Indo-European languages, the words for "anxiety" and "anger" overlap. But in the Austroasiatic language family of mainland Southeast Asia, *anxiety* is more closely tied to "grief" and "regret." The study also found that the word for "surprised" is sometimes linked to *fear* in certain languages, but not in others. There are countless words in the English language, but it can still be challenging to find the right ones to express certain ideas or concepts, particularly as English increasingly serves as the global lingua franca. As both language and culture continue to evolve, expanding the English word pantry to capture new meanings and nuances will become an ever greater challenge.

Following the murder of George Floyd at the hands of police in Minnesota in May 2020, protests were held not only in the United States but around the world, calling for an end to police brutality and for the prosecution of Floyd's murderers. Even in countries where English is not widely spoken, many handmade placards brought to these events featured English slogans relating to the Black Lives Matter movement, such as "I can't breathe," "BLM," and "no justice, no peace." Part of the reason for this may have been that these protests served a dual purpose: highlighting racism and brutality in their own country, and directly protesting the murder of George Floyd by calling for justice to be served. Because of this, some protesters may have chosen to use English on their placards to ensure that their message of solidarity with Black Americans would be understood by those in America viewing coverage of the international protests. Using the same language internationally also helps to convey the scale of the movement, creating a global bond of solidarity among its members.[6]

Overall, social media provides an open and unmediated space where users of new English can experiment with the language, enriching and innovating on the language while making it a more inclusive language capable of overcoming the ideology of English as a privileged asset for use only by the "right" kind of speakers. The spread of new English on social media further enables marginal voices to be heard by promoting the simultaneous existence of multiple forms of English, encouraging the participation of an increasingly diverse group of users.

Food Words: Reflecting Diversity

As societies across the globe are becoming interwoven at an unprecedented speed and impressive scope, so too is the world of food, allowing the English language to develop an ever widening culinary vocabulary.

The potato, a staple in traditional British cooking, originally came from the Americas. The OED states that the earliest form of the word—*batata*—comes from a Central American Indian language. The term was borrowed by Spanish colonists in 1526 as *patata,* before finally making its way into English as *potato.* Other food words of foreign origin include *carrot* and *broccoli; carrot* entered English from French, and *broccoli* via Italian. *Bacon* is a word of Germanic origin that entered English via Old French. *Celery* is of Greek origin, passed into English through a dialect of Italian and then French. *Chocolate* and *tomato* originated from Nahuatl, entering English via Spanish. *Chutney* is of Hindi origin, while *yogurt* comes from Ottoman Turkish, and *coffee* is from Arabic, reaching English via Turkish. *Ketchup* is from Malay, coming to English from Hokkien Chinese.

Food words travel quickly and widely; fusion is becoming the trademark of contemporary cuisine. The word *noodle* came from German *Nudel* and hence was originally used in a European culinary context. The OED defines *noodle* as "a string- or ribbon-like piece of pasta or similar flour paste (sometimes containing egg) typically cooked in liquid and served either in a soup or as an accompaniment to another dish; (more generally in N. Amer.) any style of pasta." However, nowadays the word *noodle* is most commonly used in an Asian culinary context. Similarly, the word *dumpling,* originally coined in reference to traditional British dumplings, is now used mostly in an Asian context. Food words of foreign origin are increasing and thriving in English, and the forms and meanings of these words reflect the transcultural nature of our lives.

In the United States in particular, many staple food names also originate from other languages. *Hamburger* and *cheeseburger* stem from German. *Hamburger* originally referred to a native or inhabitant of Hamburg. Then, in the late nineteenth century, it came to have its current meaning, referring to chopped beef that is seasoned and formed into a patty and broiled or fried. At that time, it was generally referred to as a *hamburger steak,* as in an article in the *Walla Walla Union* newspaper in 1889, and in a description of a boxing match in 1901 where "the kid had been carried out of the Ring, looking like a Hamburger Steak." A few decades later, *cheeseburger* was coined as a hybrid form of the hamburger. Now, we do not see any trace of German heritage in these words.

Babycino or *babyccino* is another word that has a complex hybrid history. It refers to a drink of hot milk that has been frothed up with pressurized steam, intended for children. The term is a combination of *baby* and *-cino* from *cappuccino*. Cappuccino derives its name from the Capuchin friars, whose robes had a color like that of espresso mixed with frothed milk. The color of a babycino has no resemblance to the color of a Capuchin robe. Words like this demonstrate the arbitrary and complex process behind the birth of words.

Fried chicken is probably less Southern than you think. According to an article in *BBC Travel*, the origin of fried chicken shows Scottish roots more so than any in the southern United States.[7] Although I will refrain from going into detail about the journey of fried chicken, I want to show how little we may know regarding our food and its border-crossing origins. Since the arrival of this chicken delicacy in North America, an increasing number of high-end restaurants in the United States are serving all sorts of varieties of fried food, which have traversed countries and continents, such as Japanese *karaage* fried chicken thighs and Palestinian fried fowl seasoned with *za'atar*. *Chimaek* has become popular in Korea, and is a meal of fried chicken (as designated by *chi*) and beer (as indicated by *maek*). *KFC* once referred to Kentucky Fried Chicken, but now it can also mean Korean Fried Chicken, as popularized in K-dramas and K-films. Fried chicken has been on a journey all over the world, just like the people in our world have.

Everyone has different taste buds, but there is a commonality in the things we can taste: sweetness, sourness, saltiness, bitterness. It is in how we combine these flavors that we create dishes to suit our own palates. Some people love stinky tofu; others hate it. Some love black pudding, but others cannot stand it. We are always innovating new flavors. Even though we have the same ingredients, we constantly produce new dishes to make our diet more diverse. Our language is like this too. Even though it might be most efficient to eat the same things every day, it is boring. Saying the same words every day is lackluster, too. Using new words is part of our expressive desire. We always want to innovate, and this is expressed in our cooking and development of new words.

Flavors often come from herbs and spices. In one of my cookbooks, a *dhana-jeera dressing* is mentioned, which is described as "India's most notorious spice duo: cumin and coriander." However, just because this combination goes by a particular name, using these two spices together—or separately for that matter—will not create a dish with a particular nation-state or regional association. Coriander is also widely used in Chinese cooking, known locally as *xiāngcài*. In the West, one contestant in a popular cooking show called *MasterChef UK* even added coriander to a pudding. Although certain flavors can be reminiscent of particular cuisines, the creative ways in which they are used make it all the more difficult to pinpoint a single place from which they originate. This is reflected in our own lexicon.

Words from the Silk Road and Beyond

When visiting a Middle Eastern or Mediterranean restaurant, you will see similar items on the menu, though the dish names will be spelled and pronounced slightly differently. Food names intrinsically demonstrate the food and people's history. The Middle East and the Mediterranean region have been intricately connected as trade partners throughout history, and their food names represent that. Shared food names echo a shared life.

Baklava is a layered dessert treat made of filo pastry filled with chopped nuts and sweetened with syrup or honey. This now widely known sweet pastry took its modern form in the palace kitchens of the Ottoman sultans, but the early history of the dish and the origin of the word remain contested topics for linguists and culinary historians of the Middle East and Central Asia. Today the dish is pronounced "ba-KLAA-wa" in Arabic and "BAA-kla-va" in Turkish. The English name *baklava* is the same as the Turkish etymon *baklava.*

The question is how should we spell, and thus pronounce, *baklava*? Even though the Arabic and Turkish names may be the most widely known, the dish's origin is uncertain, and there are many other variant pronunciations from Greek, Persian, Albanian, Bulgarian, Bosnian, Azerbaijani, and Armenian. The OED asserts *baklava* as the standard spelling, noting that it is a Turkish loanword. Here we see that very outdated style of picking the first form that English speakers encountered as the standard spelling. In the modern day, when there are people of Turkish, Arabic, Iranian, Armenian, and other origins or heritages living in English-speaking countries, is it not okay for them to spell *baklava* as *baklawa,* or however best suits their own language? They will be pronouncing it like that anyway.

Another example: *paneer.* The origin of *paneer* lies in the Persian *panir,* received into English from Hindi and Urdu *panīr,* which had been borrowed from Persian. *Paneer* is Indian-style cheese, but it just means "cheese" in many languages from West and South Asia. Someone living in Delhi may very well call what we understand to be "cheddar" as *paneer.* Meanwhile, someone living in England may view *paneer* according to its OED definition: "In Iran and South Asia: cheese (traditionally curd or soft cheese made esp. from sheep's or goat's milk, but more recently also hard cheese)."[8] This illustrates how words can take on different meanings as they cross cultures and geographic boundaries.

No single version of the word can or should be viewed as "correct," for they each come to take on a new identity as people in various speech communities reaffirm or assign new meanings.

Now, when we—"we" being any speaker of the English language—talk about dumplings, we could be talking about an innumerable number of dishes. The word *dumpling* itself dates from England in the early seventeenth century, specifically Norfolk, where the Norfolk dumpling (a ball made of savory suet dough cooked atop a hearty stew) was popularized. In modern parlance the term *dumpling* has been adapted to refer to various kinds of dough encasing a meat or vegetable filling originating in various East Asian cuisines.

I recently conducted a survey to explore the origins of the term *dumpling*. Participants were asked: "To which language or culture(s) do you think the term *dumpling* belongs?" The study was carried out with mostly British city-dwellers, 60 percent of them aged eleven to thirty, and the remainder made up of various ages and ethnicities. Sociolinguistic research always requires a look into the correlation between the results and the demographic makeup, but these days this kind of variable is becoming less relevant to such studies because the generational divide and digital literacy are generally more influential than conventional variables. As society becomes multilingual and multicultural, ethnicity does not tell as much anymore. Just like a physical dumpling, the word *dumpling* can be enjoyed by everyone. We no longer eat Chinese food from a takeaway because we are ethnically Chinese, for example, but rather because it has become integrated into our own unique culinary life—and our usage of words reflects this.

Out of the 208 respondents in the survey, the majority associated dumplings with an Asian country. Specifically, more than 50 percent believed dumplings originated in China. Respondents were allowed to select multiple answers, resulting in a diverse range of responses. Some participants suggested that dumplings

"Dumpling"
208 responses

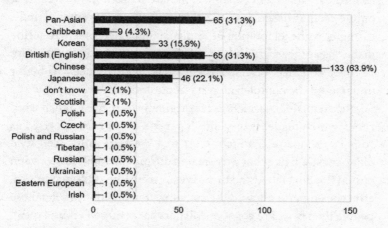

Answers given for the question "Which language or culture(s) do you think the term *dumpling* belongs to?"

were of Caribbean origin, while 31 percent believed that the term was of English origin.

The term *dumpling* has been adapted to all kinds of Asian cuisines and is used with a certain ubiquity. It has come to describe any rounded dough-based item either containing a filling or empty, cooked by almost any method (the most popular being steaming, boiling, or frying). When describing items that are given different names in their original languages (such as Chinese *baozi,* "steamed buns," and *shui jiao,* "boiled dumplings"), the term *dumpling* has also come to cover all manner of hybridized and westernized dishes. A Google search for dumpling recipes online results in a wealth of hybrid dishes, including "bacon cheeseburger dumplings," "Mom's special vegan dumplings," and "Asian vegetable dumplings." Dishes like this suggest two things. First, English speakers in the West are comfortable enough with the term *dumpling* that they see fit to adapt it to their own tastes.

Second, using one word for a variety of distinct East Asian dishes has led to "pan-Asian cuisine." This can be seen in the wealth of online recipes described as "Asian style x" or "Oriental y," indicating how the adaptation of English language terms to describe dishes has exacerbated a lack of awareness of the distinct nature of these cuisines. Perhaps, then, there is also a need to better understand the complex identity of our food and words.

Next, consider *katsu*. *Katsu* is originally from the English word *cutlet*, which made its way into Japanese. *Katsu* is categorized as *yoshoku* in Japanese, which refers to a Western-influenced style of Japanese cuisine that was created during the Meiji Restoration period (1868–1912). At the time, Western cuisine was encouraged, after the emperor allowed the consumption of red meat. Japanese people then began to consume dishes that centered around meat, and *katsu* was one of them.[9] Other examples of *yoshoku* dishes include *omurice* ("omelette" + "rice"), *kareraisu* ("curry" + "rice"), and *korokke* ("croquette"). Since then, *katsu* has been imported back into English to refer to deep-fried cutlets, as used in Japanese cooking. *Katsu* is now used to refer to a specifically Japanese-style cutlet dish and is frequently used in English and other languages.[10] Looking at restaurants and recipes both online and offline, many compounds with *katsu* are found. There are references to pork cutlets as *tonkatsu*, *donkatsu*, *pork katsu*, or *katsu don*. Notice the variation in the romanization of the dish not just in the letters but also in the word order, as *don* (meaning "pork") can come before or after *katsu*. There's even a dish known as *mille-feuille katsu*, which draws from English, Japanese, and French. How would one define the identity of this food? Would Japanese people think it's French? Would French people think it's Japanese? How about English people? As we can see, on entering the English language—and others—this hybrid word took on various forms, none of which are definitively correct and, instead, all seem to highlight their translingual nature.

Fika differs slightly from the words discussed thus far, but it is very much related to food and drink culture. *Fika* can be traced to Sweden and is often translated along the lines of "a coffee and cake break." In Swedish, however, the word means much more than this loose translation; it is a concept, a social institution, an attitude, and an important part of Swedish culture, which involves the practice of taking a break with a beverage and a snack. As the word makes its way into the Anglophone world, the depth behind it is also slowly being adopted. Indeed, culinary words are very much reflective of our multilingual and multicultural realities.

Fusion Cuisine

Certain words are born hybrid; I call them "hybrid words." Two examples are *sushi tapas* (Japanese and Spanish origins) and *sushi gourmet* (Japanese and French origins), but even then we cannot say exactly where the dishes are from. They draw from cuisines, but they are inherently a fusion, a mix, a hybrid, and they reflect the increasingly cross-cultural reality that we live in.

In my house, we have a family recipe that goes by the name "Daddy Dish." When I asked my husband how he came to create this Daddy Dish, the story was: On the radio he heard a woman talking about beans and how they can absorb the flavor of lots of other ingredients. He immediately thought of chorizo, and was inspired. He fried together chorizo, onion, and garlic. This was when he had the idea of a lentil-chorizo dish. After recalling the importance of cumin as one of the key spices in Middle Eastern cuisine, he added a teaspoon of cumin. Next came spinach and tomato for color, plus coriander and chili for flavor. With Spanish chorizo, Middle Eastern spices, Indian lentils, among other things, what would the nationality or ethnicity of this dish be? When I asked my husband this question, he simply answered, "There's no one nationality or ethnicity of this dish."

Thinking about this further, Daddy Dish is an apt example of how our everyday food goes beyond nation-state boundaries. Even if one were to follow a recipe, tracing the journey and discovering the origin of different ingredients and spices points toward a global cuisine. Linguistic and cultural interactions among diverse groups of people across the world, and subsequent cultural hybridization, make the creation of etymologically or structurally hybrid words inevitable. We come across hybrid terms daily, and many of these have complex layers of meaning that are testimony to the words' translingual journeys taken across their lifespans.

Curiously, the term *dirty* started to be widely used to describe specific types of food, although its exact meaning can vary depending on the context, and it remains a source of debate. "Dirty" foods tend to be indulgent, rich, and a little bit messy. They may incorporate unconventional or unexpected ingredients or be prepared in nontraditional ways. "Dirty fries," for instance, are commonly made by topping French fries with cheese, gravy, and other decadent ingredients, while "dirty burgers" might feature toppings like mac and cheese or fried eggs. Another popular dish is "dirty rice," which usually consists of rice cooked with meat, vegetables, and spices for a flavorful and filling meal. The term *dirty* is used to describe food intended as a special treat or indulgence—similar to the colloquial usage of *naughty*. Words like this are ubiquitous in our lives and add to the richness and complexity of our language.

Furthermore, flavor combinations that cross nation-state borders are prevalent in our society, and as tastes are innovated, flavor words are too. With the rise of veganism in recent years, many flavor words now include fragments related to veganism. This has led to the emergence of a new range of creative culinary terms, including *vegan sashimi*—a vegan alternative to thin slices of raw fish, often made with tapioca starch. In one sense, the meaning of this term is contradictory, as *vegan* means vegetable-based, while *sashimi* usually refers to raw fish. A lot of vegan food adopts conventional food names, however, instead of inventing new words, and simply puts *vegan* at the front. Even though *vegan* has English roots and *sashimi* has Japanese roots, when combined, their identity is neither solely English nor Japanese. Rather, this term is by its very nature international, multicultural, and translingual.

Another example that combines culinary contexts is the sushi burrito. Japanese sushi and Mexican burrito are combined in an Anglophone context. English speakers are likely to be more familiar with the term *burrito* than the Japanese *ehomaki*, which is used to describe long sushi rolls. *Burrito* also implies a fusion cuisine, and some varieties of sushi burrito include Mexican ingredients alongside the traditional Japanese flavors. Much like vegan sashimi, sushi burrito also has a complex linguistic and culinary identity.

Though born slightly differently, *mint chocolate chip* is another term that can be perceived as the result of a fusion of sorts. Mint chocolate chip ice cream was invented in 1973 by a culinary student, Marilyn Ricketts, while studying at South Devon College in England. She entered a competition to provide an ice cream dessert for Princess Anne's wedding to Captain Mark Phillips at Westminster Abbey. Many of us now use this term to describe a general flavor without an intentional reference to its origins. Lots of flavors are invented through fusion—just look at your local supermarket, and you'll find many more examples.

Food for Thought from the Word Pantry

One of my Ph.D. students moved from America to Britain to study at Oxford, and when he did, he felt like he had to learn English all over again. When he went to the supermarket, he found that the American and British terms for pantry items were completely different. A *cookie* became a *biscuit*; *zucchini* became *courgette*;

and *cilantro* became *coriander,* to name a few. *Biscuit* in British English was first used in 1330, imported from Old French. *Cookie* was first used in 1703 in American English, stemming from the Dutch word *koekje,* the diminutive form of *koek,* meaning "cake." *Zucchini* originates from Italian, first used in 1921; *courgette* comes from the French meaning "to ground," which was used in 1931. *Cilantro* stems from Spanish, and *coriander* is also French.

I had a similar experience when I first came to live in the United Kingdom. After living in South Korea, learning American-style English, I discovered differences in the nuances of the language in the United Kingdom. *Quite,* for example, has a different meaning there than it does in the United States. My father-in-law once cooked something for dinner, and he asked me what I thought of it. "It's quite good," I replied, meaning I really liked it. To my surprise, he replied, "Only quite?" In the United Kingdom, *quite* means "fairly," but in the States it is closer to "very." This was another difference between British and American English that I, and I'm sure many others, had to learn the hard way.

Another lesson is that, for words adopted from Latin, a lot of people assume that you must use Latin grammar to form the plural. In some cases, English adopts the Latin plural, as we see with *bacteria,* from the singular *bacterium,* and *media* from the singular *medium.* But not always. *Octopus* and *cactus,* for example, can be properly made into plurals with English grammar rules. Thus, *octopuses* and *octopi* are both correct, as are *cactuses* and *cacti.* Newer words in English do not follow clear pluralization rules. Though adding an "s" seems like a straightforward way to pluralize a word, with collective nouns such as *sheep* and *fish* in existence, should we even be adding an "-s" to new foreign words? For example, is *gyoza* (a Japanese-style dumpling) a plural noun, or should it be *gyozas*? Or how do we pluralize *qipao*? In Mandarin, there is no pluralized form of *qipao*—it could be singular or plural depending on context. To add an "-s" to words such as *qipao* and *gyoza* sounds almost infantile. The OED, half-heartedly, notes *qipao* and *qipaos* as being acceptable; it does the same for *gyoza*. However, for *jiaozi,* the Mandarin spelling of *gyoza,* the OED states that the plural is unchanged. For *sushi,* there is no note on pluralization at all. There are no clear grammar rules for these new words in English. This is because English's existing grammar rules are not ready to cater for these words. As there are so many English speakers, grammar is becoming less and less important. It is inevitable that grammar will become ever more user friendly as it fails to keep up with the influx of new words. Irregular plurals are disappearing, and our language foundations are shifting to become simpler. The future of English is simpler and more ubiquitous than it has ever been before.

Culinary words in particular show how languages and cultures are interwoven and reflect the realities of our lives. In one way, we are entering a new Babelian age. When we take inventory of our word pantry, we can see how it has changed over time. Echoing back to Frederick Furnivall and James Murray, all words are welcome, and all of them are English, in spite of their origins. Just as we are all moving around the globe and settling in various places, starting new lives and beginning families, new words enter English and then generate even more new words from there. Hybrid words therefore have great power to multiply and create even more new words. The new generation of our word pantry is bursting with flavorsome, mouth-watering words for us to try.

Chapter 5

USING WORDS

Word Stylistics

Our words were once governed by strict grammar rules and linguistic authorities, limiting freedom of expression in word choice. With the emergence of modern technology and cultural diversity, however, the hold of these traditional rules and authorities has weakened, leading to a more flexible approach to language usage. Now, global corporations often own words and hold power over them, making words like a free market commodity.

In today's world, selecting the right words is akin to choosing fashion styles. Word choice is affected by the occasion, but it is the individual's style that matters most. With the exponential growth of virtual and online lives, words are constantly expanding, and new words and phrases are being coined at an unprecedented rate. However, this expansion has also led to a growing word divide. The divide is not just limited to generational differences but also encompasses social media literacy and one's attitude toward digital literacy. The divide can make it challenging for individuals to communicate effectively with people from diverse backgrounds or age groups, as language evolves at a rapid pace, and the nuances of usage can vary widely between different communities.

When we choose our words, it is a conscious decision, and word stylistics involves selecting appropriate words, speech styles, intonation, gestures, posture, and more. Each individual has a unique set of language stylistics, much like their clothing style. We can view our word pantry as a language wardrobe, and choosing speech styles is similar to selecting an outfit for a particular occasion. We wear a suit to work and pyjamas (or pajamas) to bed, for instance, not the other way around. Similarly, we may dress more formally when meeting someone for the first time, such as on a first date, and then more informally as a relationship progresses. External factors can also influence our style, such as meeting a friend who inspires us to dress well. Choosing words can be similar, and people may use them even for decorative purposes, not necessarily considering their meanings. The names of Asian-fusion restaurants, for instance, might not make much sense in terms of their meanings, but people consume them for the atmosphere. Take Wagamama, for example, a well-known Japanese fusion restaurant in Britain. The name roughly translates to "self-indulgent," "self-centered," "selfish," and "naughty" in English and is commonly used in Japan to describe a child's misbehavior. Few will be aware of or interested in its meaning.

We use numerous words on a daily basis, and words are our most basic commodity. We have so many words, and we may already have words for objects, but still we yearn for new words and thus make them. If words are used too much, they become less valuable. At our breakfast table, I asked my husband about the hidden meaning of a word I received in an email. Ian told me it was a cliché, but our youngest child, Jessie, didn't know what that meant. Sarah explained to her that it's an overused word, and Ian added that it's a meaningless word. When words are used too often, we become a bit tired of them and seek out new ones. Let us compare this to our wardrobe. The fact that we have a few pairs of nice jeans does not stop us from buying another pair. Someone may ask why we would buy another pair of jeans when we don't need them, and we might answer that we don't need them but we like them. This is the same with words.

When I first arrived in the United Kingdom, I was very conscious of how I spoke English. I wanted to make myself sound English, simply because I was living in England. I tried to erase all my American English. At the time, I was living with my father-in-law, who spoke English exactly how I dreamed of sounding. One thing that I still remember practicing was the word *absolutely*. I practiced the intonation over and over, but I couldn't make myself sound like an English person. After despairing for a while, I came to find the value in "my" own English. Why should I speak English like everyone else? The English language that my family and I speak mixes Korean and English in creative, fun, and useful ways. I call this way of speaking Bare Speak. It consists primarily of an English lexicon with a simplified grammar, meaning you use available words to fit your context, without being limited by the standard language usage and grammar of the nation where you happen to be. I can be most creative when I take away the grammar rules. When I don't feel the anxiety of trying to sound like someone who learned English as their first language, my own voice and creativity are able to break through in my second language. When speaking, texting, or emailing with friends and family I often use Bare Speak like this. In certain settings, such as an academic book or presentation, an audience expects that this Bare Speak will be dressed up and beautified in certain ways. To extend the analogy, in these settings I am expected to put a certain amount of makeup on my speech that distorts the identity of what's underneath. When I feel the need to dress up my speech in this way, old anxieties return and I find it difficult to believe my speech expresses my own voice and creativity. That's why I choose Bare Speak whenever possible.

Bare Speak is increasingly popular with both native speakers and the growing ranks of speakers of English as a second language. This may become more plausible when generative AI such as ChatGPT becomes very accessible. When typing a message on your phone or computer you might express it in the simplest and most abbreviated form, allowing iMessage or Gmail's autocorrect software and predictive text generation to fix spelling and grammar and fill in missing words. So, if you type "haven't see," you might be helpfully prompted to accept "Haven't seen you in a while." Similarly, you no longer need to remember irregular plurals because you will always be prompted to change *hoofs* to *hooves*. Grammatical complexities still exist in English, but they have never really impeded oral communication, and the rise of computers means they're now largely unnecessary to remember for communicating effectively in written English. It seems likely that as a result of this, and our ever more rapidly increasing lexicon of global words, grammar will play a smaller and smaller role. Instead, it is possible to imagine a time when knowing the English language will mean little more than familiarity with a grammatical skeleton and will have much more to do with knowing its massive lexicon. Further, as English grammar grows more simplified it will eliminate noticeable differences between the speech of native and non-native English speakers and the border between these distinctions will cease to have meaning. Instead, there will be many local variations of English using different sets of words from a wider global lexicon.

Now, if British and American English users can't agree on a single spelling standard and the world's premier English dictionary, employing etymological and linguistic arguments, falls somewhere in between the two, what actually motivates decisions to select one spelling over another? Well, much like pronunciation, it is a marker of identity. The dons of the University of Oxford have chosen to favor British spelling conventions in their spelling guidelines in part because of the university's long-running association with British identity. In much the same way, the late queen always used *recognise* regardless of the OED's suggested spelling. Similarly, some American expatriates in the United Kingdom will never come around to their children calling them "mum."

In fact, numerous scholars have traced the codification of a formal distinction between the two standard Englishes to the period of the American Revolution. In this time, some Americans gripped by a revolutionary fervor began to espouse a form of linguistic patriotism. One anonymous pamphleteer on the eve of the revolution self-satisfiedly announced: "The English language has been greatly improved in Britain within a century, but its highest perfection, with every other branch of human knowledge, is perhaps reserved for this Land of light and freedom. As the people . . . will speak English, their advantages for polishing their language will be great, and vastly superior to what the people in England ever enjoyed."[1]

The job of promoting, justifying, and codifying this new standard of English was undertaken by the American lexicographer Noah Webster (1758–1843), the progenitor of the distinctly American Merriam-Webster Dictionary that we know today. He laid out the patriotic ideology underpinning his efforts in the introduction to the 1789 treatise *Dissertations on the English Language*, declaring the following: "As an independent nation, our honor requires us to have a system of our own, in language as well as government. Great Britain, whose children we are, and whose language we speak, should no longer be our standard; for the taste of her writers is already corrupted, and her language on the decline." Later in the same text, he demonstrated just how tightly he connected an American standard of English to the project of American independence, stating, "a national language is a band of national union."[2]

In the treatise, Webster, drawing on the work of the founding father Benjamin Franklin, proposed a radical set of orthographic reforms to separate the two Englishes, including new orthography for the consonants "ng," "sh," and "th" that would have the letters at the very least connected by a line to indicate they were to be read together. Such an ambitious reform program obviously did not succeed, but Webster, even in the confines of the same text, was aware that it did not need to succeed in order to successfully separate the two Englishes: "The alteration [of orthography], however small, would encourage the publication of books in our own country. It would render it, in some measure, necessary that all books should be printed in America. The English would never copy our orthography for their own use and consequently the same impressions of books would not answer for both countries."[3] The situation came to pass exactly as Webster predicted: small changes in spelling, grammar, and vocabulary between the two Englishes have become intrinsically linked to their respective national identities, and in turn have spawned an entire industry of publishers and copy editors who perfect works for these rival markets.

In fact, Webster made his greatest contribution to the codification of a new American English standard a few years before he articulated his arguments in 1783 in *The American Spelling Book; Containing, the Rudiments of the English language, for the use of Schools in the United States.* The text employed already existing American variant spellings like *center* and *color* as standard in place of their British equivalents, with Webster justifying this on the basis that they better "exhibit the true pronunciation" and made acquisition of the language easier. Despite provoking controversy in some quarters, the text swiftly replaced older British textbooks in American schools, as Webster had hoped, and then went on to be a massive success, with some estimates claiming more than 100 million copies sold.[4] Ultimately, it was the widespread adoption of these small spelling changes that formed the backbone of American English as we know it today.

Thus, for many English speakers, the choice of spelling convention is linked to how we enact our identity. For British and Australian English speakers, spelling *organise* and *organisation* with an "s" demonstrates their identification with their country. For American English speakers, a "z" in *organize* and *organization* demonstrates their regional belonging. But how do other English speakers choose whether to use American or British spelling? Other English speakers may adapt their use of spelling to suit the audience of their writing, or they may pick a preference and stick to it. Spelling can be used as a stylistic tool.

Commercial Words

Words consume words. They serve as verbal imprints of the products and items we consume daily, and they are closely tied to our daily usage. In a capitalist society, the production and circulation of words are closely linked to the market, where trends and technologies dictate the creation of new words and the obsolescence of old ones. Technology has given birth to many new words, but as technology progresses, words that were once new soon become outdated, such as *walkie-talkie, Walkman, floppy disk,* or *VHS,* which were once ubiquitous but have been replaced by newer technologies. I asked my two daughters, born in 2008 and 2012, respectively, about these words, and they replied that they didn't know any of them. For younger generations, words like *pager* are entirely unfamiliar, and even *DVD* may soon disappear. This fact was brought home to me when I received a set of film DVDs from the Korean Film Archive, only to realize that I no longer owned a DVD player. These constantly changing super words reflect the changes in society and technology, and their rapid evolution serves as a reminder of the ephemerality of our cultural artifacts.

Thanks to technological advancements and the breadth and depth of information shared around the globe in online and virtual interactions, the speed at which words are shared and word shifts occur will continue to accelerate, surpassing anything seen before. The word *metaverse* has become trendy in recent years. Although first used in Neal Stephenson's novel *Snow Crash* in 1992, this term has recently entered the mainstream as a buzzword in the tech industry, particularly after Facebook's rebranding as Meta. In a video presentation released on October 28, 2021, Mark Zuckerberg stated his desire for Meta to be "seen as a metaverse company," catapulting the term into even greater popularity. The presentation featured interviews with Zuckerberg and CGI concept videos of what Meta's metaverse product might eventually look like when fully realized. However, as Meta has become more closely associated with the concept of the metaverse, the word *metaverse* itself is now less frequently used. Instead, terms such as *virtual reality* (VR) and *augmented reality* (AR) have become the latest buzzwords. Indeed, the lifespan of words is getting shorter and shorter.

Now, if I were to mention the word *Amazon* in an ordinary conversation, it's unlikely that images of a lush green landscape and diverse wildlife would be the first to come to mind. Instead, a few black letters with an orange arrow underneath, packages, and perhaps a website would be your initial thought. A quick search in the Oxford English Dictionary would define *Amazon* more in the former sense, but it does not stop an ordinary person associating the word more with the company. What is more, a quick Google image search for "android phone" provides you with results that are heavily Samsung-biased and less faithful to what *android* really means. According to the OED, *android* is "an automaton resembling a human being."[5] The way we use this word today, however, is generally associated with Samsung and the mobile operating system. Corporations are changing the meanings of words that have been established in the English language at an unprecedented pace, and this does not seem to be slowing down anytime soon.

Over the decades, we have witnessed the rapid rise of commercial words—words that enter our vocabularies through companies and branding rather than traditional linguistic routes. Rather than belonging to a certain language or nation-state, many commercial words belong to the company that created them and, by extension, its customers. Most of these commercial words spring from the tech industry, as they forge linguistic pathways into an entirely new area of human understanding. Words like *iPad* and *Twitter* may be trademarks, but by naming an entirely new phenomenon that has become part of the everyday, they form the basis of a vocabulary for new forms of being and communicating. George Orwell, in his essay "Politics and the English Language" (1946), wrote: "Never use a foreign phrase, a scientific word, or a jargon word if you can think of an everyday English equivalent." The reality, however, is that this Orwellian ideal is simply not possible. Language has an explosive power to generate new words constantly, and given that a significant number of people in the world speak English in addition to at least one other language, life with such a limited set of local words would be unimaginable. Propelled by globalization, consumerism is settling itself into the heart of our language.

Consider the internationally popular fast food chain McDonald's. The trademark for the name "McDonald's" has been a subject of various corporate disputes over the years. In the Philippines, McDonald's sued MacJoy, a local fast food restaurant, for using a similar trade name. MacJoy argued that it was the first user of the name, but the Philippine Supreme Court upheld the right of McDonald's to its internationally recognized trademark. Similarly, McDonald's forced Elizabeth McCaughey of the United States to change the name of her coffee shop "McCoffee" after operating under that name for seventeen years. McDonald's lost a legal action in the United Kingdom against Frank Yuen, owner of McChina Wok Away, a small chain of Chinese takeaway outlets. The court ruled that the McChina name would not cause any confusion among customers and that McDonald's had no right to the prefix "Mc." In Denmark, Allan Pedersen, a hotdog vendor, won a legal battle against McDonald's to keep his shop name McAllan. In Malaysia, McDonald's sued a small restaurant named McCurry, which serves Indian food, for using the "Mc" prefix. McDonald's won an initial judgment in the High Court, but the decision was later overturned by the appeals court and upheld by the federal court. These disputes show that although McDonald's has trademarks for the name "McDonald's," the use of the "Mc" prefix in other contexts can be a contentious issue, with different outcomes in different jurisdictions.

The trademark for the name "Apple" has also been at the center of several corporate disputes involving Apple Inc. and Apple Corps, the record label and holding company founded by the Beatles. These disputes arose from Apple Inc.'s expansion into the music industry, which Apple Corps viewed as infringing on its trademark for the name "Apple." Through multiple settlements and legal battles, the companies ultimately reached an agreement in 2007, with Apple Inc. owning all of the trademarks related to "Apple" and licensing them to Apple Corps. These disputes underscore the importance of trademarks for our words. They are more commodified than we may first think.

Word War

In the world of words, there is a constant battle for survival. The competition is fierce, and only the fittest survive. The ability of words to endure and be remembered is closely related to human physiology and memory. In the pre-modern era, people relied on songs to preserve and transmit information, as writing materials were scarce. Songs were an optimal form for retaining information, with short, rhythmic patterns that could be easily repeated to create a collective memory. However, as we enter an age of heavily mediated communication, accompanied by AI, this tradition is beginning to change. In the future, competition between physical and digital words will be more tense, and digital words will prevail.

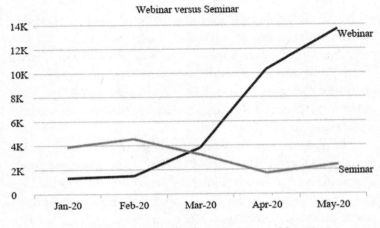

Use of the words *webinar* and *seminar*, January–May 2020.

In the war of words, some thrive and endure, while others dwindle and fade away. Of course, the demand for words plays a crucial role. Words are created in response to societal demands, and new words emerge as new demands arise. During the Covid-19 pandemic in 2020, the usage of the word *webinar* was triple that of *seminar*. This reflects the reality that we could not physically meet and had to rely on virtual platforms to connect and communicate.[6]

There are countless words in the English language, and it's a battle for survival of the fittest, which often means the shortest. Many factors can predict the lifespan of a word, but one that is consistent across languages is length. Simply put, words that are too long often can't survive. This isn't always the case in English, but it is true for many other languages. This is partly a result of limitations of our memory, as pointed out in George Miller's concept of the "magical number seven," which suggests that humans can typically hold around seven (plus or minus two) items or pieces of information in their working memory at any one time.[7] This is one of the reasons that acronyms survive and thrive.

In English, the average syllable length is 3 letters, while the average word length is 1.66 syllables and 5 letters. The average sentence length is 17 words, 29 syllables, and 87 letters. According to the *Wall Street Journal*, the average word length is 4.8 characters per word, even when covering the most complex business topics. The BBC averages slightly lower, at 4.7 characters per word.

Language is complex and varies depending on the context. Some words have staying power, while others are relatively short-lived. Once a word is born, it competes with other words to remain in our mental lexicon. On top of this word war, we recognize that words can be complex and confusing. Magdalene College in Oxford, where C. S. Lewis, the author of *The Chronicles of Narnia*, was a fellow, is pronounced as "Maudlin," but the nearby church in Oxford City Centre, St. Mary Magdalene, is pronounced "Magdalene." The pronunciation of the college's name often confuses visitors from around the world who say "MAG-da-leen." In the Middle Ages, the word's pronunciation became anglicized as "maudlin," and this pronunciation has stuck for the name of the college, even though the spelling has been revised to reflect the Greek origin; the college, regardless of what happened, wanted to keep the original anglicized pronunciation. The usage of words is often decided by their makers and users, leading to inevitable inconsistencies.

The existence of silent letters in English words can be traced to the language's historical development and its borrowing of words from other languages. They are a visual record of history. Many English words come from French, Latin, and other languages that use silent letters, and these have been retained in English even though they are not always pronounced. Particularly in French loanwords such as *hour, honor,* and *heir*, the "h" can be silent. Similarly, "k" is usually silent when it appears before an "n" at the beginning of a word, as in *knee, knit,* and *knob*. The letter "b" can be silent when it appears after "m" at the end of a word, as in *comb* or *lamb*. A "g" can be silent when it appears before an "n," such as in *sign, gnat, gnocchi,* and *foreign*. These silent letters may be inconvenient, but they serve as a reminder of the history of English and its borrowing of words from other languages.

Still looking through these historical lenses, since the emergence of personal computers in the 1980s, spell checkers and their modern cousin, autocorrect, have exerted considerable force on English conventions and accepted vocabulary for all of its users, throughout the world. These programs come installed and activated by default on the computing products we have purchased for decades, and increasingly, much of global writing in English is now processed by the spell check and autocorrect software of just a few global technology companies. Microsoft, with its Word and Outlook applications, controlled 87.5 percent of the global market for word processors and email programs in 2018, encountering significant competition only from Google Docs and Google's Gmail.[8] At the same time, the vast majority of desktop computers, laptops, tablet devices, and mobile devices in use today employ either a Microsoft or Apple operating system, which also have built-in spell checking and autocorrecting tools.

Many of these systems provide users with the choice to select between American and British English conventions, as well as a host of other languages, but the frequency with which we interact with these tools on a range of platforms means that inevitably preferences are not always set or maintained. Further, Microsoft, Apple, and Google are all U.S.-based technology companies, so their spell check and autocorrect tools often default to American English conventions. A student at Oxford intending to follow the university's style guidelines to employ British English conventions may inadvertently slip into using American English ones simply because of the default settings in their Outlook mail client.

The power of these technology monopolies in determining conventions is larger than their inadvertent promotion of American English. The algorithms that run in the background while you type to determine whether a word is misspelled, and to suggest or to automatically replace it with an alternative, corrected spelling, are more complex than simply running every word you type against a list of known words in a dictionary. Not only would this method be extremely slow, but such a system would fail to identify when you typed a relatively rare word but intended a more common one, or when a word was incorrectly inflected for the grammar of the sentence. As a result of this added complexity, we often have no clue what list of words or dictionary our spell check and autocorrect systems are checking our typing against. Instead, these decisions are made by an unknown team of programmers who may or may not have a full understanding of various English language conventions and their potential impact on users.

By controlling these programs that process much of written English, Apple, Google, and Microsoft have assumed another major role in setting conventions. They can decide when a new word is widely enough known to merit a conventional spelling and capitalization regime. In this way they exercise considerable power over our lexicon. This is particularly the case with their ability to normalize corporate words and spellings in our vocabulary. In this way, *to google* was swiftly accepted as the transitive verb to describe searching for something on the web, but also a less widely used word like *GPay,* for Google's payment system, on certain software platforms is already accepted as a correctly spelled proper noun. But perhaps the word *iPhone* is the greatest example of a word created in Silicon Valley that defies known English capitalization conventions but has its spelling rules enforced by spell checking systems.

Ordering from Starbucks can be a stressful experience for some of us—particularly because of its unique sizing conventions. Excluding "short" and "tall," the coffee chain makes use of Italian words: *grande* (a sixteen-ounce drink), *venti* (twenty-four ounces), and *trenta* (thirty-one ounces, reserved for iced drinks). Even if you do not agree with the cup size words at Starbucks, you have to use those words to order coffee there. The story behind this decision involves the time when the founder of Starbucks, Howard Schultz, first traveled to Italy in 1983 and fell in love with the "the romance and theater of coffee." *Grande* is Italian for "large," *venti* is "twenty," and *trenta* is "thirty." You may be wondering why the sixteen-ounce size isn't *sedici*, the Italian for "sixteen." Well, according to an article on Dictionary.com, possibly "the less-familiar *venti* and *trenta* may help consumers forget the cost—or calorie count—of what they are about to drink." Thanks to Starbucks, ordering a cup of joe requires knowledge of some Italian—or at least, a commercialized, anglicized version of the language. Along with other examples, one can indeed say that commercialism is rooting itself in our everyday language.[9]

Words are also born through products. Though they are not born in physical worlds, they can be considered real and enter English. The OED defines *minion* as "Originally: a (usually male) favourite of a sovereign, prince, or other powerful person; a person who is dependent on a patron's favour; a hanger-on. In later use (without the connotation 'favoured'): a follower or underling, *esp.* one who is servile or unimportant; a servant, officer, subordinate, assistant; a henchman."[10] However, if you ask a child what comes to mind when hearing the word *minion*, it will probably be a small yellow cartoon character in blue dungarees and goggles. Thanks to the Disney Company, the power of memes, and social media, the *Despicable Me* franchise has led to the child's image overpowering the traditional understanding of what a minion is.

What's more, who knew that Google would have such a notable global influence? Ditching its initial name "BackRub," "Google" came about during a brainstorming session when Sean Anderson suggested the word *googolplex,* and Larry Page countered with the shorter *googol.* (*Googol* refers to the digit 1 followed by 100 zeroes, while *googolplex* is 1 followed by a googol zeros.) However, when Anderson checked to see if that domain name was taken, he accidentally searched for "google.com" instead of "googol.com." Luckily enough, Page preferred that name, and registered the domain name for Sergey Brin and himself in 1997.[11] Who would have thought that a typo would have such international commercial power and catch on across geographical, cultural, and linguistic borders to the extent that it takes on more than just a noun form. This is the reality we live in; large companies have a bigger impact on our language than we may initially think.

The Generational Word Divide

The art of word stylistics doesn't depend solely on one's personal background. Sometimes, decisions are made on a word-by-word basis. My American friend Ben once told me that he felt more at home with British pronunciation and spelling, so much that he preferred them to the American way. He still found it challenging to pronounce the word *tomato* as the British do, however. Ben always used the American pronunciation "tomayto," rather than the British "tomaahto"; he confessed that he didn't know why. The American pronunciation was deeply ingrained in his speech patterns, and he found it hard to break away from it.

In the past, there was a noticeable Western skew in cultural capital. This has changed over the decades, as relative scarcity determines value. Before a meal, it used to be common to say the French phrase *bon appétit;* nowadays more people are saying the Japanese equivalent, *itadakimasu.* Perhaps this can be linked to the growth in popularity of Japanese cuisine in the West, which only developed after the popularization of French cuisine. The French language was commonly associated with well-made and desirable cosmetic products in the past. These days, driven by the force of globalization that allows people to access more media and cultural objects from other countries, some consumers' prefer-ence has shifted toward South Korea. You may have heard of the increasing popularity of K-beauty, which seems to be reflected in how makeup and skincare lines market their products, as they create unique words that could appeal to different tastes. In an era of cultural saturation being more prevalent than ever because of technological innovations and ever growing social media use, so too is it being reflected in our language.

In the past, nationality, ethnicity, gender, and educational and socioeconomic status were used to describe a person's word choice. In today's world, these traditional categories have lost their relevance, and personal taste has become the determining factor in choosing one's words. There are many words specific to social media that young people use and older people probably wouldn't understand: *finsta, stan, woke, fleek,* to name a few. There are also words familiar to older generations that younger people do not recognize. A YouGov survey in 2018 found that only 14 percent of children from six to eighteen knew what a "pager" or "teletext" was, and just 36 percent for a "floppy disk."[12]

Scholars have called these differences in communication trends "asymmetry" and have highlighted how this can socially isolate older adults.[13] All social media demographics show that elderly people (roughly those who are sixty or older) make up the smallest demographic of users. There are several reasons. One recent study determined that people who are now older did not see a need to start using internet technology when it first began to spread, and following its rapid development over the past few decades they now feel overwhelmed by the idea of beginning to use it. Instead, the elderly tend to prefer socializing face to face or via telephone calls.[14] Young people tend to use social media platforms for communicating, and "build empathy and social con-nectedness" by sharing photographs, activities, or comments with emotional content on these sites.[15] In this way, younger "digital natives" are communicating in a manner that may be completely outside an older person's experience. There is a clear barrier caused by social media.

Adding to this idea of asymmetry, there are several factors that may cause problems when younger and older people try to interact on social media. Finding the right time for communication may be difficult. Young people tend to be busy during the day, working or studying, and then very active on social media in the evening or at night. Older people may be retired and tend to have free time during the day and be less inclined to socialize during the evening.[16] Moreover, how younger and older people communicate on social media varies linguistically. The number of emoticons, internet acronyms, and words not in the dictionary decrease as age increases.[17] Hence, when a younger person receives a message from an older person, it will be in a style that seems unnatural to them (and vice versa), another source of dissonance between them.

If you ask a twelve-year-old these days whether they've heard of "MySpace," the answer will probably be "no." The same could be said for other once-popular online platforms like Tumblr. Indeed, social media can change at an unprecedented pace—both in decline and growth. In recent years, TikTok has established itself as one of the top online platforms for American teens, while the share of them who use Facebook has fallen sharply.[18] According-ing to a report by the Pew Research Center, YouTube stands out as the most common online platform that teens use, with 95 percent saying they have used the site or app. A majority also use TikTok (67 percent), Instagram (62 percent), and Snapchat (59 percent). Since 2014, Instagram and Snapchat use has grown. Even though teens today don't use Facebook as much as in previous years, the platform still boasts widespread usage among adults, as seen in other studies by the center.

Minecraft is a popular video game that has become a phenom-enon among young children and teenagers. It is a sandbox-style game that allows players to build, explore, and create in a virtual world made up of 8-bit square blocks. According to statistics, up to 54 percent of boys between the ages of three and twelve play Minecraft, while 46 percent of girls in the same age range do. The game captures the attention and imagination of young children, regardless of gender. The disparity in these statistics becomes even more pronounced when looking at the six-to-eight age group, where 68 percent of boys play Minecraft, and 32 percent of girls. Despite its popularity among young children, many parents may not be aware of Minecraft's significance beyond being a simple "computer game." It's worth noting that many of the terms associated with Minecraft, such as *mods, redstone,* and *biomes,* may be familiar to young players but not necessarily to their parents.

If you've ever used TikTok for more than an hour, I would be surprised if you haven't come across the terms *e-girl* and *e-boy.* Combined, *e-girl* and *e-boy* encompass a Gen Z youth subculture that became popular in the late 2010s, particularly with the help of TikTok. Originally the "e" stood for "electronic," for the association with the internet and digital landscapes. In fact, *e-girl* used to be a pejorative term that would target women who were perceived as seeking male attention online. These days, however, it is related to more of an aesthetic that draws from emo, mall goth, and Japanese street fashion—though in more recent years it has come to incorporate K-pop fashion too. TikTok played a significant role in the spread of these words, notably through a trend that started around 2019 in which people would create transformation videos—transforming themselves into an *e-girl* or *e-boy.* Many Gen Z-ers would argue that being an *e-girl* or *e-boy* is more than just dressing a certain way and eye-rolling at the camera.

On the topic of platform words, you may have come across the word *cap. Cap* means lying, and *no cap* means telling the truth, so these phrases are being used on all sorts of social media platforms to call out people on whether they are lying or not. An example of it in use: "I'm sick today no cap." The word *cap* is also sometimes replaced by the blue cap emoji. The phrase, which first emerged in African American vernacular English and was popularized through hip-hop music, derives from shorthand for gold teeth, of which there are two kinds: permanent gold teeth ("perms") and "caps." Caps can easily be taken off, but permanent ones cannot. Hence, *cap* suggests something is fake, whereas *no cap* suggests honesty and truth. The phrase reached new levels of popularity in 2021 to 2022 through social media. Indeed, social media plays a powerful role in adding to and changing the meanings of words that were perhaps more niche, as well as the spread of such words.

Digital Words

Globalization and digitalization when combined catalyze the process of word generation. Yet this comes with its drawbacks. Words intricately linked with technological innovations, such as *Touch ID* and *Face ID*, are essentially determined by the shift of technology. However, as this process speeds up, technology leaves verbal traces that are increasingly difficult to track. The Covid-19 pandemic has intensified the digital divide between not only generations but also different socioeconomic groups.[19] There may very well come a time, if it has not already begun, when we find a clear word divide in our global English between those who have access to certain technology and media and those who do not.

The British famously love to queue but are now faced with the virtual alternative. Many stores, restaurants, and service providers implemented digital queuing software that allowed clientele to join a queue via QR code, app, or text via their smartphone and receive a notification when it is their turn to enter the store. The technology had the advantage of ensuring social distancing by allowing customers to wait in their car or carry out other business nearby without losing their spot in the queue. If it took a pandemic to make this convenient service more widespread, the term *virtual queuing* is more than two decades old and was first implemented for inbound call centers where long wait times led to upset customers and a high number of abandoned calls and redials for agents to sift through. To solve the problem, answering systems were designed that allowed customers to input their phone number and receive an automated call back when they reached the front of the queue, freeing customers to do as they please while a virtual placeholder waits in line for them.

Digital queueing is yet another example of how the virtual world and consumerism in the physical world are increasingly interacting and producing new terms and words. It increasingly appears that these will be the two main forces driving the development of our lexicon and the coining of new words. The rapid speed of technological innovation and its commercialization also mean that just as a computer or phone requires regular updates to its operating system to continue to function, our lexicon will also require updating with whole suites of new words as technology changes. To some extent this has already occurred.

For earlier generations the critical period for language acquisition, the first twenty years or so of life when much of one's lexicon is formed, occurred before the terminology of personal computing was widespread, and many Generation X-ers and Baby Boomers had to update their lexicon on the fly in order to remain functional in work environments that have demanded increasing levels of technological fluency. Similarly, as virtual reality and the metaverse become more central to our everyday lives we will likely see a new suite of related and unfamiliar vocabulary, which even those currently proficient with the present "update" of technological and consumerist language will have to pick up.

Think about tech terms like 3G, 4G, LTE, and 5G. You may or may not know that the "G" in these terms stands for "generation," that LTE stands for Long Term Evolution, and it is almost certain that unless you work in telecommunications you don't know the technical specifics that define each of these technologies. Instead, you likely have an intuitive understanding from seeing them in the upper corner of your mobile phone screen that they mean your phone has broadband internet access and that the higher the number the faster the internet will be. In fact, the hyper technical definition of these various standards is not much use to the average user of these terms. Instead, their use seems to come from how easy they are to intuitively understand and the fact that as they travel rapidly across borders their simple composition of just a few letters and numbers means they do not require translation. 3G in English is the same as 3G in Turkish and Korean. What's more, the alphanumeric nature of the terms means they aren't associated with a particular national origin, and are instead truly transnational and easily made native in any language. Given the dominance of technology in our daily lives it seems that handy tech vocabulary like this, offering users an intuitive understanding and able to travel without translation, will become an increasingly common part of global vocabulary.

Chapter 6

MOVING WORDS

Migration of Words

Words are constantly traveling, much like we do. They settle and form new connections, as do we. As they journey, their meanings, forms, and identities undergo change. Words are a mirror of the realities and memories of our lives. Even amid Covid-19 and subsequent lockdowns, words persisted in their travels. Wherever you may be, young or old, tech savvy or not, virtual migration has affected us all. Before Covid-19, few could have fathomed socializing online or gathering in virtual spaces, let alone attending hybrid conferences. Teachers would have never imagined instructing young children on Google Meet. As the effects of Covid-19 subside, we are not entirely reverting back to in-person modes of communication. Rather, we assess each situation and select the most fitting meeting option. Hybrid meetings may ultimately become the norm.

From a communication standpoint, face-to-face conversations are undeniably valuable. They deepen relationships, which is vital for effective communication. Nevertheless, face-to-face communication does have limitations. Just today, I booked a flight to visit my elderly mother in Korea and was alarmed to discover, according to my ticket, that this one-way trip alone would emit 696 kilograms of carbon dioxide. Despite my efforts to justify the trip, I could not help but wonder if large international conferences should be held primarily online or in hybrid formats. I have had to withdraw from some conferences because they were exclusively "in-person," leaving me feeling disheartened and excluded. For many who cannot afford to travel, attending such events would be impossible. For working mothers, for instance, attending a conference in person may be beyond their means. Hybrid formats will become more prevalent, and words will continue to traverse boundaries between physical and virtual realms to suit our lifestyles. One does not need to physically carry words anymore; the internet and online channels have become the space for word traffic. The internet serves as a modern Silk Road where words from all over can travel to different places and encounter each other. Before, words accompanied the physical objects we carried, and we had to go places to spread words. Now, you can do all of this from the comfort of your own room through social media.

Let's imagine words as people. The migration of words resembles the migration of people. First-generation words are parallel to first-generation immigrants. It often takes them a while to settle, and they may maintain their homeland identity as well as their new identity in their new land. Words that are foreign-born remain italicized or capitalized for some time and receive special treatment in their new language. If they settle as translated, localized forms, they may be more easily assimilated; in transliterated form, more time may be needed for assimilation. In novels set in an Asian context or translated from non-English backgrounds, the number of transliterated words is often limited to around a dozen per book, as more transliterated words can decrease familiarity. Whether to keep the original word or adopt a new word is not an easy decision. When I introduce myself as June, it's easy for my English neighbors to remember, but I don't feel like that name truly represents me. On the other hand, if I use my Korean name, Jieun, people may find it hard to remember and pronounce, but it feels like me. Choosing which name to use is often a decision that many of us encounter, especially those who move or travel frequently.

Second-generation words resemble the lives of second-generation immigrants. They often have dual identities and belongings, and many words are hybrids between English and local languages. These words have gradually become a strong asset of the English language. In Asia, for example, locally born English words or English-Asian hybrid words make up a significant part of the contemporary word pantry. It's important to note that contemporary words in Asia and Africa are not the same as they were in the past, as modernization has brought a new set of words that often take on an English form. Words that existed before the twentieth century in Asia are diminishing, and English words are increasing in daily use. In Japan, for example, young people tend to prefer the "cooler," more international, more professional katakana loanwords from English, as opposed to the conventional kanji compound equivalent. Nevertheless, language purification policies are often at the heart of national activities, but it's important to know that deleting words considered impure or mixed may leave the language with fewer useful words.

Sociolinguists working in the "third wave" explore how people come together in shared interest groups that over time contribute to shared linguistic practices, which identify them as belonging to that specific group. Such groups are labeled as "communities of practice." Communities of practice are created, maintained, and adapted by the people who create them, making them very diverse, interactive, and fluid compared with the previous wave's more traditional determiners such as class or race.

One of the key works in the third wave is Penelope Eckert's study of two opposing social groups in a Detroit high school: the "Jocks" and the "Burnouts." This study helped demonstrate how communities of practice develop their own individual linguistic repertoire to identify them as belonging to the group. Eckert argued that we can look at linguistic style in a way that is not too dissimilar from personal style, suggesting that we are actively involved in a process of bricolage by which we add different elements to tailor our own personal linguistic style. Much as we put together clothes and accessories when choosing an outfit, individuals take linguistic influence from a variety of different places. Subcultures, local dialects, and communities of practice all play a role in our linguistic repertoire. Eckert spent several years observing the Jocks, the Burnouts, and a larger, less polarized middle group. She looked at where they smoked, where they ate, the width of their jeans, how they spoke, and where they hung out after school. As a result, she was able to develop a highly detailed picture of social groupings that naturally emerged at the school and how they were defined through their everyday practices.

There were substantial differences in linguistic practices between the Jocks and the Burnouts. Primarily, this was highlighted by the different pronunciation of the "u" vowel sound in words such as *hut* and *but*. Differences like this essentially reinforced the notion of linguistic practices playing an important role in in-group membership.

Eckert's research illustrated that our position in society and membership of certain common interest groups can shape aspects of our linguistic behavior. This chapter is concerned with moving words. Moving words often begin in the idiolects of a diaspora community. They are words retained from their original or heritage language, usually because a certain nuance of meaning cannot be found in English. From there, words might outgrow their idiolects, either by prolonged usage or growing interest in a certain culture and move into a wider sociolect, or the broader vocabulary of English speakers in general. Words move via a variety of paths, and this is just one of the ways they might travel and evolve. The internet especially is breaking down sociolinguistic barriers and the influence of age, class, ethnic background, gender, and other characteristics.

In the past, ordinary words were often confined to their place of birth, as people tended to live and communicate locally.

First- and second-generation words also tended to stay within their place of origin; most ordinary words were specific to their respective regions. With the increase in travel and mobility, however, the boundaries between languages and cultures have become more porous, allowing ordinary words to easily cross those borders. Global mobility has allowed more and more overseas words to become local words. For members of the third and fourth generations, who are mostly from Generation Z or Alpha, words are mostly used in some form of online interaction, unconstrained by geography. The internet is a new pathway for words of the world.

I took my first flight at the age of twenty-five, which would perhaps now be considered unusual, given how airplane travel is far more common than it was then. Today, international travel is more accessible than ever before. In the current age, aside from the pandemic, traveling and living abroad have become easier for many. Over the past decade, we've seen a significant increase of about 250 million tourists in Europe alone, before the pandemic. Additionally, it's not just tourism that has seen an uptick. Migration has increased globally. An estimated 281 million people were living in a country other than their place of birth in 2020. This number is double the amount in 1990 and triple the estimated number of 1970.[1] More young people are traveling and moving abroad for work, with 85 percent expressing the desire to do so, up from 40 percent ten years ago. Physical mobility is doomed to decrease due to climate change, but this doesn't mean that the mobility of words will decrease—online and virtual mobility will increase as this happens. Words have been traveling and now travel more and more. As they travel, they carry with them rich histories. This process has rapidly sped up in past decades thanks to the arrival of social media platforms and other online spaces. People from opposite sides of the world are able to communicate with one another no matter their distance, resulting in what I call a "word big bang."

When people move, they carry their words with them. They may not use these words in exactly the same way as before, but they still hold them dear and adapt them to fit new situations. These words are a part of the verbal identity of the diaspora and remain within their community for a long time. These words often describe emotions or are strongly tied to the diasporic community's cultural heritage. They may include interjections, terms of address, or even food-related words. In the United States, Mexican food words such as *taco, burrito, enchilada, guacamole,* and *salsa* remain as a reflection of the culture where they originated. Even words like *churro* have made their way into the English language, representing the delicious fried dough pastry enjoyed in Mexico and other Latin American countries.

The Asian diaspora also carries calling words, or terms of address, with them wherever they go. Asian communities have delicate and complex ways of addressing those in their close community that reflect warmth, solidarity, respect, and hierarchy.[2] For diasporic Asian communities, terms of address are particularly important. Calling an elder by their first name would be inappropriate and could damage a relationship. In Vietnam, for example, younger people address older men as "Ong" (grandfather) and older women as "Ba" (grandmother). Non-elderly men and women are addressed by older individuals as "Anh" (older brother) and "Chi" (older sister), respectively. Very young or unmarried men and women are referred to as "Chu" (younger brother) and "Co" (younger sister). Nobody calls each other by their given names. These terms of address are just one example of the verbal traces, remnants, and reminders that remain with the diasporic community, connecting them to their cultural heritage.

In the British Filipino community, it's still very common for children and young adults to refer to an older woman (who may not be blood-related) as "Tita." The equivalent term for older men is "Tito." This term of address can be used by itself (it comes in handy if you don't know their first name!) or with their first name, like "Tito Boi." Not referring to them as such would be considered disrespectful; calling them by their first name alone is considered rude. This is also seen with terms of address for older people in general (blood-related or not), with "Ate" (for an older female) and "Kuya" (for an older male); children and adults use these terms to show respect. Often, younger siblings are not even allowed to call their older sibling by their first name even when talking to their non-Filipino friends. These relational words are difficult to translate and integrate into new languages, particularly in English and European languages where interpersonal terms are less commonly used. Even if the second and third generations of Asian communities do not speak their home languages fluently, they still know how to properly address people in the community using the appropriate calling terms. Many Asian people in the second or third generation diaspora find the use of these complex ways to show respect toward their elders not only linguistically challenging, but also uncomfortable due to the hierarchical nature of the language.

Perhaps the most famous Asian-origin calling terms in recent years are Korean ones, thanks to the popularity of K-pop and K-drama. In 2021, the OED included twenty-six Korean wave-inspired words in the dictionary. I worked as the Korean consultant for this project. Three of these words are terms of address, *oppa, noona,* and *unni.* It is expected that more address terms, such as *hyung, ajeossi,* and *ajumma,* will enter the OED in its upcoming updates. As Korean culture continues to spread, more words from the K-wave are expected to be included in English.

Words with Multiple Identities

Yerba mate is consumed by the likes of Pope Francis and Lionel Messi, as well as being a popular drink in South America in general. The term reflects the drink's immigration history (it was introduced to me by a Syrian colleague). Its origins date back to the Guarani people of Paraguay and Brazil, and in the mid-1800s, Arab immigrants in South America were introduced to it by indigenous people, and then brought the drink back to the Arab world. However, it was initially consumed only by immigrant communities and not widely known among the general population.

In recent years, yerba mate has gained wider popularity in the Arab world, especially among health enthusiasts and those seeking a caffeine alternative. The drink is often shared as a symbol of hospitality and friendship in the Arab world, and it has become popular in such countries as Lebanon, Jordan, and the United Arab Emirates. Cafes and restaurants throughout the region now offer it alongside traditional Arabic beverages.

Waves of immigration, primarily to Argentina and Brazil, resulted in the sharing of traditions, and starting in the 1860s up to the 1960s, immigrants from Syria and Lebanon arrived in South America and began to exchange customs, including the habit of drinking yerba mate. Immigrants did not start to return to the Middle East in large numbers until the 1970s, when economic conditions in South America, including Argentina and Brazil, took a downturn, and some even became politically unstable with coups and military dictatorships. Meanwhile, Middle Eastern countries were experiencing an oil boom and a subsequent economic high. Many immigrants from the nineteenth and twentieth centuries decided to return to their homeland, bringing yerba mate with them. In the 1970s and beyond, we see the greatest spike in yerba mate exports to Syria and Lebanon, accounting for the returned emigrants who wanted to continue drinking it. *Yerba mate* is also a term in English, carrying a complex history of immigration and emigration. English now has a lot of these immigration words.

Moving slightly further afield, the Vietnamese noodle dish *pho* gives a lot of English speakers difficulty when it comes to pronunciation, with users varying between saying "foe" and "fuh."

Determining a correct pronunciation for the word is made even more complicated by the complex origins of the dish itself. Born in Vietnam, *pho* first emerged when the country was occupied by France, with the dish thought to have been inspired by the wealth of French broth-based dishes. Although there is no definitive etymology, the name is probably adapted from the French *feu* (as in *pot-au-feu*), a quintessentially French thin beef stew.

The migration of *pho* aptly reveals that the pronunciation of words imported or migrated into the English language, alongside forms and spellings, can be wide and diverse as a result of the lack of hard and fast rules about such terms. Consequently, there are no right and wrong ways of pronouncing such words, and it is instead up to the individual to determine how to pronounce each word according to their personal style and the context. Determining how a word should be pronounced is hardly something that falls under the domain of a nation-state of language—particularly when a word is being used in the context of another language and culture. Wide-ranging rules cannot be applied to situations such as these, and it is not as if international lawsuits over the proper pronunciation of words and phrases are a realistic option. In such instances, it is inevitably up to an individual or organization to determine how to pronounce the words they use for their own purposes. Far from being a problem, this diversity imbues the language we use every day with an excitement and playfulness that we otherwise may not be able to enjoy.

Border-Crossing Words

Nowadays, a word's habitat extends beyond borders, encompassing social media spaces that transcend geographic boundaries. These words are translingual, as they live beyond the borders of languages. As they settle and take root in a new language, they adapt to their new local reality by acquiring a fresh orthography, pronunciation, and even new meanings. The words we use are a reflection of our own identity. We are constantly interacting with other spaces and other cultures and learning new words through these experiences. Words are more interactive, dynamic, and fluid than ever, and are entering our everyday lives exponentially. In a globalized time, words are becoming translingual, transcultural, and transnational. Border-crossing is the defining characteristic of the life of a word, which will cause nation-state language borders to lose their validity and power in the near future. The English language, as the common language of our time, should be inclusive and reflect the heritages and dwelling places of diaspora writers, overcoming the prejudice and prestige around the English language. We should accept that English is not only the language of English people, but a language for everyone. Rather than being hierarchical and prescriptive, it should be inclusive and open to a diversity of spellings and pronunciations.

As language becomes ever more translingual, we need to respect, preserve, and protect the heritage of words with diverse backgrounds—including names. Although some spellings may look strange, such as the name of a market town in Buckinghamshire, England, "Princes Risborough," where the word *Princes* seems to be missing its second "s," we see in this chapter that names can be exempt from typical grammar rules and traditional ideas. This is especially true for foreign names. Many dictionaries anglicize foreign words, presenting the English version of pronunciation, but what if these words were also presented with their local pronunciation?

The transcultural, border-crossing nature of words is best exemplified through many food words. The word *curry* first appeared in the OED in a culinary context from 1598. At its introduction to the dictionary it had the definition of "a preparation of meat, fish, fruit, or vegetables, cooked with a quantity of bruised spices and turmeric, and used as a relish or flavoring, esp. for dishes composed of or served with rice." Hence, the noun *curry* was used to describe "a dish or stew flavored with this preparation (or with curry-powder)."[3] The compound terms *curry sauce, curry paste,* and *curry powder* all appeared in the OED via English language cookbooks from the years 1845, 1855, and 1810, respectively, demonstrating the lag between the common usage in reference to a foreign dish and the widespread knowledge of Indian cookery in the United Kingdom. The term is listed by the OED as being of Tamil or Kannada origin, where *kari* and *karil* are terms for a sauce or relish for rice. It is most likely that the term entered British English via French and Portuguese usage. The use of the word *curry* in the English lexicon has come to mean almost any sauce-based Indian dish, and hence is not used to describe any particular flavor beyond the distinctive spices of the Indian subcontinent.

Curry (or *kari*) in its indigenous usage has a meaning roughly equivalent to gravy in English, and hence is rarely used to refer to a specific dish. For example, where an English menu may say "Chicken curry" or "paneer (cheese) curry," a local speaker's description would be more inclined to distinguish between the specific dishes or flavors, instead referring to them as "chicken masala" or "matar paneer." The adaptation of the term *curry* into the English language, and the accompanying fondness for Indian cuisine (as homogenized under this term), has spread to other languages, most clearly seen in the Japanese adaptation of curry (or *kare*). Curry was introduced to Japan by the British during the Meiji era (1868–1912). India was under the colonial rule of the British raj at the time, and the use of boxed "curry powder" as a flavoring or seasoning had become popular among British troops, hence its spread to Japan via the military. Authentic Japanese *kare* recipes differ greatly from their Indian originators due to their consistent use of curry sauce mix or boxed curry powder, and often feature the addition of sweet seasonings such as ketchup or apricot jam.

Meanwhile, chicken tikka masala is believed to be the first curry recipe published in Britain, appearing in Hannah Glasse's book *The Art of Cookery Made Plain and Easy* in 1747. Surprisingly, many classic curries, such as balti, jalfrezi, madras, and chicken vindaloo, were actually invented in Britain. What's interesting is that the terms used to describe these dishes are also English in origin and have no direct translation in Hindi, Bengali, or other Indian languages. Despite their clear cultural heritage, these words are unique to the English language and were not borrowed from India. They are, in a sense, second-generation English words, born of the fusion of Indian and British cultures.

Accompanying food, we have drink. The word *tea* has its earliest English usage cited as 1655 in the OED and has a very complex etymology. In English it is a cognate for the same word in many European languages, including the Spanish *té*, French *thé*, Italian *té*, and Dutch *thee*, all of which are thought to have been born from the Malay term brought back from Bantam by the Dutch, or the alternative word in the Amoy (Xiamen) or Fujian dialects (*te*) as spoken in what was then Formosa (modern-day Taiwan).[4] *Tea* in the English language is accompanied by the parallel term *cha*, which originates from the same Chinese word in its Mandarin and Cantonese pronunciations as *chá*. This most likely traveled from Macau via the Portuguese colonies, showing up in the now obsolete cognates of the Spanish *cha* and Italian *cià* and the still-existing Arabic *shay* and Turkish *chāy*. The word *tea*, therefore, has a long transcultural history. It is unique in being relevant to so many cultures across the globe while sharing the same root name (with almost all global tea-drinking cultures using variants of the original Chinese pronounced either *cha* or *te*), making the examination of the cultures associated with the term *tea* in English very interesting.

Along with the word *tea*, there's another word in English, *cha*, referring to the hot drink. Although *cha* has the earlier citation in the OED, from 1616, compared with 1655 for *tea*, it has since become a less common term, appearing only in British English, and even then only in a slang context.[5] This is probably because its strong links to Britain's colonial past make the term seem outdated, which suggests that the terms *tea* and *cha* both exist in English, yet exhibit different connotations.

A similar root is seen in the word *chai*, an adoption from a Hindi term, which also originates from Chinese. This term is thought to have traveled from Chinese into the Persian *chay*, from which point it spread into the Russian, Hindi, Arabic, and Turkish languages. Rather than entering English alongside the variant *cha*, the word *chai* did not appear until the twentieth century, according to the OED, where it is listed as military slang. Since then, it has had additions proposed listing it as a word dating to 1957 describing tea drinks associated with Arabic- or Hindi-speaking regions. In this context it is linked to the compound term *masala chai* (1977), denoting "spiced tea, typically brewed with a mixture of milk and water and sweetened."[6]

Draft additions to the OED also include the term *chai latte*, listed as "a hot drink similar to *masala chai*, made with spiced tea or a commercially produced concentrate and steamed milk," dating to 1994.[7] Consequently, the term *chai* (as distinct from *cha*) has developed different connotations for *tea* and is arguably no longer a mere slang term, with most modern English speakers associating it with a spiced, sweet, or milky drink originating in the Indian subcontinent.

Let's think about another drink that has rapidly risen in popularity across the globe over the past decade or so. You consume it with the aid of a larger-than-average straw. It consists of a milk tea and some chewy tapioca balls. What's it called again? *Bubble tea*? *Boba tea*? *Boba*? Another example of the linguistic diversity described above is the trajectory of the terms *bubble tea, boba tea,* and *boba* on social media. Interestingly, the linguistic heritage of the term *bubble tea* differs from its cultural heritage. While the words *bubble* and *tea* are from English, the term *bubble tea* itself has its cultural roots in Taiwan, where it was adopted to refer to a sweet fruit- or milk-based cold tea drink with tapioca pearls that became popular on the small Asian island. A not-insignificant debate emerged on social media in recent years over how best to refer to this drink in English, as the terms *bubble tea, boba tea,* and *boba* are often used interchangeably to refer to it. The relatively high-profile online debate about which term should be used demonstrates the unique ability of social media to give agency to English speakers to shape the language and determine which terms should or should not be used.[8] Dictionaries and encyclopedias have served to prescribe "proper" varieties of English in the past, but online English allows ordinary users to debate and decide among themselves, regardless of whether they are language experts, or even fluent speakers of English in a traditional sense.

This new form of global English is not only of interest to linguists, however. The wide adoption of English around the world also has political significance and already affects how social movements coordinate and gain traction. Social media English has become a powerful tool capable of turning local social movements into global ones, which can then attract international coverage and recognition.

Do you remember the viral trend of making *dalgona coffee*? Dalgona coffee is a whipped coffee drink consisting of two tablespoons each of instant coffee, sugar, and hot water, producing a frothy and thick coffee topping that can be added to hot or cold milk to make a latte-style drink with minimal ingredients. This sweet treat first became popular in South Korea, supposedly after a well-known South Korean actor visited a cafe in Macau where he was served a similar drink, saying it reminded him of "Dalgona." Dalgona is a kind of Korean sweet made of sugar and baking soda, similar to honeycomb, and often served as a street snack in South

Korea. Its popularity began in earnest in late January 2020 when *dalgona coffee* emerged as a diversion for South Koreans in quarantine, who were encouraged to replace their trips to the coffee shop with this easy homemade version. As more and more global citizens were put under quarantine measures by their respective governments, the TikTok trend for dalgona coffee continued to grow, becoming one of the largest of the year.

Despite having clear origins in South Korea and the Korean language, *dalgona coffee* appears to have become a truly global phenomenon. Although many articles and social media posts mention its Korean roots, many others do not, and the majority of global citizens are not aware of the specific origins of the drink or the honeycomb-like snack that the term *dalgona* originally referred to. This may have changed, however, since the airing of the popular Netflix show *Squid Game* in late 2021, in which characters played variations of traditional Korean games in order to survive, one of which included successfully cutting out a shape on a piece of *dalgona* using a needle. Once a trend or term has spread far beyond its original locality and become popular worldwide, can we really say it belongs to any one culture or language? Or does it then fall under global ownership? Dalgona coffee has developed and found its full identity in the transnational and transcultural space of social media, meaning we must think twice about which culture, if any, may stake a claim to its ownership. What the use of the word *dalgona* shows is that even though the etymology may not be clear, we can still use the words and their users (not their makers) can give meanings to the words. This is a more common practice in the world of social media.

Time for cheers, but what do you say? Listed in the OED as either *chin chin* or *chin-chin*, this word is defined as a phrase of salutation, and can also be used as a drinking toast; it is described as being of Anglo-Chinese origin.[9] *Chin-chin* has an OED-listed first use in 1795, making it a very early example of a second-generation Chinese-origin word in English. Despite entering the language via the colonial route, *chin-chin* originates in Mandarin Chinese, dating from a period in which the British government sent multiple missions to Asia, particularly China, in order to set up early diplomatic and trade routes.

The first cited use of *chin-chin* appears in *An Account of an Embassy to the Kingdom of Ava sent by the Government-General of India in* 1795, written by a diplomat, Michael Symes, and published in 1800. Symes was an envoy to Burma, modern-day Myanmar, and he wrote a diary of his travels and encounters in South Asia. He describes *chin-chin* as "the Chinese term of salutation." By the early twentieth century, however, the term appeared in usage entirely without reference to any Chinese context. In *Passing English of the Victorian Era: A Dictionary of Heterodox English, Slang, and Phrase,* from 1909 by James Redding Ware, *chin-chin* is defined as "(Naval—passed into club society) Hail! Good health! Here's to you." As we can see from this definition, during the course of the Victorian era *chin-chin* had become completely subsumed into English, holding its own in a British cultural context entirely removed from its Chinese origins. This is exemplified in J. B. Priestley's use of the word in his novel *The Good Companions* in 1929: "chin-chin, Effie my dear, and all the best for X-mas!" Here the term is used without reference to its Chinese origins or any explanation of its meaning, so by the early twentieth century it had made itself entirely comfortable in U.K. English.

Chin-chin may be considered a secondary word because its English usage bears a distinct difference from its original Mandarin meaning and context. The word comes from the Chinese *qīng qīng,* a repetition of a Chinese verb for a request, which can roughly be translated as "please" or "please may you." Repeating a one-syllable word in Chinese acts as an intensifier—hence *qīng qīng* is used as a polite term to request someone to join in an engagement, partake in food or drink, or make themselves comfortable. First appearing in the context of Symes's diplomatic mission, this term was clearly picked up by British diplomats listening to Mandarin-speaking hosts welcoming and entertaining them during their visit. The nuanced meaning of *chin-chin* in English, used to greet one another or as a toast, has become somewhat removed from its original Mandarin meaning. So despite strongly resembling the Chinese word from which it is derived, it possesses a new meaning unique to the English language.

In the same domain but focusing on utensils, *chopsticks* (or *chop-sticks*) is an early example of a second-generation word in English gone global. Defined by the OED as "The two small sticks or slips of bone, wood, ivory, or the like, held between the thumb and forefingers of one hand by the Chinese in place of a fork for conveying food to the mouth," and given a first use date of 1699, the word *chop-sticks* is derived from a combination of Chinese and pidgin English. In Chinese, both Mandarin and Cantonese, the two characters of the word for chopsticks, *kuàizi* or *faai3 zi2*, literally translate as "quick" and "diminutive suffix." Hence, it would be more akin to an English translation of "quick little things" or "nimble boys." Instead, the English term *chop-sticks* originates in the Chinese pidgin English phrase *chop chop*, meaning "to hurry up." This phrase is most likely rooted in Cantonese, where the term *chok chok* (*cuk1 cuk1*), meaning "to hurry" (literally "quick quick"), was picked up by British seamen from Chinese workers in the South China Sea between the seventeenth and nineteenth centuries. The Cantonese *chok chok* is used in a similar context to the Mandarin *kuai kuai*, a very similar character with exactly the same Mandarin pronunciation as the first character in *chopsticks*. Hence, it is believed that *chop-sticks*, much like *chop chop*, is adopted from the Cantonese pronunciation of a character with a similar meaning to that used in the Chinese *kuaizi*, before adding the word *sticks* for descriptive quality and thereby resulting in an English term literally meaning "quick sticks."

Although we often think of *ketchup* as an English word, it actually started out as a foreign term. Specifically, it was a word used in Malay before being introduced to the English language. Over time, as ketchup became more widely used in Western cuisine, it gained a reputation as an English word. Today, it is recognized as such around the world. The definition of *ketchup* given in the OED is "In early use: a type of piquant sauce produced in southeast Asia, probably made from fermented soybeans or fish. Later: a sauce made in imitation of this, typically made from the juice or pulp of a fruit, vegetable, or other foodstuff, combined with vinegar or wine and spices, and used as an ingredient or condiment (frequently with modifying word indicating the main ingredient). Now usually: a thick red sauce made chiefly from tomatoes, vinegar, and sugar, and used as a condiment or relish."[10] The word is first dated to 1682 and given a potential etymological origin in various forms of the Hokkien language, pronounced either *kê-chiap* (Zhangzhou Hokkien), *kôe-tsap* (Quanzhou Hokkien), or *kôe-chiap* (Amoy Hokkien), where the first syllable refers to a kind of fish and the second syllable refers to a juice or sauce. This origin is disputed, however, with alternative theories suggesting origins in the Malay *kecap*, or *kicap*, meaning soy sauce, and even some suggesting the combined influence of European languages and Arabic. The Hokkien Chinese theory appears to be the most convincing, however, particularly given the introduction of the term in the late seventeenth century and early eighteenth century, dating to a similar time as other early linguistic contact between the Chinese- and English-speaking worlds.

Born into the English language as a transliterated second-generation loanword with apparent Chinese origins, *ketchup* has solidified its global nature through both its changed meaning and its presence in various languages. The thick tomato sauce we now think of as *ketchup* became popular in the late nineteenth century, and since then it has been the dominant form and almost synonymous with the term *ketchup* alone. The current use of the word in English is far removed from its origins in the fermented fish sauces of Southeast Asia. Tomato ketchup is now generally considered a quintessential element of traditional British sandwiches and fry-ups as well as American-style fast food, showing how the word has become entirely naturalized into a worldwide English discourse.

Traveling around in London's Chinatown, one can see several signs advertising *jianbing* (a popular Chinese breakfast or snack dish) as *Chinese crepes*. One could suggest that the term is translated into English rather than transliterated, as it has only recently come onto the radar of trendy Western cities. However, the choice to use the French origin term rather than the traditional English *pancake* deserves further exploration.

Although *crepe* is a firm part of the English lexicon, the English term *pancake,* originating in approximately 1400, is clearly a more native sounding term. So it is curious that a word with mainland European connotations should come to define an Asian item.[11] From a purely culinary perspective, the term *crepe* better describes a *jianbing,* as it is cooked on a large round cast iron plate much like a traditional French crepe, and often uses similar utensils. *Crepe* is also useful in distinguishing *jianbing* from the thicker rolled scallion pancakes (*cōng yóubǐng*), or the thin wheat flour pancakes Westerners have come to associate with Chinese roast duck, two of the most well recognized Chinese dishes in the English-speaking West. Indeed, Google Trends suggests that the terms *Chinese pancake* and *Chinese crepe* coexist at a similar level of usage, but the Google search results for *Chinese crepe, Chinese pancake,* and *Chinese duck pancake* show that they refer to different items. Furthermore, *crepe* is being used for more than its semantic meaning. French terms generally have connotations of sophistication and excellence, particularly in a culinary context, so using the word to introduce a new Asian food trend to the West is also an attempt to suggest exoticism with sophistication. This certainly ties in with the use of French in Asian brand names and restaurants to imply a trendy or sophisticated atmosphere.

Despite its common translation as *crepes* in English, the term *jianbing* seems to be gaining popularity online, most likely a result of increasing awareness of international foods on social media. An increase in searches for *jianbing* since 2014 suggests that the item itself has become more popular in food trends, an example of how terms transliterated from Mandarin Chinese have become more common over the past few years. The freedom of the internet is allowing users to either transliterate or translate at will, resulting in new words developing more easily.

Word Immigration

When words move, their meanings and forms can also change. By *form*, I mean specifically how they are written and pronounced. In order for a word to enter and settle in the English language, it goes through several steps of anglicization, including receiving an alphabetic spelling, a new pronunciation, and sometimes even a new meaning. Should the word then enter other European languages such as German, Spanish or French, it will also be assigned a gender. A word acquiring an alphabetic spelling is sort of like an immigrant receiving a visa. It is an arduous and complicated process, but it is necessary for the word to enter and settle into the English lexicon.

Many different forms of a word can inevitably coexist. In the past, each nation-state's linguistic authority dictated how words should be romanized. Now, whatever the majority of users choose becomes the standard. How words are romanized also changes over time. Peking in China is now called Beijing, and Pusan in South Korea is now called Busan. Some people adopt these changes, while others don't, which is why the university in Beijing is still called Peking University. For words from languages that do not use a roman alphabet and have a different vowel system, there will be additional hurdles to overcome in romanization.

To highlight some of the issues that surround word immigration and settlement in English let's take a closer look at something everyone has, a name. It will not surprise you that most names employed today, even by native speakers of English, are not of English origin, and at some point in the past were introduced to English. A good example is the last name of a well-known Russian author: Достоевский. Can you read this name? And if you can, would you know how to romanize it? The answer to the first question hinges on whether you can read the Cyrillic script, and even if you can, your answer to the second question could depend on the language you know and the variety of Cyrillic alphabet it employs. It could also depend on the transliteration scheme you selected, or perhaps your attempt to select vowel combinations familiar to English speakers that will best recreate the sound of the original name in Russian. Thus, when romanized, the name can be spelled Dostoevsky, Dostoyevsky, or Dostoyévskiy. If you don't speak a language that employs the Cyrillic alphabet, would you know which spelling is most accurate? And if you were asked to spell the name off the top of your head, would you be able to remember the correct spelling? We likely can't ask a Dostoevsky how he would like his name romanized, but for millions of immigrants and their descendants who speak languages that do not use a version of the roman alphabet, romanization offers another avenue for the expression of personal identity.

The use of accents in English-adapted terms of foreign origin is also very interesting to look at, having become more of a stylistic flourish than a genuine pronunciation aid. For example, the French accent aigu (acute accent) symbol, which is not natively used in the English language at all, is used in the English spelling of certain words, such as *crème* (distinguishing it from being pronounced like *cream*). However, accents are also used in occasions where the pronunciation is not of such importance. For example, the world-famous West End musical production *Les Misérables* may be pronounced in a variety of forms, including contracted forms such as *Les Mis,* meaning that the accent itself is not used to enlighten readers as to the correct pronunciation, but rather to suggest the French heritage of the word and potentially to add an interesting foreign flavor to its presentation.

In addition, many names of American cities, such as San Jose, draw from other languages—Spanish, in this case. Even though anglicization for such words may seem straightforward, as the roman alphabet is used across the board, there are still questions of pronunciation: is it "j" as in *jellyfish,* or "j" as in the Spanish *jardín* ("garden")? Now, given the great pressure on Latinate words that enter the English lexicon, imagine the case for terms from a non-roman alphabet.

In the case of a person's name, many of my Korean friends have chosen to pick up English names like Hannah or Pauline, thereby reserving their Korean names for themselves and for Korean friends. Recently, I had an online call with a lady whose screen name read "Juliana." I wasn't sure how to pronounce the initial J: in the English way or the Spanish way? Or maybe it was Norwegian? This made me think, if you met a person living in England with a Norwegian mother, how would you know how to pronounce her name?

Names can be especially tricky—not only because of the challenges in correctly producing an unfamiliar name, but also because of the social impact of getting someone's name right or wrong. Sometimes the speaker is aware of the variants that exist with a particular name; sometimes they are not and may be faced with spellings and phonemes that do not correspond to their native tongue. Individuals may choose to offer alternative names to avoid the hassle of continual misnaming; however, this is a personal matter that has complex interactions with registers and relationships.

For some names, the variation in pronunciation is relatively small, and marked for particular regions. *Graham* can be "gray-um" in British English but "gram" in American; *Martine* can have two syllables in British English as "mar-teen" but three in Dutch as "mar-tee-na"; *Lucia* can be "lu-see-a" or "lu-chee-a"; *Xavier* can be "zay-vee-er" or "ha-vee-air." Further complications can come where the spelling does not match the speaker's orthography. Gaelic is a classic example here, with *Siobhan* ("sha-vawn"), *Cao-imhe* ("kee-va"), *Oisin* ("osh-een"), and *Aoife* ("ee-fa"). Even more challenging is when sounds in the name are not present in the speaker's language, such as the uvular fricative in Ghadeer and the pharyngealized consonants in Ghattas. Tone can also cause mistakes that speakers may not realize they are making, such as the Chinese name *Mei*, which with the second tone means "plum blossom" and with the third tone means "beautiful." Differences in stress systems can also pose difficulties. The Bengali name *Aditi* is pronounced "Oditi" with initial stress, but to British English speakers this is homophonous with the word *oddity*, and rather different to the British medial stress placement.

As shown above, pronunciation of names is not always faithful to the original sound. Some names may be spelled with a recognizable orthography and contain phonemes from a speaker's language, yet errors are still made, such as "zey-noob" for *Zaynab*. Some names not native to English have become more familiar and appear regularly, such as Tchaikovsky and Dostoyevsky. There is a large difference between initial errors and acceptance of corrections, and persistent errors in spite of correction. This may in some cases be a challenge of articulation, but often it is rather a matter of respect.

I experienced pronunciation dilemmas first-hand when I served as a pro-proctor at the University of Oxford. One of my duties in this position was reading out the names of new graduates at the university's degree ceremonies. It is a high-stakes task; the ceremony represents the culmination of a student's accomplishments at our university, and it takes place with their families looking on. The global nature of Britain and the university means that at each ceremony, I saw names from all over the world. I couldn't help but wonder as I gazed at the list of names whether students and their families wished for their names to be pronounced in a local or in an English way. You might think I could request to know a student's nationality or ethnic background to help me make these decisions, but the reality is that names are a matter of unique personal identity, and just like every person, every name has a unique trajectory that makes selecting pronunciation extremely difficult. Because the best solution to this dilemma is simply to politely ask each student how they would like their name pronounced, many schools have started to allow students to upload a digital recording of them pronouncing their name.

Of course, the solution devised by universities is not as practical in everyday life. In the face of constant pronunciation errors, whether accidental, careless, or malicious, some people just use a different name. This can take several shapes: using a middle name that may be more familiar, such as someone named Vidar Benjamin using "Benjamin" in the United Kingdom, rather than the less familiar Norwegian name "Vidar"; providing an anglicized version of your name, such as "June" for Jieun, or permitting an adaption of your name, such as "Aditi" for Oditi; or choosing a new name altogether, such as "Amy" for Chenxi. Different choices may be made based on register and relationship, as one's birth name is generally used in official and legal settings, an accessible anglicized version with friends and acquaintances, a more accurate version used with close friends, and the birth name or native diminutives used with a lover.

In 2016, when Kamala Harris was running for the U.S. Senate, she even filmed a campaign video explaining how to pronounce her first name.[12] In the video, children said, "It's not Camel-uh. It's not Ka-MAHL-uh. It's not Kar-MEL-uh," with each incorrect variation being spelled out and crossed off on the screen. Most people now know that her name is pronounced "Comma-la," like the punctuation mark. In the preface of her memoir from 2019, *The Truths We Hold*, Kamala wrote: "First, my name is pronounced 'comma-la,' like the punctuation mark. It means 'lotus flower,' which is a symbol of significance in Indian culture. A lotus grows underwater, its flower rising above the surface while its roots are planted firmly in the river bottom." Even if most of us will not have to make a campaign video explaining how to pronounce our name, many of us can relate to the struggle of getting people to say our names right—in other words, to say our names in a way that honors and respects our cultures and identities.

Emma Raducanu is a professional tennis player who plays for Britain. She was born in Toronto to her father, Ion Răducanu, who is from Bucharest, Romania, and her mother, Renee Zhai, from Shenyang, China. Emma was raised in London, England. Based on her first name alone, which is very common in English, particularly in the Anglophone world, it is difficult to discern her heritage. Like many second-generation persons, names can be a reflection of identity that mingles both where they were born and raised with their heritage.

Meanwhile, the well-known artist Vincent van Gogh's last name is pronounced in several different ways by native English speakers, none of them accurately reflecting the Dutch pronunciation, which is now so removed from these English varieties that it has been rendered unfamiliar. As a result, the official BBC pronunciation unit was forced to recommend a "compromise between the ... English pronunciations and the Dutch pronunciations."[13] This is a reality for most people using romanized names. We live with multiple identities, represented by multiple forms of pronunciation.

My late father-in-law was of Danish descent; his parents had immigrated to the United Kingdom from Denmark. That said, he was British. He didn't speak Danish; English was his first and only language. He went to boarding school and read Classics at Cambridge. His English was the first English I was exposed to in Britain, and at the time I believed this was how one should speak. He used to tell me how to pronounce *Copenhagen*, but he didn't teach me the Danish way. He said it's not "Copen-hah-gen," as in the song "Wonderful Copenhagen." He said, "That's wrong— it should be 'Copen-hay-gen.' " In my head, I would think, "But in the original Danish it's pronounced 'Copen-hah-gen.' " For a very long time, I wondered if it should be pronounced closer to the Danish way. Similarly, think of Häagen-Dazs, a popular American ice cream brand. Although Danish has no umlauts, many people think this brand has some sort of Danish link and pronounce it "Hah-gen-dass." Some people pronounce it "Hay-gen-dass." Nobody really knows how to pronounce Häagen-Dazs correctly—so how can we say one is right and the other is wrong?

Perhaps we need to pause when passing judgment on who is right and wrong in the pronunciation debate, and hear each side, acknowledging their differences. Nowadays we have social media, operating beyond the borders of languages and cultures. In the freedom of these online spaces, words are constantly being invented and reinvented. Despite the diversity and freedom in online spaces, English pronunciation is still policed. My father-in-law tried to help me by teaching me the correct pronunciation, but for many words, a single correct pronunciation does not exist. As has been mentioned throughout this book, who gets to decide which English is the proper English? Is there even such a thing at all?

On the subject of names, as a brief aside, we can see the pressure to conform to Anglocentric standards in name order. All East and many Southeast Asian nations put the family name(s) first, before any first or middle names. This is also the case in many other nations, such as Hungary.[14] It seems then that not only are the spelling, pronunciation, and form of foreign-heritage words under duress in anglicization, but even word order.

Another interesting example of a European-origin food word is the Italian foodstuff *bruschetta*. The Italian combination of the letters "c" and "h" in various forms can be difficult from the perspective of an English speaker, and this word is no exception. Pronounced in the Italian as "broo-SKEH-ta," the spelling results in a large proportion of English speakers (mis)pronouncing the word "broo-SHEH-ta," eliding together the "s," "c," and "h" sounds as makes the most sense from a native English perspective. Although many multilingual speakers of Italian and English, or dedicants of Italian cuisine, might correct English speakers on their pronunciation, who is really to say that this alternative, anglicized pronunciation is not correct? Given that the word exists in the OED and is used commonly in a purely English language context, with many non-Italian speakers of English being familiar with the word, could it not be argued that the anglicized pronunciation is a legitimate way to use the word in an English language context? Hence, we can see that context really is everything, allowing each person to use their own judgment when using ambiguous terms such as these.

With a dictionary definition of "a Spanish dish of rice, chicken, fish and vegetables, cooked and served in a large shallow pan," the Oxford English Dictionary also gives the pronunciation of *paella* as 'pai-AY-ya.' The common debate surrounding this term is whether we should pronounce the double letter "l" in the word as it would be in a Spanish-language context (like a "y" sound in English) or as it would sound in a native English context (the same as a single "l"). Here we see an example of the most common issue facing the pronunciation of imported words: do we pronounce it as it would be in the original language, or as it would be in the imported language? There is, of course, no right or wrong answer to this question.

The word *mojito* is another example of the same quandary originating in the Spanish language. Where some people may choose to pronounce the "j" like an "h" in English, more like the original Spanish, others may prefer to pronounce it as a hard "j" as it would be in English. Due to the inconsistencies and lack of set rules in the translation of foreign-origin words into English, there is no single way of doing this, making it each person's individual choice as to what makes them comfortable and fits their sense of style.

A further issue in this area is the borrowing of names from other languages into English. Should the name of the French capital city be pronounced in its established anglicized manner, or as it is in the original French? Naturally, the anglicized pronunciation of *Paris* must exist as a part of the English language, but given that our modern linguistic climate includes so many world Englishes, should we instead pronounce it as part of a French-inspired variety of English? I find it curious just how *Paris* is pronounced in English. The pronunciation suggested by the OED, "Pa-ris," is not the same word the French use for their capital, "Pa-ree," with a guttural (uvular rhotic) "r." This is a particularly common conundrum when pronouncing Spanish and French names—both for locations and people—given the proximity and historical relations between France, Spain, and the United Kingdom. In these languages, names are pronounced in a variety of different ways, sliding from entirely anglicized to heavily influenced by their original term in the native language. In Spanish, "z" sounds are frequently pronounced as a "z" in English rather than a "th" sound as in European Spanish (such as in the U.K. English pronunciation of *chorizo*).

Foreign-born words or those with foreign heritage are a living and growing population in the British English lexicon. These words are also sometimes referred to as loanwords or borrowings, but these terms can be misleading, suggesting that terms are borrowed temporarily rather than being fully adopted as part of the English language. Not only are there a huge number of international influences in British English, but the native language itself is made of various dialects present in the British Isles.

There is also a large population of locally born English words, which have made their way into the OED and other major English dictionaries, with their geographical and partial linguistic roots in languages other than English. This is a whole other group of words for which it is very difficult to determine a proper form and pronunciation. These words could be thought of as expats, with their genetics coming largely from English but their location, usage, and connotations potentially being wildly different in their new contexts. I uphold the basic idea that local pronunciations should be respected as entirely legitimate forms of the English language. Dictionaries such as the OED contain only British and American pronunciation notes, a situation that I believe should be remedied in order to respect and celebrate diversity in the pronunciation of world Englishes. Fundamentally, pronunciation is a matter of style rather than an essential part of a language's grammar, and thus should be open to diversity and change.

In addition to *dalgona coffee*, coffee words in general present us with a unique example of cultural borrowing and hybridization that is often forgotten and merits greater examination. The word *coffee* itself began its life as the Arabic word *qahwa*, which medieval Arabic lexicons record as one of a number of epithets used for wine. The word was coined from the tripartite Arabic root *q-h-y*, which carried the idea of "lessening one's desire for something," because it was thought that wine removed a drinker's desire for food. Historians now generally agree that *qahwa* acquired a new meaning as the name of a drink produced from the seeds of the *coffea* plant in the third quarter of the fifteenth century, when

Sufis based in Yemen discovered that the beverage helped them remain alert during nighttime rituals and began to regularly consume it. *Qahwa* application to the drink likely stemmed from the fact that while wine was associated with reducing one's desire for food, coffee helped lessen one's desire for sleep.[15]

It took some time for medical works and dictionaries in the Arabic-speaking world to reflect this new and increasingly dominant usage, but the drink itself spread like wildfire. By the early 1500s, coffeehouses were recorded across the Arab world from Mecca to Cairo and Damascus, and by 1551–1552 they had arrived in the Ottoman capital of Istanbul.[16] By 1575, we find the first printed reference to coffee in a European work, by a French medical scholar. It took only another quarter century for coffee to spread across Europe and begin to be consumed in England. It took less than 150 years from the emergence of the earliest recorded coffeehouses in the Arab world for the first coffeehouse in the British Isles to open in the city of Oxford in 1650.[17]

How did *qahwa* become coffee in such a short time span? The success of the Ottoman sultan Selim I's campaign against the Mamluk Sultanate brought the central Arab lands of Syria, Egypt, and the Hijjaz under Ottoman control in 1516 and 1517, cementing Ottoman Turkish as the language of administration in the eastern Mediterranean. Ottoman, which incorporated Arabic and Persian vocabulary and grammar wholesale, rendered the "wa" in *qahwa* with the voiced labiodental fricative "v" and mid-front unrounded vowel "e" making the word *kahve*. Among European languages the Turkish word was borrowed first into Italian, as *caffè*, because this language was a lingua franca among Mediterranean merchants, and the early Italian maritime republics were important in trade between the Ottoman Empire and the rest of Europe. It seems likely that the primary change upon adoption into Italian was replacement of the voiced labiodental fricative "v" with the unvoiced labiodental fricative "f."

From Italian *caffè* to English *coffee*, the story is less well understood. James Murray, the first editor of the Oxford English Dictionary, attempted to justify the emergence of "o" for the vowel
"a" in the Ottoman word as a result of English travelers hearing
the combination of the letters "ahv" as "au" and rendering it "o."
However, in 1909 the suggestion prompted a heated debate spanning several issues of the scholarly journal *Notes and Queries*. Murray's critics pointed out that the solution presupposed an imagined
Ottoman pronunciation *qahv-ve* because the sound produced by
the letter "v" in "ahv" was already represented by the double "f."[18]

Today, English etymological dictionaries often suggest the
word *coffee* is a borrowing from Dutch, which employs the similar
word *koffie*. This might be a satisfactory explanation if use of the
substance had spread slowly and sequentially across Europe from
east to west and Anglo-Dutch trade had played a role in making
coffee popular in Britain. However, scholars of coffee's consumption in England have highlighted how outside the Ottoman Empire
nowhere else was coffee drinking so intensely adopted as in the
British Isles.[19] By 1700, the Dutch capital, Amsterdam, had merely
thirty-two coffeehouses. What's more, the proprietors of the earliest
commercially successful coffeehouses in Oxford and London were
often themselves migrants from Ottoman lands with knowledge of
the local languages, and the trade in coffee beans was overwhelmingly handled by the British East India and Levant Companies,
which held monopolies on their respective trade routes.

In not much time at all, European views of coffee transited
from derision, describing it as a bizarre Turkish beverage that was
"blacke as soote, and tasting not much unlike it," to almost total
appropriation; it became a drink "which nearly everyone finds
good." Today, the first words that come to mind when you think
of coffee are likely borrowings from Italian like *latte* and *cappuccino*. These terms reflect a distinctly European innovation in the
preparation of coffee: the addition of milk, although this was not

in origin an Italian invention. The process of adding milk to coffee is attested earliest in 1684, in France, where it swiftly garnered the name *café au lait* ("coffee with milk"), and not long after in Italy, where the same concoction gained the name *caffè e latte* ("coffee and milk") and later was just called *caffè latte*.[20] The English term *latte* is a much later shortening of this Italian phrase.

A similar time frame is often given for when the coffee craze seized Vienna, on the other side of Europe. According to a likely apocryphal story, Georg Franz Kolschitzky, a Polish nobleman who had worked for some years as a merchant in Ottoman lands, became a Hapsburg spy during the second siege of Vienna in 1683, because of his unique linguistic capabilities. Using his knowledge of the Ottoman Turkish language and attire he was able to exit the besieged city and cross the Turkish lines unhindered and secure a promise of imminent military relief from Christian forces amassing outside the city. The arrival of this relief broke the siege, and the Ottomans retreated leaving behind many of their supplies, including numerous bags of coffee. Recognizing the value of these beans, Kolschitzky requested they be granted to him as part of his reward for his heroism during the siege. Loosely familiar with the Ottoman preparation of the drink, he began to hawk it around Vienna with great success. At some point shortly after this, the Viennese began to sweeten the coffee by adding a few drops of cream or a dollop of whipped cream on the top. The color of the drink was thought to resemble the distinctive red-brown color of the robes worn by the Capuchin order of Franciscan friars. As a result, the drink was called a *kapuziner,* an Austrian calque of the Italian word for a member of the order, a *cappuccino.* This was in fact the Italian word for "hood" in the diminutive form, a reference to the order's distinctive hooded cloak and the fact that they were a newer branch of the Franciscans. It was not until several centuries later that the drink and its name spread to northern Italy—then part of the Austro-Hungarian Empire—whose Italian speakers translated it back as *cappuccino* and helped introduce the concoction to the rest of the country. It was in Italy in the second half of the twentieth century that it took on its modern form as a drink made of espresso and steamed fresh milk topped with milk foam.

As for the *latte,* it assumed its now ubiquitous form as an espresso mixed with more milk than a *cappuccino,* not in Italy but in the United States, as part of the process that introduced these coffee words to languages the world over. According to specialty coffee enthusiasts, *latte* in this form was first served in 1959 at Caffe Mediterraneum, an Italian cafe in Berkeley, California.[21] This cafe was a countercultural hotspot frequented by the Beat Generation. The patrons of the cafe, unused to the strong coffee flavor of the cappuccino, frequently asked the barista to add additional milk, until it developed into a new menu item.

The Bay Area played a unique role in making these drinks popular with a new generation of entrepreneurs initially fascinated with sourcing, roasting, and selling the more artisanal coffee beans that these Italian drinks required. It was there that the original founders of Starbucks had met as college students, although it was not until a decade later, in 1971, that they opened the first Starbucks on the West Coast, in Seattle. For the first decade and a half of the company's existence it sold roasted beans and coffee equipment, not espresso, a marker of just how unfamiliar these drinks remained to American consumers at the time. It was not until 1987 that the brand was sold to Howard Schultz. Schultz was the one-time marketing director who had become convinced of the wisdom of introducing Italian-style coffee shops to the U.S. market after a trip to Milan. The brand then refocused on selling espresso drinks and rapidly expanded into a national chain. The company was almost singlehandedly responsible for introducing Americans beyond the bohemian haunts of the West Coast to espresso drinks and their lexicon.

Less than a decade later, Starbucks began expanding outside North America—first into the East Asian market, opening stores in Japan and Singapore in 1996, but perhaps most importantly in China in 1999. In East Asia, Starbucks pursued a business-savvy strategy of mixing local flavors with its espresso concoctions to appeal to its consumers' palates, a process that also helped give birth to now well-known hybrid terms like *matcha latte*—where *latte* practically returns to its original Italian meaning of "milk," since the drink contains no coffee.

If you had been asked to name where coffee consumption was first popularized before reading the above, you would not have been alone in thinking of Italy, elsewhere in Europe, or perhaps even Seattle. The slow process that started from the European appropriation of coffee by adding milk three centuries ago has been supercharged by the global spread of coffee chains like Starbucks, which have warped how many perceive the origins of coffee consumption. As a result of the proliferation of American and English coffee shops, the meaning of the word *kahve* alone has changed and is now most closely associated with the European and American versions of the drink. Although the drink of their forefathers is still wildly popular, Turkish speakers refer to it with an additional adjective as *Türk kahvesi* ("Turkish coffee").

The fact that coffee chains overwhelmingly maintain their English menu terminology as part of their branding further demonstrates the power of corporations in today's globalized world to singlehandedly reshape our vocabularies. In Turkey, the practice has produced a growing lexicon of hybrid terms for coffee products often made up of two or three separately borrowed words. Now, at a trendy coffee shop in Istanbul you might receive a friendlier reception from your barista if you order an "iced filtre kahve" than if you substitute the Turkish term *buzlu*, meaning iced, while at a Starbucks there would be absolutely no confusion over your request for a "buzlu chai tea latte."

Chapter 7

MORE THAN WORDS

Word Politics

"Beneath the rule of men entirely great, the pen is mightier than the sword" is a phrase that was first used by the English author Edward Bulwer-Lytton in his play *Richelieu; Or the Conspiracy* in 1839. Words hold immense power indeed. This may be most evident these days in social media. Seemingly ordinary words can have a huge impact all around the world.

An old Korean saying goes, "A single word can repay a thousand debts." This highlights the significance of a word in human interaction. Some words have more power than others. Once upon a time, standard words were much more powerful than words found only in certain dialects. "StopAsianHate," "Black Lives Matter," and "#MeToo" are all expressions that have become the driving force and source of power for their respective social movements. Sometimes people want to possess words, cover them away and keep them for themselves. Sharing words and languages hasn't always been the aim of everyone. The educated and the powerful have often wanted to keep words to themselves, reluctant to share them with the poor and uneducated.

Word share happens through the process of translation and transliteration. This has never been a straightforward task. Historically, there has been a great struggle between those who have power and those who do not in this complex issue. Throughout history, sharing information has been a tense affair because words and languages have always been valuable assets. As a result, translation has never been widely encouraged. One of the prime examples of this is the translation of the Bible.

William Tyndale's translation of the Bible from Hebrew and Greek texts is considered a milestone in English language translation. However, his efforts led to his condemnation for heresy, and he was executed by strangulation and burned at the stake in 1536. This event came after concerns expressed by the Archbishop of Canterbury, Thomas Arundel, in the Constitutions of Oxford in 1408. Arundel believed that unauthorized translations of the text could result in a loss of meaning, stating: "It is a dangerous thing, as witnesseth blessed St. Jerome to translate the text of the Holy Scripture out of one tongue into another, for in the translation the same sense is not always easily kept. . . . We therefore decree and ordain, that no man, hereafter, by his own authority translate any text of the Scripture into English or any other tongue . . . and that no man can read any such book . . . in part or in whole."[1] Although religion may have been the primary motivator for discouraging translation, it's also worth considering the possibility of human selfishness and the desire to monopolize knowledge as the underlying reason for resistance against translation. The situation has since changed. With the advent of social media and large language models like ChatGPT, the words of our time have become widely accessible and the language of the ordinary can now be known to all. AI empowerment has the potential to promote fairness in word sharing, but there may also be downsides, such as the risk of word monopolies and the manipulation of language by corporations or social media influencers.

It may not always seem obvious, but pronunciation matters too. It tells so much, and it can lead to some terrible injustices. The Bible contains a story of Israelites who killed each other based on different pronunciations of the word *shibboleth*. In

September 1923, thousands of Koreans were killed in Japan's Kanto area following a devastating earthquake. The Japanese phrase *ich-ien gojissen* ("one yen and fifty sen," a monetary unit) would typically be pronounced by Koreans as "ichien koshissen." Many of the victims were identified and murdered based on their Korean pronunciation, and so "the tongue became a dividing point to decide who would live and who would be killed." Although it is not always a matter of life or death, pronunciation continues to cause upset and conflict. In a more recent example of the pitfalls of pronunciation and word choice, a debate erupted on a campus of the University of Southern California in 2020 when a professor used a Chinese word that sounded like a racial slur in English. He apologized and was temporarily removed from teaching, but was later defended by a group of mostly Chinese students supporting his use of the term.

Words are a reminder of our own past and history, with the transformation of words mirroring our own transformations. That said, there is still a need to combat the traces of colonization, Westernization, and imperialism in our verbal footprints. After all, a word is more than just a word—a word can carry the soul of people and their cultures.

In the wake of the collapse of the Soviet Union, the Ukrainian government came to associate the spelling and pronunciation of its capital as *Kiev* with Russian domination, and instead preferred the spelling *Kyiv*. Transliterating the name as *Kyiv* was legally mandated by the Ukrainian government in 1995, and since then it has tried to make *Kyiv* more widely used abroad. Although this movement began before the current war between Russia and Ukraine, it was really during this time that this spelling and pronunciation choice became a way of expressing solidarity. In fact, *KyivNotKiev* was an online campaign started by the Ukrainian Ministry of Foreign Affairs in October 2018. Its goal was to persuade English language media and organizations to use *Kyiv* exclusively instead of *Kiev*. Since the invasion of Ukraine by

Russia in 2022, international political opinions surrounding the use of *Kyiv* versus *Kiev* have only intensified. Natalia Khanenko-Friesen, director of the Canadian Institute for Ukrainian Studies at the University of Alberta, said in an interview that the *Kyiv* spelling and pronunciation are particularly significant during this "time of aggravated assault on the sovereignty and integrity of the Ukrainian state."[2] She continues, "Using, right now, the Ukrainian pronunciation of . . . the capital is a very small choice one can do in recognition that Ukraine does have the right to exist as an independent nation, contrary to what Vladimir Putin has been stating in his recent statements and addresses to his nation." Indeed, words are loaded with meaning—some more than others—and *Kyiv* is an apt example of this.

Turkey, too. "Turkey": is it a country or a bird? Should one be referring to the former, we can see traces of Anglocentric biases in its romanization, which first occurred centuries ago. Recently, however, there have been some rumblings in the Turkish government: a thirst for change in the way their country is viewed. President Recep Tayyip Erdogan wants to start with the basics: the name of the country. The idea is to change the English language name of Turkey to "Türkiye." As part of the campaign for change, a series of advertisements promoting travel in Türkiye—and not Turkey—have been released by Go Türkiye. Go Türkiye works with the Ministry of Culture and Tourism. Originally named Go Turkey, it was rebranded to adopt the *Türkiye* spelling in 2021.

President Erdogan has said that the name "Türkiye" best represents the country. Others speculate that it is to distance Turkey from the bird with the same name and its meanings of "flop" or "failure," as used in theater terminology and elsewhere. There is a strong nationalist rhetoric in the country, and the government is becoming more and more sensitive to how it is being received internationally. The government argues that "Türkiye" conveys the nation's "eternal spirit" more than its English counterpart.

The OED has yet to change the official spelling of "Turkey" or add the new name to the dictionary, noting that Turkey has had a variety of spellings throughout the ages: *Torke, Turkie, Turky, Turkye, Tokey, Turquey, Turkeye, Tyrkye*.[3] In June 2022 the nation registered the new spelling with the United Nations, which accepted the change with immediate effect. Perhaps this will prompt the OED to change its spelling?

Possibly more compelling than the political concerns driving the adoption of the name Türkiye are the issues underpinning the name and spelling of another Turkic language speaking country: Kazakhstan. Since the mid-2000s, Kazakhstan's leadership has been contemplating how to switch the country from a modified Cyrillic script imposed on the Kazakh language by the Soviet Union in 1940 to a modified roman script. In 2021, the Kazakh government finally cemented a process that will see the switch finalized by 2031. The change will undoubtedly produce some literacy issues in a country where most people's second language, if not their first, is Russian. So why the eagerness to switch? In part it reflects local leaders' desire to shift perceptions about the country's alignment with Russia and make it easier for the country and its population to compete in the international economy. But the transition is also motivated by a desire to seize one's own identity back from a legacy of Russian imperialism and Soviet domination.

The existing romanization of the word *Kazakh*, both the ethnonym for the country's primary ethnic group and the name of their language, and *Kazakhstan*, the name for the country, reflect a romanization and anglicization based on the Russian Cyrillic spelling of these words, where the first letter "k" and the digraph "kh" are differentiated. However, in the modified Cyrillic alphabet presently used for Kazakh, and the Perso-Arabic script that preceded it, the "k" and "kh" letters are not differentiated. Thus, adopting a modified roman script for the Kazakh language allows for a differentiation between "k" and "q" sounds that the dominant Russian Cyrillic alphabet does not have and eliminates the differentiation between "k" and "kh," which does not exist in Kazakh. In this new roman script, the Kazakh language words for *Kazakh* and *Kazakhstan* would be rendered *Qazaq* and *Qazaqstan*. Although the switch does not guarantee world-wide adoption of a more Kazakh spelling and pronunciation of the word, it offers an opportunity for Kazakhs to take back possession of a word fundamental to their identity and potentially revise the legacy of Russian domination embedded in its present anglicization.

Travelling farther west from Kazakhstan, have you ever wondered why the Middle East is called the "Middle East"? Geographically, there is very little east in this region. Well, the history of the term can be traced to British imperialism. The term *Middle East* is actually a political construct, coined in the 1850s by staff in the British India Office, and during this period, the *Orient* (a term used to describe the East) was split into three distinct areas: the Near East (including the Ottoman Empire—much of today's Turkey—and the Balkans), the Middle East, and the Far East (which included Asian countries along the Pacific Ocean).[4] British colonization of India made this space of critical importance to the empire at the time, and reflects a very Eurocentric view of the world. Toward the mid-1900s, the name "Middle East" firmly established itself beyond the British Empire and the designated region itself. That said, many people argue that the Eurocentricity of this term makes it valid only from a Western perspective. Hence, it should be replaced with a term that is more appropriate. Jawaharlal Nehru, the first prime minister in India, for example, argued that the term should be replaced with *West Asia*.[5] To this day, *West Asia* continues to receive a great deal of support among both academics and non-academics. Much like *Kyiv* and *Türkiye*, the use of *West Asia* is saturated with political meaning, and often its use helps to convey that the speaker or writer has a certain set of beliefs.

When in Turkey, however, or Türkiye, how would you exchange greetings with someone? More devout and conservative members of society will often say *selamünaleyküm* ("peace be upon you") as a greeting, which should receive the response *aleykümselam*. More secular individuals, though, prefer to use the greeting *merhaba* (from the Arabic *merhaban* of the root "r-ḥ-b"), which means "hello" or "welcome." Notably, both greetings have Arabic roots, and Arabic speakers can and do use versions of both depending on their dialect.

Another example from Turkish is that more secular individuals say *iyi akşamlar* ("good evening"), which was coined after the language reform, while more conservative speakers might more often use *hayırlı akşamlar* ("good evening"). Here *iyi* (meaning "good") has a Turkish root, whereas *hayırlı* mixes the Arabic root for "good" with the Turkic suffix -*lı* meaning "with/of/from."

Finally, there is the use of *kutlu* (from the old Turkic root *kut*, originally meaning "luck" or "lucky" but now meaning "blessed, or auspicious," or just "happy") versus *mübarek* (now meaning "blessed," "sacred," or "good," originally from the Arabic *mubarak* meaning "blessed" or "fortunate" from the Arabic root "b-r-k") for holidays. In a sentence, this would be formed as either *bayramınız kutlu olsun* or *bayramınız mübarek olsun*—both literally meaning "may your holiday be blessed/happy" or as it is more often translated nowadays "happy holiday." However, this usage distinction is less strictly divided between groups and has more to do with context. More conservative individuals use *kutlu olsun* for non-religious holidays, so a birthday greeting would be *doğum gününüz kutlu olsun*, but they would use *mübarek olsun* for religious holidays, so a typical Ramadan greeting would be *Ramazan bayramınız mübarek olsun*.

There are many words that are used to refer to cultural items shared by Turkish, Persian, Arabic, and Hebrew communities. These common words show the extent to which lexical items are crossing geographical, cultural, and linguistic boundaries. It is becoming increasingly difficult to associate a word with a sole nation-state. Even as they show similarities, they also exhibit differences, thus helping to affirm a shared social identity and bring about a sense of belonging.

Şiş kebap in Turkish and Crimean Tatar (commonly romanized as *shish kebab* in the West) refers to cut cubes of meat served on a skewer. One variety made with chicken is known as *tavuk şiş*. The Turks of Iranian Azerbaijan have popularized *şiş kebap* in Iran, but the Persians also have a similar although not identical dish, called *Kabâb-e bargh* (sometimes pronounced and spelled *kebob* and meaning "leaf kebab"), where slices of meat are grilled using a skewer. In addition, in Iran, *Jujeh Kabâb* is the term for *chicken şiş kebap,* utilizing the Persian word for "young chicken." In Israel, an identical dish to the Turkish *şiş kebap* is widely prepared and eaten; it is known as *Shishlik* (in Eastern Europe this is termed *Shashlik*). The dish was popularized in Israel by Eastern European and Russian Jews. The term first spread in eighteenth- and nineteenth-century Russia thanks to Cossaks who coined the term from the Crimean Tatar *şiş.* Among the Levantine Arabs, a dish is prepared called *Lahem Meshwi,* which consists of lamb cubes grilled on a skewer. In Greece, the same dish of chunks of skewered meat is known as *Souvlaki.* While some words show more noticeable similarities, they all refer to a similar—or even identical—dish, which reflects a shared culture in which certain people may, figuratively or literally, choose to highlight a particular flavor that is specific to a subgroup they identify with.

In Turkey, meat cooked on a vertical rotisserie from which shavings are sliced was popularized in the nineteenth century. This method of preparation is known as *Döner* (meaning "rotates," from the verb *Dönmek) Kebap,* which has since spread to Europe via Turkish migrants in Germany as *Döner Kebab* (with or without the umlaut). In the Arab world and Israel, the same food is known as *shawarma* (apparently an Arabic rendering of the Turkish word *çevirme* meaning "turning'). In Greece and America, the Greek term *Gyro* (from the Greek *Gyros,* meaning "turn") is preferred for the same dish. In Mexico, this dish is served in a taco shell and known as *al pastor*. It was introduced to Mexico by Lebanese immigrants in the nineteenth and twentieth centuries. In spite of the variations in the exact term, again we see how a certain culinary item is shared with new names across the borders.

Words and Belonging

In data I have collected through personal communication, an American student from Chicago, studying at Oxford, in England, reported:

> I am using UK spelling while living here. At first it was definitely uncomfortable, but there was also a certain amount of excitement and fascination with the differences. So, we were eager to learn the spelling differences. Now, we have all our devices set to UK spelling, and I'm writing my dissertation using it. So, we're pretty used to it now. So much so that when we see American spellings for words like "favor," it feels wrong. But there are other words we use less like "tyre" that look very wrong to us in UK spelling still. In the end it feels like you don't belong anywhere, and you're stuck between the different systems!

A word can carry much more than just its semantic meaning; it can create solidarity or ignite disputes. It shows who we are and where we belong. It carries memories. When my daughter Sarah was a baby, her Korean nanny Mrs. Jung left a small memo each day for me with the words that Sarah had learned to say that day. Each word was special for me and brings back memories of her childhood.

When I arrived in the United Kingdom in the 1990s, some of my friends suggested that I choose an English name. While I understood that it might have made communication easier for my British friends, the idea of changing my name made me uncomfortable. My name was given to me by my parents at birth, and it is a fundamental part of my identity. In the past, immigrants didn't have a choice and had to adapt to the locals by anglicizing their names. However, things are changing now, and diverse voices are being heard more thanks to social media. We should have the freedom to choose whether or not to adopt a new name and not feel pressured to conform to our new surroundings. Our words have gained the independence to stand on their own two feet, without the need for validation from linguistic authorities or the wider society.

In the digital era, names and words that describe ethnicity may be less needed. As our lives migrate into virtual reality, we will be represented by avatars more and more. We can design our avatars as we wish and give them whichever name we would like. We may no longer be able to know people's ethnicity or national background. We may only know their username, rather than their real name. The digital world that we are moving into will not need the same words as the physical world.

Representing words is not always a neutral act. Spelling often goes beyond a mere grammatical rule; it serves as an identity marker. Why do some Brits in America continue to use the spelling "civilisation" instead of "civilization"? It remains up to the individual to decide whether to change their spelling and vocabulary depending on where they live or where they feel they belong. Do people from Birmingham, Alabama, change their pronunciation of "Birmingham" when they move to Birmingham, England? The way you spell and pronounce certain words is akin to an accent. An increasing number of words carry political connotations that can lead to significant divisions among different groups. It can be a potent marker of one's personal identity, indicating a sense of belonging or alienation. Words can be tools, but they are much more than that. Our lexical choices are an ongoing process of constructing and negotiating our social identities.

Words like *Black, foreign,* and *ethnic minority* are often used to describe people's backgrounds, but they are not always easy or comfortable to use. The term *African American* is commonly used to refer specifically to Black people who are U.S. citizens or residents and who are descendants of enslaved Africans. This term reflects the unique history and experiences of Black Americans and has gained broader acceptance as an inclusive term. In the United Kingdom, *Black* is often used more broadly to refer to people of Black African or Caribbean descent, regardless of citizenship or nationality. However, there is a growing recognition of the importance of acknowledging the specific experiences and histories of different Black communities in the United Kingdom, and using more specific terms like *Black British, Black African,* or *Black Caribbean* to reflect this diversity.

David Olusoga, in his book *Black and British,* explains how in the past *black* simply meant "other" and was unquestionably the opposite of "British." In principle, terms like *black, foreign,* and *ethnic minority* can be seen as prejudiced language, highlighting the negative implications of labeling people based on their background. In today's hyperconnected, multilingual, and multicultural age, it's important to consider the negative connotations these words may carry. Instead, we should strive for more inclusive language that celebrates diversity and avoids reinforcing negative stereotypes.

African American Vernacular English (AAVE), also known as Black English or Ebonics, is a dialect spoken by many Black Americans. It has its own unique grammar, vocabulary, and pronunciation, and has often been stigmatized and criticized in mainstream society. However, linguists and educators have recognized this vernacular as a legitimate and valuable form of language, with its own rich history and cultural significance. Its recognition as a valid form of communication is an important step toward acknowledging and valuing the language and culture of Black communities.

The umbrella term *BAME* (Black, Asian, and minority ethnic) categorizes Asians as a minority, which is inaccurate. Asia is home to more than 2,300 languages, accounting for more than a third of the world's languages, spoken by more than 4.5 billion people.[6] The ranking of the top ten most spoken languages, according to *Ethnologue,* has Mandarin Chinese as the second most spoken language globally, behind only English. Hindi and Spanish follow, but Mandarin Chinese and English are much more widely spoken in comparison.[7] In 2016, Chinese, Arabic, Japanese, and Malay ranked among the top ten languages on the internet by number of users, so Asian languages clearly have a wide sphere of influence, at least in pop-culture and internet-aided communication.[8] Southeast Asia alone is home to more than a thousand languages spanning five language families, with around 2.6 billion speakers, which is much higher than the number of speakers of European languages in Europe.[9] In light of the vast linguistic diversity and widespread nature of Asia's languages, it feels inappropriate to label Asians as a minority—"undervalued by the West" may be a more accurate rephrasing.

Hybrid English Injustice

Children who are born outside their parents' home countries as part of expatriate communities or diasporas may encounter challenges related to language and cultural barriers. Unfortunately, the English spoken by diaspora communities can sometimes be viewed as less esteemed and underrated. Children who grow up speaking a hybrid variety of English as a result of their exposure to multiple languages and cultures may face criticism or negative attitudes about their speech. This is especially true for those who were born outside the United States or the United Kingdom and are not native speakers of either country's English. Hybrid English is an issue of identity, language, and belonging. It highlights the struggles that children of U.S. and U.K. citizens born abroad face, as well as the challenges they encounter in their language development. But it's important to recognize the richness and diversity that these hybrid varieties of English bring to the language, and to appreciate the unique perspectives and experiences of those who speak them.

Hybrid words are not subsidiary or temporary words but are a crucial linguistic currency for those who are constantly exposed to multiple languages. Often the language that a diaspora community finds most useful and comfortable is not their original home language, or the new home language, but a hybrid language made from elements of both. For people living at the border of two regions with different languages, it is often hybrid words that are most expressive and communicative. Spanglish words are a daily reality for those living in the Mexican-U.S. border area, while Filipinos in Canada communicate not in Tagalog, Canadian English, or standard Filipino English, but a combination of all three. As a result, hybrid languages become the new home languages for such communities.

Terms such as *foreigner* and *minority* can be particularly divisive, as they carry echoes of colonial and imperial pasts. Words are a double-edged sword. They can help to bring about a sense of unity and belonging, but they may very well deepen divisions among individuals and groups—thereby feeding into an "Us versus Them" narrative. This is especially the case with more global English words that are born through hybridization and innovation. Such words are often an important part of forming a shared social identity and lead to different hybrid varieties of English, such as Spanglish, Hong Kong English, Singlish, and Chinglish.

Let's think of Spanglish first. Writers who use techniques that involve hybridizing languages in their works often do so with a purpose in mind. The purpose could be sentimental, it could be political, or it could simply be reminiscent of the culture and speech patterns of the specific area they are trying to portray in their literature. The author Junot Díaz described some of his complex influences: "In the United States we have a Spanish that is deeply affected by each other's Spanishes . . . . a Dominican may use Mexican words, Cuban words, Puerto Rican words. . . . [I]n any U.S. Latino there are going to exist multiple Spanish registers." As Díaz says, the Spanish that is spoken is a mixture of Spanish from all the various cultures of people from all parts of the Spanish-speaking world. He goes on: "I have absolutely no problem with being Latino as long as it doesn't eliminate the fact that I'm also Dominican, and African diasporic, and from New Jersey. We can use these names strategically, sentimentally, politically, collectively, and I don't see any problem in this."[10]

In an interview about the writer Malin Alegria's works, the librarian Nora Galvan said: "The way she writes is the way we speak in this area. We do Spanglish all the time."[11] Alegria, like other writers in a similar vein, writes in a way authentic to the actual people her work describes. Readers who know both English and Spanish are common in the United States, and it would make sense for those with this wide linguistic repertoire to want to read works that appeal to a larger portion of their lexicon.

Another Mexican American author, Cristina Rivera Garza, says: "We not only have Mexican readers on this side of the border, but Mexicans who've been reading both in English and Spanish."

> Very often I realize that I'm writing material both in English and Spanish in the original version, and that gets into the very DNA of the writing. There is no special side or special compartment for each of these languages, they come in waves and are totally

intertwined. I'm not talking about mastery of both languages, I'm talking about . . . borrowing aspects of English and aspects of Spanish, and combining them in ways that are even to me ways that I am not necessarily expecting. I'm taking what is more useful, what is more truthful to the kind of things I want to convey.

. . . When we write, we are not concerned about matters of mastery . . . or power. When we write, we're talking about a deeper sense of communication.[12]

Indeed, there are countless writers who break down the socially constructed walls between languages when they craft books, songs, poems, and other forms of literature. In doing so, they are able to encompass what it means for a person to make use of their linguistic experience and resources. These authors are helping to bring greater awareness to the widespread existence of people with multiple language repertoires. Their texts create a template of hybridizing language for others to accept and follow, thereby forging a deeper sense of communion and communication among their related social groups.

"No sabo kids" is a slang phrase that originated in the Latinx community in the United States. It is a play on words using Spanish and English and translates to "I don't know kids." The phrase is often used to admit a lack of knowledge or understanding about a particular topic or situation, particularly when it comes to popular culture. It has gained popularity on social media platforms and in online conversations, particularly among younger generations. Despite its wide usage, "No sabo kids" is not a widely recognized expression and is not found in traditional dictionaries. It is only listed in the Urban Dictionary, which is a user-generated online collection focused on slang and informal language.

Meanwhile, in Hong Kong English, some words are used to describe aspects of life and culture unique to Hong Kong and have limited currency in other varieties of English.[13] Other words are also used in other countries in the region that have large Chinese communities, such as Singapore or Malaysia. Some such words are formed through coinage, which includes analogical constructions, clippings, abbreviations, total innovations, new compounds, prefixed compounds, and hybrid compounds. You will come across the term *batchmate,* for example, in both Hong Kong English and other Southeast Asian Englishes, meaning "a colleague recruited at the same time as others to a company or organization." Clippings are also common, as in the word *aircon,* meaning—you guessed it—"air conditioner." Abbreviations, however, are arguably one of the most common ways to form Hong Kong English terms, such as the following: *ABC* ("American-born Chinese"), *BBC* ("British-born Chinese"), and *HKSAR* ("Hong Kong Special Administrative Region"). Some additional examples of Hong Kong English terms include *Anglo-Chinese,* relating to Britain and China or English-medium schools in Hong Kong; *foodstall,* an open-air pavement (or sidewalk) restaurant; and *street hawker,* an unlicensed street trader.

The historical background of cross-Asian words, in the context of Hong Kong English and a wider sense of Asian English words, involves India. A number of words are of Anglo-Indian origin— such as *brinjal, bungalow, chit, chop, congee, coolie, mango, monsoon,* and *shroff.* This was a result of historical connections between India and Indian communities in Singapore, Malaysia, and colonial Hong Kong. At the beginning of the colonial period, there were also South Asians arriving in Hong Kong as soldiers, sailors, merchants, traders, and recruits for the police force. However, the number of Anglo-Indian words used today is relatively small.

A substantial number of Hong Kong words are also used in Singapore and Malaysia, in addition to *aircon* and *batchmate: Chinese New Year, fishcake,* and *kowtow,* to name a few more examples. This has a number of historical and contemporary reasons. Historically, Hong Kong was a transit point for many Chinese emigrants from the Guangdong and Fujian provinces who were recruited as unskilled workers in the "coolie" trade system in the nineteenth and early twentieth centuries. Chinese merchants and traders in Singapore and the Straits Settlements (Malacca, Dinding, Penang, and Singapore) had strong contacts with Hong Kong traders. More recently, many Hong Kong families have relatives living in Singapore, and there is also a great amount of business transacted between the two cities, and with Malaysia. There are many Malaysian Chinese who visit Hong Kong every year, as well as Hongkongers who go to Singapore or Kuala Lumpur. English is used alongside or instead of Chinese in communication.

English is important as a means of international communication in the fields of education, banking and finance, business, and the tourism and hospitality industry in Hong Kong. The language is so deeply integrated into Hong Kong life in various ways that it has resulted in a thriving and developing variety of English. For those living in Hong Kong, new words are constantly being made based on the needs of local people; often this involves combining English with Cantonese. Although there are without doubt traces of colonial history, the change in lexicon also helps to reflect the changing, more globalized reality of Hong Kong society.

Singlish is also essential in maintaining social life among local Singaporeans. James Wong, a Japanese person who grew up in Singapore, commented in a BBC article that not being able to hold a conversation in Singlish had posed a problem for him—stall owners at local food centers, for instance, could not understand his English.[14] The article also describes the Singlish term *play play,* frequently found in the phrase "Don't play play," which was popularized by the sitcom character Phua Chu Kang in 1990s. It roughly means "don't mess around with me," and is more accurately written as "*Don(ch) pray pray*"—a spelling that more closely reflects the Singlish pronunciation. This is a more self-deprecating, rather than self-aware, joke that can be used among friends.

Here are a few more examples that show this unique intimacy expressed through Singlish. First off, you ask someone to go *makan* with you, instead of grabbing food. This is one of the most commonly used and heard words in daily life in Singapore. *Makan* literally means "food" in Malay; you ask someone for *makan* when you want to know if they have eaten or to invite them for a meal. After you accept this invitation and arrive at a local hawker center with your Singaporean friend, you may decide that you want takeaway after all. To the stall owner who is bringing you food, you may ask if you can *dabao*. *Dabao* is a colloquial Cantonese word meaning to wrap or pack, but frequently used as a verb to refer to the act of takeaway. When you finally get to taste the meal that you have *dabao*-ed, you might exclaim: "*Shiok!*" *Shiok* is also a Malay expression, conveying a feeling of sheer pleasure and excitement. To emphasize the heightened pleasure, one might then say: "This *Nasi Lemak* damn *shiok!*" ("Damn" is often also placed in front of adjectives to underscore the sentiment—such as "damn nice" and "damn tired.") Another example can arise when you tell a third friend about the Nasi Lemak you have just had, and they could answer with: "*Walao eh*, so *bojio*." The Hokkien and Teochew term *walao* (other forms being *wah lau, walau*) is a broader expression of surprise, disbelief, or amazement. An English equivalent of *walao* would be "OMG" or "what the hell." The use of *walao* adds onto the expression of *bojio*. A Hokkien word, *bojio* consists of *bo* ("no/didn't") and *jio* ("call/invite") and can be summed up as meaning "not invited," or the feeling of not being invited. It generally translates to: "Where is my invite?" or "Why wasn't I invited?" In this specific case, your third friend is expressing his disbelief that he was not invited to try this amazing *Nasi Lemak* that you and your friend have discovered, and wishes he was present as well.

There are several other exclamation phrases like *walao* that are commonly used among local Singaporeans. Perhaps the most heard is *aiyo* or *aiya,* originally from the Chinese *āiyā.* This is a multi-purpose term that is often used as a lament, or an expression of surprise, frustration, and annoyance. Let's say you are supposed to treat your friend to lunch, but you realize upon payment that you had forgotten your card. Your friend may remark, "*Aiyo,* never mind. I'll buy lunch today." Then there is *alamak,* a Malay expression of surprise and shock. It is somewhat similar to *walao,* but it leans more toward "oh no" rather than mere surprise like "OMG"; it is typically used in a difficult, troublesome situation. (One example is, "*Alamak!* Forgot to water my plants.") There are more unique linguistic combinations, such as *abuden,* constituted by the Hokkien *a-bo* ("if not") and the English word "then." *Abuden* is often used as a sarcastic remark to an obvious question to which a response is unnecessary. An English substitute would be "obviously." If you notice someone dropping their wallet on the street and ask your friend if you should alert him, your friend might exclaim, "*Abuden!*" In addition to these exclamations, there are also endearing ways of calling to close friends, instead of a simple "hey." This may come in the form of *wei,* from a Chinese character or the Tamil words *dei* and *macha,* which mean "dude" or "mate." Such words are incorporated into English sentences and phrases. Where you might say "idiot," you could instead use *goondu*—a word that means "fat" in literal translations but is used as a derogatory name for someone who is acting stupid and idiotic.

Like the examples above, the following Singlish words also represent a specific feeling or sentiment unique to the local setting. *Sian* is the Hokkien word for feeling bored and tired of something. (One example is, "Next class is history. So *sian.*") You may say *kiasu* (a Hokkien word that originates from vernacular Chinese *pàshū*) instead of "fear of losing out." This word somewhat resembles the English slang *FOMO* ("fear of missing out"), but it refers more to the general feeling of anxiety arising from the possibility of losing out rather than being related to a social event, often leading to extreme measures to prevent loss and achieve success. For instance, if the latest version of an iPhone is to be showcased at the X branch at 12 p.m., some would show up and start queueing for hours before. In Singlish, you would call this behavior *kias*. Another example is *paiseh*. Say you run into Ryan Gosling at a shopping mall, but you're too shy. Rather than "embarrassed," you might say you are *paiseh*, which is a Hokkien expression, delivering a subtle sense of embarrassment or shame; you can use this in various contexts, such as "*Paiseh*, I was late because the traffic was heavy." Similarly, there is *jialat*, from the Hokkien word *chă-lát*, which literally translates into "sapping energy." Almost as an opposite to *shiok*, *jialat* means to be in a state of trouble or a negative situation. If an interview goes badly, you would say the interview was "damn (very) *jialat*."

The point of this discussion is to demonstrate the process of linguistic localization. Through example phrases and sentences of Singlish, we can see how English words and local words live together. Rather than there being a clear distinction between what counts as "English" and what counts as belonging to the local languages of Singapore, Singlish serves as a sort of linguistic melting pot for Singaporeans, whether living in Singapore or in the diaspora. This hybrid language is an example of how a world English can help to bring together individuals and a community, as well as showcase the beauty of living together in a more globalized world through creative language combinations.

As for Chinglish, it is defined by the OED as "a mixture of Chinese and English; *esp.* a variety of English used by speakers of Chinese or in a bilingual Chinese and English context, typically incorporating some Chinese vocabulary or constructions, or English terms specific to a Chinese context." Also: "The vocabulary of, or a characteristic idiom from, such a variety."[15] The following can be considered Chinglish terms: *drunken chicken* (referring to a way of preparing chicken with the help of alcoholic beverages, such as marinating the chicken in rice wine before cooking it), *dragon boat, sweet and sour,* and *chopsticks.* These words, which are also used in the West, are calques. Meanwhile, words that have entered English through Western European languages are less so. If we consider the names of Chinese restaurants, too often they may sound funny or ridiculous. It seems that there is still a need to decolonize and de-Westernize modern world Englishes in order to overcome prejudices and preconceptions that may be associated with them.[16]

"New Chinglish" includes ordinary English utterances that are reappropriated with different meanings for Chinese speakers of English, as well as creations of words and expressions that generally conform to the morphological rules of English but with Chinese twists and meanings. Li Wei offers the following examples:

Shitizen (pì mín)= shit + citizen, reflecting how ordinary citizens in China feel about their status in society.

Democrazy (chī xīn wàng xiǎng) = democracy + crazy; mocking the so-called democratic systems of the west and in some parts of Asia where certain legislations such as the ownership of firearms can be protected due to political lobbying and, in the case of Taiwan, parliamentarians get into physical fights over disagreements. The occurrence of the word was prominent after the news of Trump's victory in the US presidential election broke.

Harmany (Zhōngguó tèsè héxié) = The Chinese Communist Party's discourse on "harmony" has been turned by the bilingual netizens into harm + many, as many people felt that the social policies imposed on them brought harm rather than cohesion.[17]

The other side of Chinglish, then, is that it allows a means of escape from nation-state censorship and criticism. The terms mentioned above exhibit a satire-like element and contain political sarcasm, as these words are not used solely for pragmatic purposes and daily survival; they convey feelings and attitudes beyond such basic needs. Chinglish words can convey sentiments that are difficult to express in Chinese or English alone.

The Problem with Calling Everything Chinese

Words are often reflections of our identities, and in many cases, they have multiple identities. This can sometimes lead to nationalistic debate and even spark a war of words. For example, there has been a heated discussion between China and Korea on the etymology and origin of words. In mainland China, it is not unusual to hear even an academic say that Korean culture is Chinese culture. There is of course a heritage of cultural and diplomatic ties, but Koreans seek a more nuanced understanding. One word that caused a clash was *hanfu,* the Chinese umbrella term for dynastic traditional dress. Korean has an equivalent word, *hanbok,* which stems from the same Chinese characters, but has its own pronunciation. The Chinese promotion of *hanfu* caused frustration among Koreans, who view it as cultural appropriation and a form of historical revisionism. Korean netizens argued that *hanfu* is worn by other East Asian cultures and was not widely worn during the dynastic periods of China. Debates like these have intensified in recent years. One *Global Times* article that heralded the "international standard for the kimchi industry led by China" sparked fury in South Korea. In an effort to calm the disputes, Professor Kyungdeok Seo from Seoul took out an advertisement in the *New York Times* stating that Korea's kimchi is not just for Koreans but for everyone.

One of the questions that I most frequently encounter is "Are you Chinese?" When it comes to East Asia and Southeast Asia, China is often the country that people default to. The term is not well understood either. How does one define China? Ming China is hugely different from Qing China, which is hugely different from the People's Republic of China. What about Hong Kong and Taiwan? How many people can name Chinese dialects beyond Mandarin and Cantonese? Are they aware of the diverse ethnic groups living in China? In Xinjiang, Uyghur people speak Uygur, while Han Chinese speak Mandarin. Up until recently, Mandarin was a second language learned by Uyghur children at school or in community spaces. How many people understand the multiplicity of China when they ask me whether I am Chinese? The English term *Chinese* is an umbrella term, but all that it encompasses is not widely understood. The same issue does not exist with China's own terminology in Mandarin or Cantonese. It is only when the term is used in English that further clarification of meaning is required.

The term *Chinese New Year* can also pose problems. According to Google N-gram, this expression has been in use since the 1840s, and *Lunar New Year* only appeared in the 1930s. Google N-gram also shows that *Chinese New Year* is still more widely used than *Lunar New Year*. When I first came to the United Kingdom in the 1990s, I thought "Chinese New Year" was simply the way to say "Lunar New Year" in English. Referring to "Lunar New Year" as "Chinese New Year" overlooks the fact that this holiday is celebrated by many other Asian cultures besides China, including Vietnam, Korea, and Mongolia. Labeling it solely as Chinese New Year not only ignores diversity but can also perpetuate the erasure of Asian identities. Such terminology can also reinforce the stereotype that all Asians are the same, which can be harmful and offensive. In the United Kingdom, all prime ministers until Rishi Sunak have used the term *Chinese New Year*. Sunak was the first to use *Lunar New Year,* in 2023, mentioning not only China, but also Korea and Vietnam too.

What's more, many East Asian or pan-Asian culinary terms have Sinitic origin and are engaged in complex translingual journeys. *Soy sauce* is defined in the OED "as a sauce prepared chiefly in Japan, China, and India, from soybeans and eaten with fish, etc." In principle, then, *soy sauce* is a hybrid word. Nowadays, soy sauce is used in the global kitchen—beyond Asian cuisine. Even as the popularity of soy sauce has soared, it is fascinating to observe that not everyone opts to use the term *soy sauce* when referring to this condiment. Instead, an intriguing shift has occurred, with the growing adoption of its transliterated counterpart, *shoyu*. This linguistic divergence sparks a question: Why do individuals choose different words to convey the same concept? The answer lies in our innate yearning for change and diversity. Hence, our language does not remain stagnant but rather evolves into distinct variations. As we engage in sharing and communication, we discover that it constantly seeks avenues to diversify. The more we exchange ideas and experiences, the more our language adapts and embraces new expressions.

This is the same in the case of *tofu* and *bean curd*. The first quotation concerning tofu that appears in the OED is from 1880: "*Tôfu* is made by pounding the soy beans after soaking in water." Tofu is spelled and pronounced according to the Japanese word, but tofu equally originates from China and Korea. This means the spelling could be *doufu* from Mandarin, or even *dubu*, according to Korean pronunciation. Words like *tofu* demonstrate that cultural products rarely originate from one single country. These products often precede the modern world as defined by nation-states. The idea that this food belongs to one country alone would not have existed at the time. So, to set the spelling according to one country is quite problematic. It harkens back to Orientalist sentiments, where the Orient was one giant, exotic monolith. As more and more people of different heritages and ethnic backgrounds engage with their cultural products and speak about them in English, more and more cases like this will arise. More people will know the varied pronunciations of words like *tofu*, and they may begin to vary their spelling too. As our lexical pantries grow, our spellings become more and more diverse. As a result, our choice of words, and their forms and significance, will greatly depend on cultural context and individual taste.

Pairs of Japanese native words and translated terms that behave like *tofu* and *bean curd* include *sakura* and *cherry blossoms, bunraku* and *Japanese puppet theater, nori* and *seaweed, onsen* and *hot spring, ramen* and *noodle soup, shogi* and *Japanese chess, yakuza* and *Japanese mafia, yakisoba* and *fried noodles, zaibatsu* and *conglomerate*—and many more. As awareness continues to grow, transliterated forms are becoming increasingly prominent.

Painful and Personal Words

Words have the power to evoke emotions and can be deeply painful to those they are directed toward. Derogatory terms, slurs, and discriminatory language can not only hurt individuals but also perpetuate harmful stereotypes and prejudices toward marginalized communities. The use of offensive language can lead to feelings of exclusion or disrespect, and can damage one's self-esteem and mental health. It is important to recognize the impact of words on individuals and society as a whole and strive toward using language that is inclusive, respectful, and reflective of the diversity of our communities.

Oriental is a term that was used by Europeans to describe all lands and peoples east of the Mediterranean, reflecting a totalizing and homogenizing view of them. In this way, the word denied the important human differences that Europeans acknowledged when discussing themselves. This word offered a view of the world that lent itself well to the colonial project that underpinned British dominion from the seventeenth to the twentieth centuries, seeking unquestioned British political and economic power over a nebulous other. As a result, when this term is used today to refer to non-European peoples and lands, it is often seen as derogatory and invokes memories of these colonial policies.

In a globalized world, where a vast majority of English speakers belong to societies that were the victims rather than perpetrators of this world view, questions arise about what to do with this vocabulary. Should it be modified, changed, or replaced? Can it be co-opted by the groups it was previously used to disparage? And should those beyond the group be allowed to use it if their intentions are obviously different from those who gave birth to the word? These are questions that have animated my home department at the University of Oxford, which until the summer of 2022 was known as the Faculty of Oriental Studies and was housed in a building called the Oriental Institute.

Although some Near Eastern languages have been taught at the university since the middle of the sixteenth century, it was not until 1871, at the height of Britain's colonial empire, that the university offered a final examination in Oriental Studies. At that time, the department's students and faculty either directly or indirectly aided Britain's imperial project in the "orient." But today, many members of the department hail from places and populations that would formerly have been described by this term. The work of the department's students and faculty often provides a direct challenge to harmful and reductive narratives produced by past scholars about the Orient, and at other times focuses a light on the cruelties of colonialism and imperialism that were associated with the term.

The problem of finding a new name to cover all the regions studied by the department was complex because so much of our language for regions beyond Europe emerged from colonial projects or as a consequence of colonialism. In the end, finding a truly neutral alternative was impossible, and the department formally adopted the name the Faculty of Asian and Middle Eastern Studies. This solution is obviously not perfect or neutral, as the term *Middle East* also carries imperial and Eurocentric connotations.

Nevertheless, it avoids producing the same level of offense as the term *oriental*. Even if the solution to our department's naming problem was not totally satisfactory, the conversation around naming is an important one as it forces us to ask difficult questions about why certain regions of the world were separated into area studies departments in the first place.

Turning to the United States, Barack Obama made efforts to replace the term *oriental* with *Asian* in federal law. In 2016, Obama signed a bill into law that removed the word *oriental* from federal language and replaced it with *Asian American*. Obama's move was seen by some as a positive step toward more inclusive language and recognition of the diversity and contributions of Asian Americans. However, replacing *oriental* with *Asian* does not accurately capture the full range of ethnicities and cultures that were historically referred to as *oriental*. Using *Asian* in the place of *oriental* is simply replacing one umbrella term with another.

There are always two sides to a story. There have been movements across the world for the promotion and preservation of more local languages. One extreme example is the story of Massimo Lecas, the owner of an Italian restaurant in Quebec that was known for its celebrity clientele, including Leonardo DiCaprio, Robert De Niro, and Rihanna.[18] One day, Lecas received a letter from the Office Québécois de la Langue Française (Quebec Board of the French Language)—a group within the regional Quebec government that seeks to protect the French language from the rise of English—informing him that his establishment, Buonanotte, had broken the law by including the words *pasta* on the menu and *bottiglia,* the Italian word for "bottle," instead of the French word *bouteille.* Affronted, the owner turned to social media and posted the letter on Facebook for his friends to see. This led to a political storm concerning one of the most hotly debated topics in the province. Eventually, the Quebec government was forced to rein in its language inspectors and ensure that exceptions to the rules are made for ethnic food and restaurant menus. They were also ordered to review their handling of public complaints.

When interviewed, Lecas stated: "I think that when they circled the word pasta that was the sensitive spot. It wasn't an anglophone thing so right away the francophones jumped in [to support the restaurant] because it was an Italian word." Lessac, and others involved in this controversy, experienced first-hand how charged words can be, socially and politically. The history of words—like *pasta*, which has crossed borders, cultures, and languages—can be complex and, if poorly understood, may lead to conflict.

When words are not painful, they can be a source of expression and enjoyment, capable of bringing pleasure and comfort, and eliciting laughter. In fact, words are essential not just for the exchange of facts and ideas, but also for our emotional and psychological well-being. As a personal example, after spending an entire day speaking English, I find solace in watching a Korean television show in the evening. Listening to my native language is an indulgence that brings me great pleasure. Pleasurable words, sometimes referred to as pleasure interjections, are typically brief and uncomplicated expressions that evoke feelings of happiness and joy. They are best expressed in the language that is closest to one's heart, and as a result, can be difficult to translate into other languages. Interestingly, such words tend to be spontaneous and effortlessly uttered in our daily lives. Pleasure words tend to be short, often just one or two syllables, regardless of the language being spoken. Even speakers whose native language is not English will inevitably use these words repeatedly, demonstrating the workings of our language instinct. Japanese speakers may spontaneously use the word *sugoi*, for instance, while German speakers may use *wunderbar,* even in an English-speaking context. Words like these, including familial terms of endearment, are often untranslatable. For me, my late father will always be an "appa." No other word can capture the depth of meaning and sentimentality that this personal word carries.

Chapter 8

AFTER WORDS

Never Ending Words in the World of AI

What lies beyond words? As we become increasingly interconnected, it may seem that we will soon arrive at a universal set
of words. The truth is that the more we share words, the more
diverse our language becomes. This is how language evolves.
With the expansion of digital cultures and their influence on
our physical world, the use of visual and image-based words is
becoming increasingly prominent. People use both alphabetic
and visual words, and even punctuation marks can have emotional or stylistic meanings like images. Using memes as words
is popular not only among young people, but people of all ages
are engaging with this new practice. While some may argue that
image words could create misunderstandings, their usage is on
the rise. Compared with alphabet words, which can be dry and
unengaging, visual words like memes are fun and expressive.
Image words, like emojis, are the future of our language. Mixing languages in English is common and adds to the language's
versatility, but even with this mixing, letter words alone are not
enough. Emojis and memes have become integral parts of our
daily interactions, used to express our likes, dislikes, and more.
The absence of image words in one's digital communication can
carry negative connotations and may be perceived as a lack of
digital literacy. Nowadays, people are speaking and writing less

than ever. With all this diversity and new technology, it may seem that we are losing our words, but in reality, we are only changing how we communicate.

According to some research, infants as young as six months may already possess knowledge of everyday words, suggesting that vocabulary learning begins well before this age. Language acquisition continues to progress rapidly throughout childhood.[1] By the time children reach eighteen months, they typically have a vocabulary of around 200 words, which then expands to about 2,600 words by the time they enter school.[2] Although word acquisition happens rapidly in the early years, the process slows down as we get older. In today's fast-paced world, this slowing appears to be less pronounced. I find myself learning and acquiring new words constantly, not necessarily because I want to, but because I feel I need to in order to navigate and function in this ever evolving world. Recently I stumbled on a new word—*smartify*—from the Ashmolean Museum at Oxford. An announcement read: "Smartify at the Ashmolean Museum. Listen to 2 new audio tours on your smartphone." With the continuous advancement of technology, it is inevitable that new words will emerge.

Dictionaries are valuable tools for finding and recording the meanings of words, but they struggle to keep up with the rapid pace of change in language. Even crowd-sourced dictionaries can't possibly record all the words that are in existence at any given moment. As a result, the life trajectory of words—their evolving forms and meanings—will increasingly become privatized, with meanings that are only known and understood by small communities or subcultures. This privatization of language poses significant challenges for language learners and researchers who rely on traditional sources to understand the meanings and usage of words. It also underscores the need for a more dynamic and adaptable approach to language study that can keep pace with the ever evolving nature of language. As if the challenge of keeping up with new words wasn't enough, there is also the added complication of deciding whether these words even belong in a dictionary. Proper nouns, such as names of individuals or sub-groups, may not necessarily be included in dictionaries, but the same cannot be said for other words. In a world where more and more words are being privatized by individuals and companies, the future of dictionaries seems uncertain. People may soon have to resort to visiting company websites to understand the meanings of newly coined words. The proliferation of visual words such as memes and emojis has rendered traditional dictionaries somewhat obsolete. Where do we turn to decipher the meanings of image words, assuming they have any common meaning at all?

The impact of AI should not be underestimated. AI is now capable of more than just translating, as it can even produce original text. In December 2022, ChatGPT became a hot topic in social media. Developed by OpenAI, ChatGPT is a model that "interacts in a conversational way." Users can ask the chatbot to write something for them or tell them about something, and it will produce within a matter of seconds. ChatGPT can "answer follow-up questions, admit its mistakes, challenge incorrect premises, and reject inappropriate requests."[3] You can ask ChatGPT to write a resignation email, a children's short story, a song, or pretty much anything you might desire. So far, all of my requests on the program have yielded impressive responses. Even though we currently ask our AI assistants to help with small tasks like playing a song or turning on a timer, we may eventually be able to ask them to send correspondence without having to say much more than "Let HR know I'm taking a sick day." For functional requests, AI-generated writing could be of great assistance, but when it comes to songs, poems, and literature, how can AI compare? This is a question for another book, but it is worth bearing in mind that AI might one day come to endanger human creativity. In the past, it was only humans who could generate language. Now that AI can generate language too, will it have an influence on the evolution of our languages? Perhaps, in the future, we will begin using words that have been created by AI. Modern technology is one of the most influential forces on our language, and it will transform human language completely.

As digital cultures constantly move forward into our physical worlds, we are finding new ways to process documents digitally. In this process, we are interacting not just textually, but also multimodally. One change that is becoming increasingly visible is words on QR codes. Since the Covid-19 pandemic, we see more instructions telling us to "scan a QR code," such as when ordering food or paying for a meal. I wonder whether we will have more words but speak less. In the not too distant future, we may find ourselves inundated with an abundance of words, yet we may not need to use them as frequently as we do now. The reason? Automation. It's a thought that sends chills down our spines, but who knows what the future may hold? Perhaps someday soon our AI assistants will not only order food for us through QR codes but also respond to all our emails and messages, impersonating us entirely. With the emergence of generative, hyperscale AI, like ChatGPT, nobody can predict the future of our words and languages. We may see an exponential growth of words as information sharing soars, but when everything is circulated and utilized by automation, it's possible that we may not even be aware of the words that are being used to represent us.

New Online Habitat

Perhaps the most significant change in the evolution of language is the shift in words' habitat from the physical to the virtual and online worlds. In the digital age, the creation of new words and expressions has accelerated, with many unique words being coined in virtual spaces. Hashtags are a prime example, used to categorize and group content on social media platforms, but having no tangible existence in the physical world. Emojis, digital images used to convey emotions, ideas, and concepts, are another example of virtual words with no physical form. Meanwhile, words like *vlog* and *avatar* have physical equivalents, but their meanings have evolved in the virtual world to refer to specific online activities or representations. The rise of online communication has also led to the creation of many new expressions and acronyms used to convey meaning and emotion in digital conversations, such as *LOL* ("laugh out loud") and *FOMO* ("fear of missing out"). These terms have become commonplace in online discourse and have even entered offline conversations.

As our lives shift into online spaces, we are encountering new action words, such as *meet* versus *e-meet*—the latter being a virtual meeting. It can be challenging to use these terms appropriately, and there is no clear consensus on which form is correct. In email replies, using "nice to meet you" may feel awkward since the action of actually "meeting," seeing, or communicating verbally with the other person may not occur. Such new challenges are crucial, and even verbs like *come* and *go, travel* or *visit,* are being redefined, as virtual interactions become much more common. Activities including rock climbing, fishing, sailing, and skiing that were once associated with physical experiences can now be simulated in virtual reality. It's unclear, however, whether we will continue using these words to describe these experiences in VR, or whether new words will emerge. It's possible that these words may need to be reevaluated in virtual worlds, or perhaps new words may await creation.

As for ways in which we engage with words, printed books have historically outsold e-books, but the landscape is shifting. Despite predictions that digital formats would dominate the market, traditional print books still hold a strong position among consumers. In the United States, publishers earned nearly $26 billion in revenue from book sales in 2019, with print books accounting for $22.6 billion and e-books making up $2.04 billion, according to the Association of American Publishers annual report.[4] However, the increasing prevalence of digital media is changing the way people read and interact with information. Physical books will continue to hold value, but their dominance is gradually being challenged by e-books, which are advancing in functionality with the introduction of AI books. AI books differ from traditional e-books in that they are interactive, customized, and multimodal, providing readers with a more engaging and informative experience.[5] Illustrated children's e-books that incorporate movement, music, and sound are now commonplace, where just a few decades ago they would have been impossible. Moreover, as children rely on technology more and more for their education, the appeal of visual aids and interactive elements has become increasingly important. The rise of digital media in the book market is following a pattern similar to that seen in other forms of media, from the evolution of newspapers and radio to color television. As more and more words move into the virtual world, printed materials are gradually losing ground. This is only further exacerbated by deforestation and dwindling resources. It is unlikely that paper books will disappear entirely, and they will continue to have their place in the market. As a result of these changes, however, words will no longer be confined to black and white spaces but will exist in more dynamic and colorful forms. The future of books is moving toward digital, and it is only a matter of time before e-books become the norm rather than the exception.

Without doubt, words have always played a significant role in human history, leaving behind a trail of both visual and verbal expressions, from our names to ancient texts. In the twenty-first century, the definition of words is expanding to encompass not only alphabetic letters but also non-verbal visual expressions. Although the term *non-verbal* may sound marginal, it is a crucial component of human communication—only 7 percent of communication is conveyed through words alone. Human communication is intrinsically orchestrated by bodily movements, including facial expressions, gestures, and tone of voice. In this sense, words are not limited to what is spoken or written but also include nonverbal cues that contribute to the overall message being conveyed.

Memes and emojis are becoming the words of our future. The use of image words is not a new practice. In fact, images and writing have been used together since ancient times, often with blurry lines between them. The Sumerians are believed to have created one of the earliest forms of writing in human history around 4000–3000 BCE. This is called cuneiform, which means "wedge-shaped," because it was written on clay tablets using a stylus with a wedge-shaped tip. Cuneiform script consisted of a combination of images, such as pictures of objects or animals, and a set of prototypical letter-like signs that represented syllables or sounds. The Sumerians used cuneiform writing for various purposes, such as recording business transactions, legal agreements, and religious texts. They also created some of the earliest works of literature in the world, including the Epic of Gilgamesh, which tells the story of a legendary king and his adventures.

Cuneiform script was initially used mainly for practical purposes, but over time it became increasingly complex and sophisticated, incorporating more abstract ideas and concepts. Looking to the past, we can trace the evolution of writing from hieroglyphs to alphabets. The invention of the alphabet can be dated to around 1500 BCE, with alphabets around the world, including Latin, Arabic, and Hebrew, being derived from Proto-Sinaitic.[6] During the time of the Roman Empire, all the nations that fell under its rule became literate in the first centuries of our era. This included but was not limited to the Gauls, Angles, Saxons, Franks, and Germans who inhabited present-day France, England, and Germany. Over time, use of the Latin alphabet grew and became a symbol of Westernization. Image words can be just as intuitive as letter words, and they exist in a multimodal form. In her book *Drawn from the Ground,* Jennifer Green explores how sand stories from Central Australia represent a traditional form of Aboriginal women's verbal art, which combines speech, song, sign, gesture, and drawing.[7] It is difficult to separate one part from the other, as they all work together.

I recall the time I once sent a series of red hearts to my friend Anna to show that I was happy to look after her children while she and her husband were away. She then texted me to say thank you but with a row of gray hearts. I thought to myself, "What does the gray heart mean?" Thanks to smartphones and technological advancements, colors have been added to our communication. A red heart may mean nothing to some, but to others in, say, a strictly conservative culture, it could have serious consequences. In black-and-white print, it would not be possible to use a red heart, but on screen, the colors of emojis have different meanings. *Cosmopolitan* published an article titled "The Color of the Heart Emoji You Send Is Seriously Important," describing common interpretations of different colored heart emojis: red is a basic romantic heart, and it can be used as "a timeless, platonic-love, support emoji," while a gray heart "represents neutral or indifferent emotions," and a blue heart has "bro energy" and "implies a sort of shallow friendship."[8]

Since the invasion of Ukraine by Russia, however, blue hearts—particularly when used alongside yellow hearts—have come to show support and solidarity with Ukraine. This is rooted in the "Color Revolutions" of various anti-regime protest movements and accompanying (attempted or successful) governmental changes that took place in post-Soviet Eurasia during the early twenty-first century.[9] Different colors were associated with different movements and revolutions, such as orange with the Pitta Revolution in Bolivia, green with the Green Movement in Iran, and yellow with the Yellow Revolution of Philippines, Yellow Rally of Malaysia, and Yellow Vests Revolution of France. Clearly, color symbolism can be powerful. The multimodal nature of our communication permits constant border-crossing on-screen. This liberates our language from the black-and-white space, removing barriers and further expanding our word pantry to include letter and non-letter words.

Punctuation markers are additional good examples of this phenomenon. Using a full stop, or period, for instance, is hardly perceived as neutral in online spaces. As the digital world continues to evolve, the dominance of letter words may gradually give way to image words, with punctuation marks and other symbols playing a more prominent role in the way we communicate. Punctuation matters greatly. An article published by the *Guardian* in 2021 states that "full stops are dying but the exclamation mark is doing fine," as these markers all very much continue to convey feelings.[10] Suppose you ask your friend whether you can borrow her rice cooker. She says "Okay." Most of us wouldn't feel at ease with this response, because the full stop conveys something like a passive-aggressive tone.

> Jieun: Would you like to come for a cup of tea?
> Sarah: Okay.
> Jieun: Could I borrow your car?
> Sarah: Okay . . .

In this context, the full stop adds an air of annoyance to the reply, while the ellipsis expresses reluctance or hesitation. Traditional punctuation markers are now used in tailor-made ways. It's less a matter of adhering to "proper" grammar rules, and instead of relaying sentiments. The emotional impact of punctuation markers is explored in Gretchen McCulloch's book *Because Internet*; in fact, an entire chapter is dedicated to the topic of "typographical tone of voice," which examines the use of full stops, ellipses, all caps, asterisks, tildes, and minimalist typography as means of emphasizing certain words or phrases. It's important to note, however, that the meanings of these symbols can vary depending on cultural and individual differences. In Asia, for example, tilde signs (~) are more commonly used as a wave-like gesture of comfort rather than a means of emphasis. Interpreting the meanings of symbols, whether in writing or speech, is not always straightforward.

Are Emojis also Words?

Just as there is a diversity of words, there is also a diversity of emojis, and defining what constitutes an emoji is not straightforward. In my book *Emoji Speak*, I use *emoji* as an umbrella term that includes symbols of any sort, such as emoticons, stickers, or punctuation markers, as well as (moving) images like GIFs, memes, and more. Emoji speak consists of emoji words, which stand in contrast to letter words. They can be thought of as image words that primarily exist in online spaces. I also propose the term *emoji speak* as a form of newspeak that highlights how our communication has gone beyond letter-driven texting to become multimodal and multilingual. The term is inspired by "Newspeak" in George Orwell's novel *1984*. Newspeak was a simplified version of the English language intended to limit and control the way people thought and spoke. While emoji speak has no such sinister undertones, it shares similarities in that emojis represent a highly simplified and abstract form of language. Emoji speak liberates our writing from the linguistic authorities of grammar or borders of languages and cultures. It will open a new era of language where nation-state languages and their prescriptive rules may be less significant as the norms of language use come to be more determined by and seen as sets of idiolects and community practices. People think of emojis as substitutes for letter words, but rather they are their own meaningful entity that is crucial for online communication.

Let's pause to consider the term *non-verbal*. This word is interesting in its contrast to *verbal,* which is strongly associated with language produced by the vocal organs or in writing—especially in the age of digital communication. Dr. Albert Mehrabian was one of the first researchers to recognize the significance of non-verbal communication. Through his studies on body language, he developed the 7–38–55 rule, which suggests that only 7 percent of communication is conveyed through words, while 38 percent and 55 percent are conveyed through tone of voice and body language, respectively. In the digital world, the importance of non-verbal communication has only continued to grow. Memes, for example, are influential and popular. While *non-verbal* may make the term sound secondary to *verbal,* the truth is that human communication is intrinsically tied to bodily movements. Vocal aspects are crucial, but they are not everything. Communication involves much more than just words that are spoken or written; it is also performed through non-verbal cues.

Emojis have become one of the most prevalent forms of international communication: 90 percent of internet users regularly use emojis, and they are used across borders, generations, and in all world languages. Emojis are a prime example of how non-verbal cues play a critical role in human communication. Since the inception of emojis (which began as emoticons typed on the keyboard) in the 1990s, the usage rates of emojis through the years experienced a rapid increase in the 2010s, after the standardization of seven hundred emojis and the addition of an emoji keyboard in Apple's operating system. Even though the history of emojis has been relatively short, their use is greatly varied. To analyze diversity in emojis, one needs to look at the various attributes that are linked to their use, such as culture, ethnicity, and age. There is already a great variety of graphics for any particular emoji. An emoji can look different when rendered on different operating systems, as each uses a system-specific set of symbols for them.[11] Emojipedia, a website that catalogs emojis and their use in detail, lists seventeen different platforms where emojis are rendered (with many of these having unique renderings), which suggests that there may be at least seventeen different depictions of any given emoji.[12]

Linguistically, emojis can represent a wide range of concepts, from emotion to professions and race, as well as fulfill a range of functions in conversation from operating as a reply to a preceding text or as the following word in a sentence.[13] According to an Adobe study in 2021, 67 percent of emoji users worldwide perceive other people who use emojis as friendlier, funnier, and cooler than those who don't. In addition, more than half of those people claim to be more comfortable expressing their feelings through emojis rather than traditional conversations. Our word pantry is expanding its inventory to become more multimodal. However, with this shift, we see what you may call the unsearchability of emojis. Words becoming emojis makes it all the more difficult to search for them as they lose or gain new nuances—words will be more hidden. Although emojis may seem to be a common pictorial language, their use and meaning are heavily individualized, resulting from personal style developed from factors such as location, age, mother tongue, and membership in particular subcultures. An emoji may mean one thing among a group of fans and something totally different to another group of people who know little or nothing about that world. With the rise of social media and the birth of the metaverse, the language of emojis is becoming all the more valuable.

Sign, Symbol, and Gesture Words

Everywhere we look, we are surrounded by sign words. From *Wi-Fi* and *Bluetooth* to *contactless payment* and more, there are countless signs in the world of technology. Many technical terms are represented through visual forms, which are often more productive than alphabetic forms. They can be incredibly useful in everyday life—pictorial signs at airports can be life-saving for those who don't speak the language. The meanings of these signs are not always straightforward, however. Zebra crossings, for example, can be found all over the world, but their interpretations and significance can vary greatly. In the United Kingdom, cars are required to stop when pedestrians are crossing the road at a zebra crossing, but in South Korea, cars may not stop, or even slow down. In the virtual world, symbols such as emojis and memes are even more open to diverse interpretations. Even a simple smiley face can have sarcastic connotations. Understanding symbols or non-verbal communication is not always straightforward. Each culture has its own unique interpretation, and even within a culture, different contexts can change the meaning. Users can have diverse ways of using symbols, and even gestural language can be diverse and vary from region to region. In Bulgaria, for example, nodding your head means "no" instead of "yes." The most common way to show agreement and say "yes" in Bulgaria is to shake your head from side to side, which typically means "no" in many other countries. And it's not just Bulgaria—other countries such as Greece, Iran, Lebanon, Turkey, and Egypt also follow this same method of communication.

Signs, symbols, and gesture words are indeed everywhere. The hashtag (#) on Twitter was originally proposed by Chris Messina in 2007 to allow for "contextualization, content filtering and exploratory serendipity" on the platform. Originally the idea was for people to be able to "follow" hashtags to stay updated on tweets relating to certain topics. People began using the hashtag system with spaces alongside the tracking system Twitter put in place in 2007 to get updates on the San Diego fire. However, the spaces between words made it difficult to track the hashtag. So Messina suggested that hashtags have no spaces. This proved to be much more effective for following topics accurately, and the idea caught on. Later in 2007, Messina updated his blog reflecting on the use of hashtags. He acknowledged that some "just don't like how they look." Ultimately, Twitter hashtags do not have spaces for technical reasons. The "# + [term with no spaces]" format allows for the computer to recognize the classifying word without confusing it with other parts of the tweet that are not part of the hashtag. Although this may confuse some people initially, most have accepted this and understand that it has a practical purpose. Nonetheless, hashtags have been criticized for other reasons. For example, they can be "annoying adding more noise than value" and "they encumber a simple communication system that should do one thing and one thing well." Regardless of your take on #, it has become a globally accepted word used by billions of people worldwide.[14]

Another example is the @ symbol. Although it gained popularity in social media spaces, the symbol has now become widely used in formal email settings as well. While variations of @ are argued to have been found as early as several centuries ago in the writings of medieval monks and merchants, it wasn't until 1971 when the modern @ made its way onto our keyboards, thanks to a computer scientist named Ray Tomlinson. Yet think how rapidly @ was integrated into lexicons worldwide. Nowadays, we find it all over the place: in emails, in writing, and on social media platforms. It has even been added to the Merriam-Webster dictionary as a verb, commonly used in the phrase "Don't @ me," which means "Don't argue with me" when one has posted a controversial statement. Merriam-Webster defines @ as: "to respond to, challenge, or disparage the claim or opinion of (someone)." Subcultural communities and social movements will overtake the traditional meanings of many words and create new ones. Living in a digital age, words like # and @ have become so influential and convey meaning cross-linguistically, exhibiting how platform-driven words will continue to flourish.[15]

The meanings of symbols and signs change over time as their users and environments change. The rainbow has long been a powerful symbol that increasingly means different things to different people, demonstrating the versatility of non-letter words. In the Bible, the rainbow is invoked as a reminder of God's presence and power, first appearing after the great flood as a sign of God's covenant with Noah and his family that the earth would never again be destroyed in the same way. Many of the world's Christians continue to associate the symbol of the rainbow with these meanings. But meaning is not constant, so from the late 1970s, the rainbow and the rainbow flag became a symbol of pride in the gay community and the demand of its people for recognition and equality. Since its early uses in the Bay Area, the meaning of the rainbow has expanded to encompass the entire LGBTQ community, and the symbol has been invoked around the globe by local queer communities struggling for rights and acceptance.

Even if the LGBTQ community may now be the primary group that the rainbow symbol evokes for many readers, the symbol has continued to take on new meanings. In 1994, during the first fully democratic election in South Africa after the end of apartheid, Archbishop Desmond Tutu invoked the symbol of the rainbow to describe the new multi-ethnic nation and government. The concept of the rainbow nation was quickly adopted by Nelson Mandela for his cabinet, which had not just black and white members but also ministers of Indian Muslim and Hindu descent. Thus, in South Africa the symbol of the rainbow has become strongly associated with certain public figures' support for a multicultural society, sometimes at the expense of more radical post-colonialism. In the United Kingdom during the Covid-19 pandemic, support for the country's National Health Service and its employees rose to astronomical levels. While initially public support was expressed through the Clap for Carers movement, which saw members of the public come outside every Thursday at 8 p.m. to applaud for frontline workers, other symbols for displaying support for the NHS soon became popular. Beyond the use of letter-word banners that voiced support for NHS workers, the symbol of the rainbow was also adopted, in part because Matt Hancock, the then health secretary, delivered regular briefings wearing a badge that featured a rainbow flag design behind the white letters NHS. While initially Hancock had worn the badge to show his solidarity with LGBTQ workers at NHS, the pairing soon helped bring about a new meaning of the rainbow as a symbol of support for the NHS. The rainbow is just one example of how symbols, even more than letter words, can have dynamic and evolving meanings that can at times be transnational and transcultural and at other times vary substantially across subcultural and national groups.

Emojis: From the Computer to the Printed Page

The personalized lexicon afforded by emoji use comes at a price, because it is also more corporate. Just as certain letter words can be trademarked, emojis are subject to certain copyright protections that mean tech companies can require permission and payment for them to be used in certain contexts. To understand exactly how copyright laws interact with our ability to freely use emojis requires a brief foray into the technology behind emojis. When you use your iPhone to shoot a text containing the extremely popular "Loudly Crying Face" emoji to your friend's Android phone, the image you selected from Apple's emoji keyboard, and which appears on your screen in the sent text bubble, is not actually sent to your friend. Instead, the phone encodes the image of the emoji, using the Unicode Standard, which has assigned a near universally recognized numeric value for each character and emoji. This string of numeric codes is sent and decoded by your friend's phone, which then assigns characters and emojis from its own repertoire of fonts and emoji images.

Thus, although the Unicode for the "Loudly Crying Face" is not copyrighted, the way it is rendered on a particular platform, app, or website is, in much the same way that an image can be copyrighted. This is why, as you probably have noticed, emojis look slightly different depending on where you type them.

But what happens if you want to take emoji use offline to a nominally commercial product, as I did when I published my book *Emoji Speak: Communication and Behaviours on Social Media*?[16] In a discussion of the "Red Heart Emoji," if I wanted to include an image of it in Apple's style, I would need to receive special permission from Apple, and more likely than not, pay to license the image. Similarly, if I were to design a new app, platform, or website for commercial purposes where emoji images were utilized, I would need to license them from a particular vendor like Microsoft, use a free or open-source emoji pack, or draw my own. We are not as free to use emoji words as we are to use letter words that previously constituted the totality of our idiolects. When corporate forces and technological advancements collide, they are a generative force upon global lexicons and can also stimulate the uneasy creep of privatization over the languages we choose to speak.

If, by chance, you are still thinking of emojis and social media language as trivial facets of our everyday communication even after the previous section, then you might be surprised to learn what great importance social media messages can take in court cases. Social media messages are the paper trail of the twenty-first century. What someone did or did not say offline can be hard to verify, but social media messages constitute hard evidence that judges and juries can take into account. The South Korean politician and ex-presidential candidate Ahn Hee-Jung, for example, was jailed in 2019 for sexually assaulting his secretary, Kim Ji-Eun.[17] A lower court had acquitted Ahn in August 2018, but the Seoul High Court overturned the ruling, finding Ahn guilty of

ㅋ　ㅎ　ㅠ　^^

Emoticons used as evidence in a lawsuit.

nine counts of sexual assault. One key piece of evidence that affected the verdict was online messages sent by Kim to Ahn. In her messages, Kim used emoticons, as well as the word *neng* ("yes"), which Ahn's lawyers argued expressed affection. The Seoul High Court disregarded this part of Ahn's defense, stating that such expressions were routinely used in young people's online messaging without having any special significance. This was part of the reason why the Seoul High Court overruled the original not guilty verdict. From this story, which is one of countless others, we see how there is always room for interpretation when it comes to emojis, arguably more so than our traditional understanding of letter words.

The word of the year for 2015 was the "Face with Tears of Joy" emoji. However, determining what this emoji actually means isn't so straightforward. Is it intended to convey amusement? Pain? Embarrassment? Well, it could be any of them. Different people— or even the same person in different conversational contexts— have different interpretations for each emoji. The meanings of emojis are crowdsourced, with people flocking together to support a certain meaning resulting in a snowball-like effect. Unlike letter words, the meanings and interpretations of emojis can change at such breakneck speed that it's hard to keep up. To make things even more interesting, emojis can go viral, and when they do, their meaning is not always so readily deduced. The emoji of a smiley face cracking in half was introduced on the Chinese app WeChat in 2020, based on the Chinese viral expression *wǒlièkāi le* ("I have cracked open"), implying "I am having a minor breakdown." When I first saw this emoji, however, that interpretation was not the first one that came to mind. Interpreting emojis is highly context dependent, diverse, and complex. Even the seemingly obvious "Smiling Happy Face" emoji can often be used to convey a sarcastic mood by young Chinese users whom I have interviewed.[18]

Time for a quick glance back at history. In 1874, the first iteration of the Qwerty keyboard layout was created by an American inventor named Christopher Latham Sholes, who had been developing a typewriter.[19] In earlier typewriter key layouts, the first half of the alphabet was placed in order on the bottom row, and the second half in order on the top row, which led to some problems. The keys were mounted on metal arms, and they would jam if pressed in succession too rapidly. To solve this issue, Sholes separated commonly used letter pairings such as "s" and "t" to avoid such jams, allowing a typist to type faster. After having made several adjustments, Remington launched the Sholes and Glidden typewriter in July 1874. The keyboard was almost the same as the Qwerty layout we use today, with a few minor differences. Now, why am I talking about Qwerty? Well, as I'm typing, I'm glancing at my keyboard and its roman letters. We use these keys so much these days, thanks to technology developing, but the history behind them is less than two hundred years old. It's crazy to think that we're able to express deep thoughts, ideas, and feelings using a Qwerty keyboard. Yet we may need to say goodbye to it in the future, however near or far that may be. We may very well have more keyboards with tailor-made images—consider how smartphone-mediated communication has already led to the invention of emoji keyboards—that will overtake Qwerty.

When Conventional Words Aren't Enough

Turning to examine international scripts, there is a significant portion of the world population that does not use the roman alphabet. Computer keyboards around the world can be made to cater to local writing systems, such as Chinese logosyllabic characters, and the Tibetan and Thai alpha-syllabic scripts, to name a few.[20] There is an undeniable tendency to romanize internationally, but there are still plenty of languages thriving in their own respect. That said, although romanization has not occurred in every corner of the world, there is great pressure to make it happen. When non-roman words are then brought into the Anglophone sphere, exponential variations will inevitably appear due to the difficulties in regulating romanization. It is important to see this through the lens of diversity.

This shift toward online audio-visual words is already under way and becoming more pronounced every day. In fact, when we talk about writing, we often mean typing. And when we have a meeting, it doesn't necessarily mean we are meeting in person. Like many, I communicate with dozens of people through digital channels such as email and WhatsApp messaging. In these inter-actions, the use of emoji words has become increasingly common. I've found that they offer a unique and effective way to convey emotion and tone in digital communication.

According to research by Ofcom, in a post-lockdown world, social media usage has surged, with people sixteen to thirty-four years old spending over 33 percent of their curated commercial media day on social media, compared with just 12 percent spent with live or recorded TV. Memes have also become mainstream, with 55 percent of people thirteen to thirty-five years old sending memes every week, and a million memes shared daily on Instagram— double the amount shared in 2018. The growth of TikTok, with a forecasted reach of 14.8 million users and U.K. teens spending more than a hundred minutes daily on the platform, is providing a steep change in the speed and scale at which marketing memes can spread, making it a perfect breeding ground for mass meme marketing.

The word *meme* was coined by Richard Dawkins in 1976. The OED defines a meme as "a cultural element or behavioural trait whose transmission and consequent persistence in a population, although occurring by non-genetic means (esp. imitation), is considered as analogous to the inheritance of a gene." Dawkins described the word as a "replicator, a noun which conveys the idea of a unit of cultural transmission, or a unit of imitation.... Examples of memes are tunes, ideas, catch-phrases, clothes fashions, ways of making pots or of building arches."[21]

The meaning of *meme* has evolved to include images, videos, pieces of text, or other types of content that is often humorous and spreads rapidly among internet users, usually with slight modifications. Additional terms like *internet meme* reflect its use as a phenomenon of the online world. In my book *Emoji Speak,* I use the term *emoji word* as an umbrella term for all types of graphical image words, but memes have become so popular that they may deserve their own category. Unlike emojis, which are often limited to a preset repertoire provided by companies, memes offer users the ability to personalize and explore more complex emotions. They are also community based and can be difficult to censor, which makes them a unique and powerful form of expression in our digital age.

Are you familiar with the term *finger heart*? It's a small heart shape created by crossing the tip of the index finger in front of the thumb. The gesture was popularized by South Korean celebrities in the early 2010s and quickly became a regular feature of K-pop fandoms. It has slowly gained worldwide recognition, with Benedict Cumberbatch flashing the symbol to fans while promoting the *Doctor Strange* movie in Korea in 2016. Many global athletes also adopted the symbol while participating in the Winter Olympics of 2018 in Pyeongchang, an event with official merchandise featuring gloves with a red index finger and thumb to accentuate use of the symbol. The finger heart was born and proliferated as a gesture or image word, but written and spoken communication necessitated its conversion into a letter word, giving us the term *finger heart.* The rapid and multimodal nature of communication today means that this is not some streamlined and universally

The finger heart (Courtesy of Loli Kim).

agreed upon term; some websites and commentators refer to the gesture by other names, such as "mini-heart" or "baby heart." The dynamic nature of image-born words is also demonstrated by its multiple meanings. While it is often interpreted as an expression of love or affection by K-pop fans, it has also been understood as an alternative to the peace sign, a symbol of freedom and hope, a meaning that proved especially poignant when the North Korean leader Kim Jong-Un flashed the symbol for photographers during peace talks with then South Korean president Moon Jae-in.[22]

The China Challenge

As of January 2023, English remained the most widely used language for web content, representing nearly 59 percent of all websites. Russian ranked second, accounting for 5.3 percent of web content, followed by Spanish, with 4.3 percent. However, recent statistics show that China has the highest number of social media users, with more than 1 billion as of 2023. India ranks second with 755 million, and the United States is third with 302 million.[23] If Chinese users actively use romanization and export Chinese words into English, the future of the English lexicon may be altered. Transliterated Chinese words, also known as romanized, could be viewed as both Chinese and English. Of course, Chinese is not a single language but rather a collection of more than three hundred distinct languages, spoken by a total of more than

1.3 billion native speakers. Despite this linguistic diversity, the Chinese government has recently launched a campaign to promote the study and use of Mandarin across the country, with a target of having more than 85 percent of the population speaking Mandarin by 2025. This move may have a significant impact on the global linguistic landscape in the coming years.

One may not consider Chinese overtaking English in the linguistic landscape, however due to the rising power of the Chinese economy, this may not be completely unthinkable. Analogous to this, the digital yuan is also gaining significant traction as a medium of exchange. According to Bloomberg, China's yuan has surpassed the dollar as the most traded currency in Russia. This development challenges the long-standing dominance of the dollar and raises the possibility that its future may lie in a currency that is physically intangible. Similarly, the future of the dollar may share analogous characteristics with the future of the English language, evolving and adapting to new digital landscapes. As technology continues to reshape our financial systems and communication methods, both the dollar and English may undergo transformative shifts in their respective realms.

It is uncertain whether English will continue to dominate or be overtaken by another language such as Chinese. A language free from any national or geographic association may even emerge as the lingua franca in the future. The distinction between languages like Chinese and English may become less defined in the language of Generation MZ, who are growing up in a transnational era. As a result, linguistic nationalism may diminish, and we may see more multilingual and translingual individuals and communities in the future. It is undoubtedly a fascinating time for language and culture.

The growing number of speakers of English as a second language, a group that now constitutes a majority of English speakers, suggests a future for English beyond the British or American binary.

Even if the growing economic prominence of countries like China as both a major global producer and consumer may not be sufficient to launch Mandarin Chinese as a global lingua franca to rival English, it is far easier to imagine new forms of English, particularly those spoken among non-native speakers, becoming a new global norm. This version of English might be more accessible to all by focusing on effective communication rather than perfect English according to British or American standards. It might prize the use of simple words and phrases rather than the stigmatization of non-native accents and common mistakes that do not hinder comprehension. At the same time, this new version of English might more easily incorporate local lexicons that have been romanized. This is made all the more likely by steps taken by the current Chinese government, including a recent decision to replace the English on Beijing's subway signage with pinyin, the romanized version of Chinese characters. Steps like these help us imagine new ways that languages might interact with English, especially for speakers with knowledge of both. Chinglish and Spanglish are well studied—if often stigmatized—forms of English, while other hybrid Englishes like Turklish and Russlish have not received significant scholarly attention even from those working on world Englishes. Whether economic or geopolitical considerations will prompt one of these varieties or a sort of Globlish, which can accommodate the common traits of all of these world Englishes, to arise as the new dominant form of English remains to be seen but is not at all unimaginable in our near future, especially as super-digital empowerment via social media, virtual realities, and even interactive generative AI are quite literally at our fingertips.

Final Words

"Tea. Earl Grey. Hot." is an expression used by Captain Picard in *Star Trek: The Next Generation*. This phrase is his preferred way of ordering a cup of Earl Grey tea from the ship's replicator. He often uses this phrase in moments of relaxation, such as when he is sitting in his ready room or taking a break from his duties. Maybe English will look like this: no grammar, simple grammar, or even grammar of a community and many words and memes?

Words are constantly in flux—being born, migrating, falling into disuse, changing meanings and taking on new ones, much like us. The pace at which this is happening is faster than ever before. In the twenty-first century, the words we use have evolved in ways that would have been unimaginable to James Murray and his team at the Oxford English Dictionary at the beginning of the twentieth century. The English language has expanded and shifted, with new words and phrases emerging to describe the globalized world we now live in. But as we continue to encounter new realities, it's likely that we'll need even more new words—words that may take us beyond what we currently recognize as English. So, while we celebrate the rich tapestry of words that have come before, we must also remain open to the possibility of new linguistic horizons and embrace the changes that come with them.

As a result of English becoming a language for everyone—in other words, increasing its reach as the lingua franca—spelling, pronunciation, capitalization, pluralization and other linguistic practices will be used in accordance with one's personal style and communities of practice. In a paradoxical way, English is losing its "Englishness." As every human endeavor leaves behind verbal footprints, so is our language becoming more varied. Human history in an even broader sense is full of words, verbal and visual. In recent decades, we have experienced what we may call a word big bang, with commonalities and differences growing simultaneously like the head of a sunflower. We have been so used to letter words, but a time will come—or has already come—when multicolored, multimodal emoji words become more influential and powerful. We should also prepare for our new lives in the metaverse. Already, virtual immigration has begun and with this, new words will travel across borders—physical and metaphorical—to acquire (new) meanings. Soon enough, there may no longer be a need for the Oxford English Dictionary or "standard" grammar conventions as English embraces and caters to speakers with all languages. To begin with, English will be diversified but linguistic changes will spread to all languages. Words themselves will be liberated from nation-state identity. Technology enables us to keep growing our lexical pantries, but the irony is that we may very well become more confused than ever before. Much like the builders of the Tower of Babel, we may find it all the more difficult to communicate with one another given the speed at which we build our lexical towers.

As the boundary between the virtual world and the real world grows increasingly ambiguous, and the borders between languages and cultures around the world become more porous, our relationship with words and letters will also change. The younger generations, including Gen Z and Alpha, born as AI natives, constantly embrace innovative words that exist in virtual spaces and social media, many of which are unknown to their parents' generation. Our vocabulary is akin to an iPhone, requiring frequent updates that may go unnoticed until one day we realize that the words we use daily operate and appear nothing like they did when we first learned them. As our lives continue to merge with technology, and as we continue to experience the blurring of boundaries between the virtual and real worlds, the way we communicate and express ourselves will continue to evolve. Our words reflect who we are and the world around us, and it is up to us to shape and embrace their ever changing nature.

Notes

Opening Words

1. James Murray, *Lectures I, II and V to Oxford School of English* (Unpublished lectures delivered to the University of Oxford School of English, 1911), 18. I acknowledge Murray's descriptions are in part outdated and culturally offensive but I felt it necessary to include the full context of this quotation.

2. John Fitzgerald Kennedy, *A Nation of Immigrants* (New York: HarperCollins, 1964), 3.

3. NALDIC, "Languages in Schools," 2015; https://www.naldic.org.uk/research-and-information/eal-statistics/lang/, accessed May 19, 2023.

4. "Schools, Pupils and Their Characteristics, Academic Year 2022/23," GOV.UK, https://explore-education-statistics.service.gov.uk/find-statistics/school-pupils-and-their-characteristics, last modified June 13, 2023.

5. François Grosjean, *The Mysteries of Bilingualism: Unresolved Issues* (Oxford: Wiley, 2022).

6. Peter Gilliver, "Furnivall's Dictionary: 1861–1875," in *The Making of the Oxford English Dictionary* (Oxford: Oxford University Press, 2016), 46.

ONE. Whose English?

1. Jennifer Jenkins, *Global Englishes: A Resource Book for Students*, third ed. (London, 2015), 2.

2. Paul Howson, *The English Effect: The Impact of English, What It's Worth to the UK, and Why It Matters to the World* (London: British Council, 2013), 14, https://www.britishcouncil.org/sites/default/files/english-effect-report-v2.pdf.

3. Ibid.

4. David Crystal and Hilary Crystal, *Words on Words: Quotations About Language and Languages* (London: Penguin, 2000).

5. Andrew Read, "Good Practice for Pupils with English as an Additional Language: Patterns in Student Teachers' Thinking," *Research in Teacher Education* 2, no. 2 (2012): 24–30.

6. "Schools, Pupils and Their Characteristics, Academic Year 2021/22," GOV.UK, https://explore-education-statistics.service.gov.uk/find-statistics/school-pupils-and-their-characteristics, last modified June 13, 2023.

7. David Graddol, *English Next*, vol. 62 (London: British Council, 2006).

8. Braj B. Kachru, *The Alchemy of English: The Spread, Functions, and Models for Non-Native Englishes* (Oxford: Oxford University Press, 1986).

9. Jess Staufenberg, "Cameron Announces 'Funding' for English Classes Six Months After £45 Million Cuts," *The Independent*, January 18, 2016; https://www.independent.co.uk/news/uk/politics/cameron-announces-funding-for-english-classes-six-months-after-ps45-million-cuts-a6819656.html.

10. Jieun Kiaer, *Translingual Words: An East Asian Lexical Encounter with English* (London: Routledge, 2018).

11. "saké, n.2," OED Online, Oxford University Press, https://www.oed.com/view/Entry/169883?rskey=nCJu0b&result=2&isAdvanced=false, accessed May 19, 2023. Unless otherwise noted, all references to the OED are to the online version.

12. Sun-mi Hwang, *The Hen Who Dreamed She Could Fly*, translated by Chi-Young Kim (New York: Penguin, 2013).

13. Danica Salazar, "English Is Picking Up Brilliant New Words from Around the World—and That's a Gift," *The Guardian*, December 12, 2022; https://www.theguardian.com/commentisfree/2022/dec/12/english-words-world-global-speakers-language.

14. Jieun Kiaer, *The Language of Hallyu: More Than Polite* (London: Routledge, 2023).

15. Gail Shuck, "Racializing the Nonnative English Speaker," *Journal of Language, Identity, and Education* 5, no. 4 (2006): 256.

16. Noam Chomsky, "Persistent Topics in Linguistic Theory," *Diogenes* 13, no. 51 (1965): 13–20.

17. Adrian Holliday, "Native-Speakerism," *ELT Journal* 60, no. 4 (2006): 385–387.

18. Constant Leung, Roxy Harris, and Ben Rampton, "The Idealised Native Speaker, Reified Ethnicities, and Classroom Realities," *TESOL Quarterly* 31, no. 3 (1997): 543–560.

19. M. B. H. Rampton, "Displacing the 'Native Speaker': Expertise, Affiliation, and Inheritance," *ELT Journal* 44, no. 2 (1990): 97–101.

20. Vivian J. Cook, "Evidence for Multicompetence," *Language Learning* 42, no. 4 (1992): 590.

21. Rajendra Singh, *The Native Speaker: Multilingual Perspectives; Language and Development*, vol. 4 (New Delhi; London: Sage, 1998).

22. Salikoko S. Mufwene, *African-American English: Structure, History, and Use* (London: Routledge, 1998), 17.

23. Graddol, *English Next*.

TWO. Word Injustice

1. John Locke and J. R. Milton, *Literary and Historical Writings*, Clarendon Edition of the Works of John Locke (Oxford: Oxford University Press, 2020), 23.

2. Clive Probyn, "Swift, Jonathan (1667–1745), Writer and Dean of St Patrick's Cathedral, Dublin," *Oxford Dictionary of National Biography*, September 23, 2004, https://www.oxforddnb.com/view/10.1093/ref:odnb/9780198614128.001.0001/odnb-9780198614128-e-26833, accessed September 18, 2023.

3. Samuel Johnson, "Preface to A Dictionary of the English Language," in *A Dictionary of the English Language* (London, 1755), https://www.gutenberg.org/ebooks/5430.

4. Peter Thomson, "Sheridan, Thomas (1719–1788), Actor and Orthoepist," *Oxford Dictionary of National Biography*, September 23, 2004, https://www.oxforddnb.com/view/10.1093/ref:odnb/9780198614128.001.0001/odnb-9780198614128-e-25371, accessed September 18, 2023.

5. W. H. Fremantle and Roger T. Stearn, "Alford, Henry (1810–1871), Dean of Canterbury and Biblical Scholar," *Oxford Dictionary of National Biography*, September 23, 2004, https://www.oxforddnb.com/view/10.1093/ref:odnb/9780198614128.001.0001/odnb-9780198614128-e-341, accessed September 18, 2023.

6. John Pickering, *A Vocabulary, or Collection of Words and Phrases Which Have Been Supposed to Be Peculiar to the United States of America* (Boston: Cummings and Hilliard, 1816).

7. G. F. Graham, *A Book About Words* (London: Longman and Green, 1869).

8. Stephanie Lindemann, "Who Speaks 'Broken English'"? US Undergraduates' Perceptions of Non–Native English 1," *International Journal of Applied Linguistics* 15, no. 2 (2005): 187–212.

9. Jens Korff, "Aboriginal Words in Australian English," *Creative Spirits*, https://www.creativespirits.info/aboriginalculture/language/aboriginal-words-in-australian-english, last modified April 25, 2023.

10. Donna R. Gabaccia, "Migration History in the Americas," in *Routledge International Handbook of Migration Studies*, edited by Steven J. Gold and Stephanie J. Nawyn (London: Routledge, Taylor and Francis Group, 2020), 48.

11. Ying Hui-Michael, "Multicultural Education for Learners with Special Needs in the Twenty-First Century," in *Contemporary Clinical Practice with Asian Immigrants: A Relational Framework with Culturally Responsive*

Approaches, edited by Anthony F. Rotatori and Festus E. Obiakor (Charlotte, N.C.: Information Age, 2014), 87.

12. Huping Ling and Allan W. Austin, "The Asian American Experience: History, Culture, and Scholarship," in *Asian American History and Culture: An Encyclopedia,* edited by Allan W. Austin and Huping Ling (London: Routledge, 2015), 2.

13. Patrick Ongley and David Pearson, "Post-1945 International Migration: New Zealand, Australia and Canada Compared," *International Migration Review* 29, no. 3 (1995): 765–793.

14. Mustafa Aksakal, Kerstin Schmidt, Mari Korpela, and Pirkko Pitkänen, "Introduction: Temporary Migration in European-Asian Social Spaces," in *Characteristics of Temporary Migration in European-Asian Transnational Social Spaces,* edited by Pirkko Pitkänen and Mari Korpela (Cham, Switzerland: Springer, 2018), 13–14.

15. Graeme Hugo, *Migration in the Asia-Pacific Region: A Paper Prepared for the Policy Analysis and Research Programme of the Global Commission on International Migration,* Global Commission on International Migration, September 2005, 6–7, https://www.iom.int/sites/g/files/tmzbdl486/files/2018-07/RS2.pdf, accessed September 18, 2023.

16. "saké, n.2," OED Online, Oxford University Press, https://www.oed.com/view/Entry/169883?rskey=nCJu0b&result=2&isAdvanced=false, accessed May 19, 2023.

17. Kiaer, *Translingual Words,* 33.

18. Mari C. Jones and Sarah Ogilvie, eds., *Keeping Languages Alive: Documentation, Pedagogy and Revitalization* (Cambridge: Cambridge University Press, 2013), 39.

19. Jieun Kiaer, "Does a Language Have to Be European to Be 'Modern'?" Language on the Move, May 28, 2017, https://www.languageonthemove.com/does-a-language-have-to-be-european-to-be-modern/.

20. "lingua franca, n.," OED Online, Oxford University Press, https://www.oed.com/view/Entry/327283?redirectedFrom=lingua+franca, accessed May 19, 2023.

21. S. Ramesh, Channelnewsasia.com, "Choosing English as Working Language Ensured S'pore's Survival: Lee Kuan Yew," *Malaysia Today,* September 7, 2011, https://www.malaysia-today.net/2011/09/07/choosing-english-as-working-language-ensured-spores-survival-lee-kuan-yew/.

22. "Bafta Film Awards 2021: Nomadland and Promising Young Woman Win Big," BBC News, April 11, 2021, https://www.bbc.co.uk/news/entertainment-arts-56711344.

23. Dino-Ray Ramos, "Lulu Wang, Daniel Dae Kim, Phil Lord, and More Drag Golden Globes for Placing 'Minari' in Foreign Language Category," *Deadline: Breaking Hollywood News Since 2006,* December 24, 2020, https://deadline.com/2020/12/golden-globes-minari-foreign-language-film-back lash-1234661357/.

24. Kathryn Board and Teresa Tinsley, *Language Trends 2014/15: The State of Language Learning in Primary and Secondary Schools in England,* 2015, https://www.britishcouncil.org/sites/default/files/language_trends_survey_2015.pdf, accessed September 18, 2023.

25. Tracy Brown, "Bong Joon Ho's 'Parasite' Speech Marks Second Year Korean Is Spoken at the Golden Globes," *Los Angeles Times,* January 5, 2020, https://www.latimes.com/entertainment-arts/movies/story/2020-01-05/golden-globes-2020-bong-joon-ho-parasite-speech-korean.

THREE. Ordinary Words

1. Ryan Browne, "All You Need to Know About ChatGPT, the A.I. Chatbot That's Got the World Talking and Tech Giants Clashing," *CNBC,* February 8, 2023, https://www.cnbc.com/2023/02/08/what-is-chatgpt-viral-ai-chatbot-at-heart-of-microsoft-google-fight.html#:~:text=ChatGPT%20is%20powered%20by%20a,OpenAI's%20GPT%2D3%20language%20model, accessed September 18, 2023.

2. Roger Montti, "What Is ChatGPT and How Can You Use It?" *Search Engine Journal,* December 26, 2022, https://www.searchenginejournal.com/what-is-chatgpt/473664/#close, accessed September 18, 2023.

3. Dong Nguyen, Barbara McGillivray, and Taha Yasseri, "Emo, Love, and God: Making Sense of Urban Dictionary, a Crowd-Sourced Online Dictionary," *Royal Society Open Science* 5, no. 5 (2018): 172320.

4. Michael Erard, *Um . . . : Slips, Stumbles, and Verbal Blunders, and What They Mean* (New York: Pantheon, 2007).

5. Pierre Bourdieu, "The Forms of Capital," in *Handbook for Theory and Research for the Sociology of Education,* edited by John G. Richardson (Westport, Conn.: Greenwood, 1986), 241–258.

6. Kiaer, *Translingual Words;* Jieun Kiaer, *Delicious Words: East Asian Food Words in English* (London: Taylor and Francis, 2020).

7. Alan S. C. Ross, *Linguistic Class-Indicators in Present-Day English* (Finland: Modern Language Society of Helsinki, 1954).

8. Henry Wyld, "The Best English: A Claim for the Superiority of Received Standard English," in *Proper English? Readings in Language, History and Cultural Identity,* edited by Tony Crowley (London: Routledge, 1934), 207–218.

9. John Walker, *A Critical Pronouncing Dictionary and Expositor of the English Language* (London, 1791).

10. Henry Newbolt, *The Teaching of English in England* (London: HMSO, 1921), 202.

11. John Marenbon, *English Our English: The New Orthodoxy Examined* (London: Centre for Policy Studies, 1987).

12. "slang, n.3," OED Online, Oxford University Press, https://www.oed.com/view/Entry/181318?rskey=P7J2mG&result=3&isAdvanced=false, accessed May 15, 2023.

13. Hana Lee, " 'Parasite' Subtitle Translator: Comedies Are a Fun Challenge," Korea.net, June 19, 2019, https://www.korea.net/NewsFocus/Culture/view?articleId=171974, accessed September 18, 2023.

FOUR. Word Pantry

1. "Number of Words in the English Language," *The Global Language Monitor,* December 16, 2018, https://languagemonitor.com/number-of-words-in-english/no-of-words/, accessed September 18, 2023.

2. "How Many Languages Are There in the World?" *Ethnologue,* https://www.ethnologue.com/insights/how-many-languages/, accessed May 11, 2023.

3. United Nations, "International Decade of Indigenous Languages 2022–2032 for Indigenous Peoples," https://www.un.org/development/desa/indigenouspeoples/indigenous-languages.html, accessed May 11, 2023.

4. "K-pop, n.," OED Online, Oxford University Press, https://www.oed.com/view/Entry/92768206?redirectedFrom=Kpop, accessed May 19, 2023.

5. Joshua Conrad Jackson, Joseph Watts, Teague R. Henry, Johann Mattis List, Robert Forkel, Peter Mucha, Simon Greenhill, Russell D. Gray, and Kristen A. Lindquist, "Emotion Semantics Show Both Cultural Variation and Universal Structure," *Science* 366, no. 6472 (2019): 1517–1522, https://doi.org/10.1126/science.aaw8160.

6. John Leicester and Frank Jordans, "A Look at Black Lives Matter Protests from Around the World," *The Globe and Mail,* June 6, 2020, https://www.theglobeandmail.com/world/article-a-look-at-black-lives-matter-protests-from-around-the-world/, accessed September 18, 2023.

7. Adrian Miller, "The Surprising Origin of Fried Chicken," *BBC Travel,* October 13, 2020, https://www.bbc.com/travel/article/20201012-the-surprising-origin-of-fried-chicken, accessed September 18, 2023.

8. "paneer, n.," OED Online, Oxford University Press, https://www.oed.com/view/Entry/247027?redirectedFrom=paneer, accessed May 19, 2023.

9. Nancy K. Stalker, ed., *Devouring Japan: Global Perspectives on Japanese Culinary Identity* (New York: Oxford University Press, 2018).

10. Kiaer, *Delicious Words*.

FIVE. Using Words

1. Quoted in Mitford M. Mathews, *The Beginnings of American English* (1931; reprint, Chicago: University of Chicago Press, 1963), 40; John Algeo, "The Effects of the Revolution on Language," in *A Companion to the American Revolution,* ed. Jack P. Greene and J. R. Pole (Malden, Mass.: Blackwell, 2000), 595–599, https://doi.org/10.1002/9780470756454.ch72.

2. Noah Webster, "An Essay on the Necessity, Advantages, and Practicality of Reforming the Mode of Spelling and of Rendering the Orthography of Words Correspondent to Pronunciation," *Dissertations on the English Language: With Notes, Historical and Critical, to Which Is Added, by Way of Appendix, an Essay on a Reformed Mode of Spelling, with Dr. Franklin's Arguments on That Subject* (Boston, 1789), 20–21, 397.

3. Ibid., 397.

4. Christopher Dobbs, "Noah Webster and the Dream of a Common Language," *Connecticut History,* May 28, 2021, https://connecticuthistory.org/noah-webster-and-the-dream-of-a-common-language/.

5. "android, n. and adj.," OED Online, Oxford University Press, https://www.oed.com/view/Entry/7333?redirectedFrom=android, accessed May 19, 2023.

6. Hyejeong Ahn, Edgar W. Schneider, Jieun Kiaer, and Laurence Mann, "Words Going Viral: The Effects of COVID-19 on Media English," *The Journal of Comparative Media and Women's Studies* 7 (2022): 20–60 [in Japanese].

7. George A. Miller, "The Magical Number Seven, Plus or Minus Two: Some Limits on Our Capacity for Processing Information," *Psychological Review* 63 (1956): 81–97.

8. Samantha Schwartz, "Microsoft Created the Office Suite Status Quo. Can Google Grow?" *CIO Dive,* February 11, 2020, https://www.ciodive.com/news/Google-Microsoft-Office-collaboration/571740/, accessed September 18, 2023.

9. "A Dream 33 Years in the Making, Starbucks to Open in Italy," *Starbucks Stories and News,* February 28, 2016, https://stories.starbucks.com/stories/2016/howard-schultz-dream-fulfilled-starbucks-to-open-in-italy/, accessed September 18, 2023; " 'Grande,' 'Venti,' and 'Trenta': What Do the Starbucks Sizes Literally Mean?" Dictionary.com, August 15, 2022, https://www.dictionary.com/e/starbucks-trenta/, accessed September 28, 2023.

10. "minion, n.1 and adj.," OED Online, Oxford University Press, https://www.oed.com/view/Entry/118859?rskey=kT0vHm&result=1&isAdvanced=false, accessed May 19, 2023.

11. Nathan McAlone, "The True Story Behind Google's Hilarious First Name: Backrub," *Business Insider,* October 5, 2015, https://www.businessinsider.com/the-true-story-behind-googles-first-name-backrub-2015-10?r=US&IR=T, accessed September 18, 2023.

12. Matthew Smith, "Two Thirds of Children Don't Know What a Floppy Disk Is," YouGov, April 26, 2018, https://yougov.co.uk/topics/technology/articles-reports/2018/04/26/two-thirds-children-dont-know-what-floppy-disk, accessed September 18, 2023.

13. Diego Muñoz, Raymundo Cornejo, Francisco J. Gutierrez, Jesús Favela, Sergio F. Ochoa, and Mónica Tentori, "A Social Cloud-Based Tool to Deal with Time and Media Mismatch of Intergenerational Family Communication," *Future Generation Computer Systems* 53 (2015): 140–151.

14. Shivan Meymo and Kenn Nyström, "Why Do Elderly Not Use Social Media?" (Master's thesis, Umeå University, 2017), https://www.researchgate.net/profile/Shivan-Meymo-2/publication/319307162_Why_do_elderly_not_use_social_media_An_investigation_of_the_elderly%27s_attitudes_to_HCI/links/59a2a707a6fdcc1a315f30e0/Why-do-elderly-not-use-social-media-An-investigation-of-the-elderlys-attitudes-to-HCI.pdf; Muñoz, Cornejo et al., "A Social Cloud-Based Tool."

15. Raymundo Cornejo, Mónica Tentori, and Jesús Favela, "Ambient Awareness to Strengthen the Family Social Network of Older Adults," *Computer Supported Cooperative Work* (CSCW) 22 (2013): 309–344.

16. Kimberly Tee, A. J. Bernheim Brush, and Kori M. Inkpen, "Exploring Communication and Sharing Between Extended Families," *International Journal of Human-Computer Studies* 67, no. 2 (2009): 128–138.

17. Sara Rosenthal and Kathleen McKeown, "Age Prediction in Blogs: A Study of Style, Content, and Online Behavior in Pre- and Post-Social Media Generations," *Proceedings of the 49th Annual Meeting of the Association for Computational Linguistics: Human Language Technologies* (2011): 763–772.

18. Emily A. Vogels, Risa Gelles-Watnick, and Navid Massarat, "Teens, Social Media and Technology 2022," Pew Research Center, December 15, 2022, https://www.pewresearch.org/internet/2022/08/10/teens-social-media-and-technology-2022/, accessed September 18, 2023.

19. Hannah Holmes and Gemma Burgess, " 'Pay the Wi-Fi or Feed the Children': Coronavirus Has Intensified the UK's Digital Divide," University of

Cambridge, https://www.cam.ac.uk/stories/digitaldivide, accessed September 18, 2023.

SIX. Moving Words

1. Marie Mcauliffe and Anna Triandafyllidou, eds., *World Migration Report 2022*, International Organization for Migration (IOM), 2021.

2. Jieun Kiaer, *Pragmatic Particles: Findings from Asian Languages* (London: Bloomsbury Studies in Theoretical Linguistics, 2021).

3. "curry, n.2," OED Online, Oxford University Press, https://www.oed.com/view/Entry/46118?rskey=ScXoLfr&result=2&isAdvanced=false, accessed May 19, 2023.

4. "tea, n.1.," OED Online, Oxford University Press, https://www.oed.com/view/Entry/198340?rskey=MrSwCs, accessed January 4, 2023.

5. "cha, n.," OED Online, Oxford University Press, https://www.oed.com/view/Entry/30117?rskey=xKKp2w&result=1&isAdvanced=false, accessed January 4, 2023.

6. "chai, n.2.," OED Online, Oxford University Press, https://www.oed.com/view/Entry/30196?redirectedFrom=chai, accessed January 4, 2023.

7. Ibid.

8. Kiaer, *Delicious Words*.

9. "chin-chin, v.," OED Online, Oxford University Press, https://www.oed.com/view/Entry/87571316?rskey=uEuc4C&result=3&isAdvanced=false, accessed May 19, 2023.

10. "ketchup, n.," OED Online, Oxford University Press, https://www.oed.com/view/Entry/103080?redirectedFrom=ketchup, accessed May 19, 2023.

11. "pancake, n.," OED Online, Oxford University Press, https://www.oed.com/view/Entry/136689?rskey=c5ng7d&result=1&isAdvanced=false, accessed January 4, 2023.

12. Kate Sullivan, "It's 'Comma-La': How to Pronounce Kamala Harris' Name," *CNN Politics,* August 12, 2020, https://edition.cnn.com/2020/08/12/politics/kamala-harris-pronunciation/index.html.

13. David Sanderson, "Pronouncing Van Gogh the 'Real Dutch Way,'" *The Times,* February 7, 2020, https://www.thetimes.co.uk/article/pronouncing-van-gogh-the-real-dutch-way-2f6f7rwcx.

14. "Personal Name," Wikipedia, December 10, 2022, https://en.wikipedia.org/wiki/Personal_name#:~:text=of%20bureaucratic%20formality.-,Eastern%20name%20order,in%20Central%20Europe%20by%20Hungarians, accessed September 18, 2023.

15. Ralph S. Hattox, *Coffee and Coffeehouses: The Origins of a Social Beverage in the Medieval Near East* (Seattle: University of Washington Press, 2014).

16. Cemal Kafadar, "How Dark Is the History of the Night, How Black the Story of Coffee, How Bitter the Tale of Love: The Changing Measure of Leisure and Pleasure in Early Modern Istanbul," in *Medieval and Early Modern Performance in the Eastern Mediterranean* (Turnhout: Brepols, 2014), 243–269.

17. Brian Cowan, *The Social Life of Coffee* (New Haven: Yale University Press, 2005), 16–25.

18. For Murray's argument, see "coffee, n." in the OED; for the debate, see *Notes and Queries* 10 S. XII (1909), 64, 111, 156, 198, 232, 318.

19. Cowan, *The Social Life of Coffee*, 30.

20. Jonathan Morris, *Coffee: A Global History* (London: Reaktion, 2018), 77.

21. Nick Brown, "Remembering Latte Birthplace and Quintessential Counterculture Destination Caffe Med," *Daily Coffee News by Roast Magazine*, December 12, 2016, https://dailycoffeenews.com/2016/12/12/remembering-latte-birthplace-and-quintessential-counterculture-destination-caffe-med/.

SEVEN. More than Words

1. Charlie Murray, "Moynahan, Brian. God's Bestseller: William Tyndale, Thomas More, and the Writing of the English Bible—a Story of Martyrdom and Betrayal," *Library Journal* 128, no. 12 (2003): xxii.

2. " 'Kyiv' or 'Kiev'—Here's Why the Difference Is Political," CBC/Radio Canada, March 4, 2022, https://www.cbc.ca/news/world/cbc-pronunciation-kyiv-ukraine-crisis-explainer-1.6371766.

3. "Turkey, n.1.," OED Online, Oxford University Press, https://www.oed.com/view/Entry/207631?rskey=g7HyGp&result=1&isAdvanced=false, accessed May 19, 2023.

4. "Why Is the Middle East Called the Middle East?" Commisceo Global Consulting Ltd., n.d., https://www.commisceo-global.com/blog/why-is-the-middle-east-called-the-middle-east, accessed September 18, 2023.

5. Ibid.

6. "What Are the Top 200 Most Spoken Languages?" *Ethnologue*, 2022.

7. "What Is the Most Spoken Language?" *Ethnologue*, 2023, https://www.ethnologue.com/insights/most-spoken-language/, accessed September 18, 2023.

8. Florian Coulmas, *An Introduction to Multilingualism: Language in a Changing World* (Oxford: Oxford University Press, 2018).

9. Andy Kirkpatrick and Wang Lixun, *Is English an Asian Language?* (Cambridge: Cambridge University Press, 2020).

10. Brian Donohue, "Pulitzer Prize-Winning Author Junot Diaz Tells Students His Story," nj.com, October 21, 2009, http://www.nj.com/ledgerlive/index.ssf/2009/10/junot_diazs_new_jersey.html, accessed September 18, 2023; Karen Cresci, "Junot Díaz: 'We Exist in a Constant State of Translation. We Just Don't Like It,' " *Buenos Aires Review,* May 4, 2013, http://www.buenosairesreview.org/2013/05/diaz-constant-state-of-translation/, accessed September 18, 2023.

11. Librarian Nora Galvan, quoted in Nishat Kurwa, "Author Malin Alegria Builds on 'Estrella's' Star Power," National Public Radio, October 18, 2011, https://www.npr.org/2011/10/18/141428890/ya-author-celebrates-growing-up-latino-in-the-usa.

12. Cristina Rivera Garza, "Boston Calling, American Identities, the Benefits of Bilingual Writing," BBC World Service, May 22, 2015, video, https://www.bbc.co.uk/programmes/p02rz648, accessed May 19, 2023.

13. Jane Se Setter, Cathy S. P. Wong, and Brian Hok-Shing Chan, *Hong Kong English* (Edinburgh: Cambridge Core, 2010).

14. Tessa Wong, "The Rise of Singlish," *BBC News,* 2015, https://www.bbc.co.uk/news/magazine-33809914.

15. "Chinglish, n. and adj.," OED Online, Oxford University Press, https://www.oed.com/view/Entry/258885?redirectedFrom=chinglish, accessed May 19, 2023.

16. Antje Glück, "De-Westernization and Decolonization in Media Studies," *The Oxford Encyclopedia of Communication and Critical Cultural Studies,* December 20, 2018, https://doi.org/10.1093/acrefore/9780190228613.013.898.

17. Li Wei, "Translanguaging as a Practical Theory of Language," *Applied Linguistics* 39, no. 1 (2018): 9–30.

18. Allan Woods, "Quebec Language Police Try to Ban 'Pasta' from Italian Restaurant Menu," *The Guardian,* March 1, 2013, https://www.theguardian.com/world/2013/mar/01/quebec-language-police-ban-pasta.

EIGHT. After Words

1. See Elika Bergelson and Daniel Swingley, "At 6–9 Months, Human Infants Know the Meanings of Many Common Nouns," *Proceedings of the National Academy of Sciences* 109, no. 9 (2012): 3253–3258; Annette Karmiloff-Smith, "Nativism Versus Neuroconstructivism: Rethinking the Study of Developmental Disorders," *Developmental Psychology* 45.1 (2009): 56; Seamus Donnelly and Evan Kidd, "Individual Differences in Lexical Processing Efficiency and Vocabulary in Toddlers: A Longitudinal Investigation," *Journal of Experimental Child Psychology* 192 (2020): 104781.

2. See Philip S. Dale and Larry Fenson, "Lexical Development Norms for Young Children," *Behavior Research Methods, Instruments, and Computers* 28 (1996): 125–127; Donnelly and Kidd, "Individual Differences in Lexical Processing"; Anton Gerbrand, Gustaf Gredebäck, Martina Hedenius, Linda Forsman, and Marcus Lindskog, "Statistical Learning in Infancy Predicts Vocabulary Size in Toddlerhood," *Infancy* 27, no. 4 (2022): 700–719.

3. "ChatGPT" website, *OpenAI*, https://chat.openai.com/.

4. Claudia Dimuro, "Books with Covers—Gen Z and Millennials Still Love Paper Books over e-Reads," *The TYLT*, April 8, 2020, https://thetylt.com/culture/gen-z-and-millennials-love-paper-books-over-e-reads; Felix Richter, "Infographic: E-Books Still No Match for Printed Books," *Statista Infographics*, April 21, 2022, https://www.statista.com/chart/24709/e-book-and-printed-book-penetration/.

5. "Artificial Intelligence to Be Added to Customised School Textbooks by 2025," *PIME Asia News*, February 23, 2023, https://www.asianews.it/news-en/Artificial-intelligence-to-be-added-to-customised-school-textbooks-by-2025-57822.html, accessed May 3, 2023.

6. Denise Schmandt-Besserat, "The Evolution of Writing," in *International Encyclopedia of Social and Behavioural Sciences*, edited by James Wright (Elsevier, 2014), https://sites.utexas.edu/dsb/tokens/the-evolution-of-writing/, accessed January 4, 2023.

7. Jennifer Green, *Drawn from the Ground: Sound, Sign and Inscription in Central Australian Sand Stories* (Cambridge: Cambridge University Press, 2019).

8. Carina Hsieh, Rachel Varina, and Kayla Kibbe, "The Meaning of Every Heart Emoji," *Cosmopolitan*, September 8, 2023, https://www.cosmopolitan.com/sex-love/a28635219/heart-emoji-meanings/.

9. "Colour Revolution," *Wikipedia*, https://en.wikipedia.org/wiki/Colour_revolution, last modified September 3, 2023, accessed September 18, 2023.

10. Simon Horobin, "In Our War of Words, Full Stops Are Dying but the Exclamation Mark Is Doing Fine," *The Guardian*, December 28, 2021, https://www.theguardian.com/commentisfree/2021/dec/28/punctuation-complicated-full-stop-culture-war.

11. Ariadna Matamoros-Fernandez, "Inciting Anger Through Facebook Reactions in Belgium: The Use of Emoji and Related Vernacular Expressions in Racist Discourse," *First Monday* 23, no. 9 (2018): 61, https://doi.org/10.5210/fm.v23i9.9405.

12. Hannah Miller, Jacob Thebault-Spieker, Shuo Chang, Isaac Johnson, Loren Terveen, and Brent Hecht, " 'Blissfully Happy' or 'Ready to Fight': Vary-

ing Interpretations of Emoji," in *Proceedings of the 10th International Conference on Web and Social Media*, ICWSM, 2016 (AAAI, 2015).

13. Mariam Doliashvili, Michael-Brian C. Ogawa, and Martha E. Crosby, "Understanding Challenges Presented Using Emojis as a Form of Augmented Communication," *Interacción* (2020): 26.

14. Chris Messina, "Groups for Twitter; or A Proposal for Twitter Tag Channels," *Medium* (blog), August 26, 2007, https://medium.com/chris-messina/groups-for-twitter-or-a-proposal-for-twitter-tag-channels-5b8eb08adff8; Belle Beth Cooper, "The Surprising History of Twitter's Hashtag Origin and 4 Ways to Get the Most Out of Them," Buffer (blog), September 24, 2013, https://buffer.com/resources/a-concise-history-of-twitter-hashtags-and-how-you-should-use-them-properly/.

15. William F. Allman, "The Accidental History of the @ Symbol," *Smithsonian Magazine*, September 2012, https://www.smithsonianmag.com/science-nature/the-accidental-history-of-the-symbol-18054936/, accessed September 18, 2023; "@," Merriam-Webster.com Dictionary, https://www.merriam-webster.com/dictionary/%40, accessed January 5, 2023.

16. Jieun Kiaer, *Emoji Speak* (London: Bloomsbury, 2023).

17. "#MeToo in South Korea: Governor Resigns After Rape Allegations," *BBC News*, March 6, 2018, https://www.bbc.co.uk/news/world-asia-43297331.

18. Kiaer, *Emoji Speak*.

19. Michelle Starr, "A Brief History of the QWERTY Keyboard," *CNET*, July 1, 2016, https://www.cnet.com/culture/a-brief-history-of-the-qwerty-keyboard/.

20. "Non Latin Script Languages of the World," *Worldfactsinc*, https://sites.google.com/site/worldfactsinc/Non-Latin-Script-Languages-Of-The-World, accessed September 18, 2023.

21. "meme, n., sense 1," OED Online, Oxford University Press, https://www.oed.com/dictionary/meme_n?tab=meaning_and_use&tl=true, accessed September 18, 2023.

22. Elle Hunt, "Kim Jong-Un All Fingers and Thumbs in Bid for Instagram Diplomacy," *The Guardian*, September 21, 2018, https://www.theguardian.com/world/2018/sep/21/kim-jong-un-all-fingers-and-thumbs-in-bid-for-instagram-diplomacy.

23. "Why China Is Turning Away from English," *The Economist*, April 13, 2022, https://www.economist.com/china/2022/04/13/why-china-is-turning-away-from-english.

Index

Words discussed in the text appear in italics in the index.

Index

Index

Index

Index

Index

Index

Index

Index

Index

Index

Index

Index

Index

Selim I (sultan), 155
seminar, 114
senpai, 17
sentences, 61, 115
Seo, Kyungdeok, 181
serviette, 73
seven, as magical number, 114
Shakespeare, William, 50, 75
sharing of words, 160–161, 167–168
Shashlik, 167
Shaw, George Bernard, 46
shawarma, 168
sheep, 102
Sheridan, Thomas, 28, 72
shibboleth, 161
shiok, 177, 179
shish kebab, 167
Shishlik, 167
shitizen, 180
shogi, 184
Sholes, Christopher Latham, 206
shoyu, 183
shroff, 175
sian, 178
sign, 116
sign words, 199–202
silent letters, 115–116
Singapore: British vs. American English in, 50–52; hybrid Englishes in, 172, 175–179
Singlish, 172, 176–179
singular forms, 14, 22–23. *See also* pluralization
Sinitic languages, 182–183
Siobhan, 147
şiş kebap, 167
skinship, 15
slang, 18, 31, 61, 74–75

slay, 74
slurs, 162, 184
smartify, 189
smartphones: ordinary words related to, 63–64; suggested and predicted words on, 16, 62, 107
smh, 86
smiley faces, 200, 205–206
Smiling Happy Face emoji, 206
Snapchat, 121
snort, 76
Snow Crash (Stephenson), 110
soccer players, 48
social class: ordinary words in divisions of, 71–75; and pronunciation, 46, 72–73; and "proper" English, 27–28, 30
social distancing, 123–124
social media: abbreviations on, 18, 86; in court cases, 204–205; in creation of new words, 4, 6, 64, 122–123; global and new English on, 3–4, 16–18; grammar on, 18, 23–24, 79; number of users, 3, 121, 207, 209; ordinary words on, 61, 63, 64, 69, 79; rise and decline of sites, 121; word divide on, 120–123
social mobility, 30, 46
social movements, 139, 160, 202–203
socioeconomic word divide, 123
sociolects, 74
sociolinguistics, 96, 128–129
songs, 113
South Africa, 42–43, 202
South America, 132–133
South Korea: cosmetics of, 120; culture of, 181–182; food of, 139–140; social

Index

Index